Ambivalent Legacy

A LEGAL HISTORY OF THE SOUTH

Ambivalent Legacy

A LEGAL HISTORY OF THE SOUTH

Edited by
David J. Bodenhamer
and
James W. Ely, Jr.

UNIVERSITY PRESS OF MISSISSIPPI
Jackson

This volume has been sponsored by the
University of Southern Mississippi

Library of Congress Cataloging in Publication Data
Main entry under title:
Ambivalent legacy.

Bibliography: p.
Includes index.
1. Law—Southern States—History and criticism.
I. Bodenhamer, David J.   II. Ely, James W., 1938-
KF352.A78   1984   349.75   83-25928
ISBN 0-87805-210-0   347.5

Contents

Notes appear at end of chapters

Preface

NO PART OF southern history has received less attention from scholars than the region's laws and legal systems. This is ironic because few things reveal social values more clearly than does law. Joel P. Bishop, a nineteenth-century legal theorist, voiced this judgment when he remarked that "law sustains a more intimate relation to the everyday life of the community than any other institution in society." It establishes standards of social and economic behavior, defines conditions of class and caste, and reflects community attitudes toward offenses and offenders. Thus, an examination of southern law and legal behavior offers an opportunity to locate important values of the region, to gauge whether those values are traditional or modern, and to discover the extent to which they parallel attitudes found in other sections of the country.

Although historians have not totally ignored the legal history of the South, much of the existing work has been sporadic, uneven in quality, and marked by traditional questions and techniques of investigation. Many topics remain unexplored. More serious is the lack of central themes to guide the investigation of southern legal history.

Failure to develop a corpus of scholarly work on southern legal history has also hindered the effort to understand the role of law in the nation's past. There has been a rebirth of academic interest in American legal history over the past two decades, but much of what scholars know about the subject comes from intense study of only one region, New England. Outside of certain northeastern states, a body of literature from other regions still does not exist, and without such, it will remain difficult for historians to judge the appropriateness of current interpretations for different sections of the country. The study of law and legal institutions in the South, in other words, offers a valuable counterpoint for the understanding of the development of an American legal tradition.

In the hope of giving some direction for a regional approach to legal history and with the aim of providing a different perspective on perennial themes in southern history, the University of Southern Mississippi and Vanderbilt University School of Law cosponsored a three-day Conference on the Legal History of the South in early February 1983. This meeting, held at the USM Conference Center on the Mississippi Gulf Coast, brought together established and emerging scholars whose current research focuses on important topics in southern legal history. Papers presented at the conference, nine of which are published here in revised form, explored the relationship between southern law and the emergence of the regional economy, the nature of bench and bar in the South, the law of slavery and race in the southern past, and the impact of law on southern politics and society.

The essays in this volume do not attempt to be comprehensive or definitive. The paucity of published work on southern law, and the vastness of the research which remains to be done, dampens enthusiasm for such a project. Yet it is possible to sketch broader interpretations for certain topics based on what scholars have discovered about the role of law in the South. Several essays address this task, while others examine a more narrowly drawn subject. Regardless of the focus, however, each author relates his research to other work in southern and legal history, thus enhancing the value of his contribution.

Four topical divisions provide a measure of thematic coherence to the individual essays. An introductory section, "Law and Southern History," includes two essays, one by the coeditors and the other by Lawrence M. Friedman, which treat major themes in southern legal history and confront the issue of the region's distinctiveness in matters of law and legal behavior. In the section, "Law and the Southern Economy," Tony Freyer enters the debate over the nature of the antebellum southern economy by examining laws which regulated economic activity. Harry N. Scheiber analyzes the southern response to legal and constitutional changes in federalism that occurred from the Civil War to the New Deal. A third essay by John V. Orth provides a case study of some of the issues raised by Scheiber, especially the changing relationship between states and the central government in the area of debt repayment.

Few issues in southern history have received more attention from scholars than slavery and racial segregation. Three essays treat these problems in the section, "Law and Race in Southern History." The first two essays discuss the emerging law of slavery: Philip J. Schwarz examines reasons for the development of a criminal code for slaves in colonial Virginia, and Thomas D. Morris continues his study of the legal personality of the slave by focusing on the law of chattel mortgages. A third essay by Mark Tushnet sketches the legal strategy adopted by the NAACP as it mounted a campaign against segregation.

At first glance, essays in "Southern Courts, Bench, and Bar" appear to range more widely than those in earlier sections, yet each author treats an important element in the evolution of southern courts, lawyers, and judges. Peter C. Hoffer's contribution on criminal justice in Tidewater Virginia, for example, is more than a study of crime in this part of the colonial South; it is also an examination of how local courts responded to problems of criminal disorder. The response of immigrant German pietists to an English system of law in the southern colonies is the subject of A.G. Roeber's contribution. In a comprehensive survey, Kermit Hall takes a pioneering look at the impact of popular elections on the appellate judiciary of the South from the Jacksonian Era to the Jazz Age.

It is the hope of the editors that this book, and the conference upon which it is based, will stimulate interest in the legal history of the South. As legal history matures as a discipline, scholars must appreciate diversity in the development of legal institutions. Likewise, a better understanding of the southern legal tradition promises to broaden scholarly perspectives on perennial questions in the region's history. For these reasons the editors are pleased to present the essays in this volume.

In the course of preparing this book and in organizing the conference that preceded it, the editors incurred many personal obligations to individuals and organizations whose assistance facilitated our work. Special thanks are due to the National Endowment for the Humanities, Mississippi Committee for the Humanities, University of Southern Mississippi, and Vanderbilt University School of Law for grants that made the conference possible. President Aubrey K. Lucas (USM), Dean C. Dent Bostick (Vanderbilt), and Dr. Cora Norman (MCH) deserve separate recognition because of their willingness to provide the editors with financial support that helped to speed the completion of this volume. It is also proper to recognize those individuals who lent their talents to the various tasks of preparing and editing manuscripts. Without the work of Betty Lyon, Ann Herrington, and Jay Anglin, the book itself might have become a historical relic before it came to public attention.

One of the primary benefits of any conference comes from the informed comments that follow formal presentations. The Gulf Park meeting was fruitful in large measure because of the quality of the commentators for the sessions, many of whom offered valuable criticisms that found their way into the essays published here. For their unique contributions, the editors wish to thank Eugene Genovese, Harold Woodman, A.E. Keir Nash, Milton Klein, Kathryn Preyer, Charles McCurdy, Maxwell Bloomfield, Grady McWhiney, Neil McMillen, and W. Bradford Reynolds.

This book is dedicated with love to our children, Elizabeth, Kimberly, Suzanne, and James Ely; and Karen and Jeff Bodenhamer.

David J. Bodenhamer
James W. Ely, Jr.

Part I
Law and Southern History

Regionalism and the Legal History of the South

JAMES W. ELY, JR., and
DAVID J. BODENHAMER

THE SOUTH HAS long fascinated historians. For decades scholars have debated the often elusive features which define the South as a distinct region. Indeed, C. Vann Woodward has observed that study of the South "has suddenly emerged in a position of central importance in national history."[1] Yet there has been a surprising absence of focus on the legal history of the region. Many topics remain unexplored, and legal historians have not developed any central themes to guide investigation of this field. These omissions have not gone without notice. As early as 1950 J. Willard Hurst called for greater attention to regional and state legal history.[2] In 1982 Hurst declared that "it is only within recent years that students of legal history have begun to explore ways in which legal doctrine and uses of law may have shaped or responded to sectional experiences and patterns different from or in tension with interests taking shape on a national scale."[3]

It seems appropriate at the outset to question the extent to which regionalism is a valuable concept in understanding southern legal history. The entire notion of a unique, well-identified southern region is suspect. The geographic borders of the South have always been imprecise. It is debatable whether there was a distinct South before the sectional crisis that preceded the Civil War; certainly that conflict did much to define our thinking about the area. A group of border states defies easy sectional analysis. Moreover, there have been important divisions within the region. The Tidewater counties of Virginia and South Carolina were settled communities when Texas and Arkansas were frontier districts. The economy and society of the Upper South were markedly dissimilar from those in the Lower South. Whites in the region were further fragmented along class and regional lines.

The laws of the region inevitably reflected these divisions. Seaboard states, with their colonial past, clung tenaciously to traditional legal concepts and were less open to innovations. While most of the southern states adhered to English common law as the basis of their legal system, Texas and Louisiana followed in large measure the civil law inherited from their French-Spanish ancestry. Consequently, slack generalizations about southern law must be viewed with caution.

Not only is there some difficulty in ascertaining the perimeters of the region, but it is also evident that the southern states shared many common legal norms with the nation at large. Southern leaders, as committed to republican tenets as their northern counterparts, contributed significantly to the drafting of the Constitution and the formation of the national government. Southerners concurred with the central values of American legal culture: resistance to arbitrary power, popular sovereignty, and protection of private property.[4] It is important to remember that regional legal differences have existed within a general consensus of national attitudes toward the function of law. Thus, a regional emphasis can offer only one avenue for exploring our legal past.

Without overstating the significance of regionalism, it is the thesis of this essay that there are unique dimensions to southern legal history. Among the differences which define the southern legal heritage has been an unusual degree of attention to matters of race and caste, a rural culture, a hierarchical society, and a pervasive localism. Charles S. Sydnor has contended that this special social order created "within the South, even in the oldest and most cultivated parts of it, an attitude toward law that was very much like that of the frontiersman."[5] This essay will sketch these attitudes toward law as a preliminary attempt to shape the field for further inquiry.

1. Slavery and the Racial Caste System

The crucial importance of slavery and race throughout southern

history is well known. No area of the South's legal past has received more attention from scholars than the laws governing the
institution of slavery. Although much of this literature has been
concerned with the treatment of slaves accused of crime,[6] historians have started to examine the law of slavery in a wider context.[7] Slaves, with their human qualities, constituted a unique type
of property and posed special problems for lawmakers.

The place of slavery in the southern scale of values is clearly
demonstrated by the scheme of societal restrictions and protec-
tions placed upon the ownership of human chattel. Southern lawmakers early enacted comprehensive slave codes which established detailed regulations for the institution of slavery. The ability
of creditors to seize the slaves of debtors in order to satisfy their
claims was limited, while the fellow servant rule was not applied
to bar claims by masters for injuries to their slaves.[8] Owners of
slaves executed for capital offenses received financial compensation from the state. The net effect of such provisions was to ele-
vate slaves to a superior legal position in the law of property. At
the same time, however, slave owners were subject to regulations
which severely restricted their exercise of dominion over slaves.
Owners could not lawfully kill their slaves, and they faced increasing restriction on their ability to manumit their human property.[9] Slave patrols supervised the master's control of his bondsmen and could interfere with lax discipline perceived as a threat
to public order.[10] The property rights of individual owners were
subordinated to the larger societal need to defend the institution
of slavery.

The predominant position assigned to the protection of slavery
is further illustrated by the Negro Seamen's Acts. Concerned that
the presence of free black sailors might disrupt slavery and spread
abolitionist sentiments, several southern states enacted laws to require that black seamen be detained in jail while their ships were
in port. Such legislation hampered both coastal and foreign trade
and prompted serious diplomatic protests from Great Britain.[11]

The Civil War and the subsequent emancipation of the slaves
transformed the nature of this problem. Southern lawmakers became preoccupied with the maintenance of a racial caste system.
Post-Reconstruction legislation restricted employment opportun-

ities for blacks and eventually eliminated their political participation. Vagrancy statutes reduced many blacks to virtual peonage,[12] while segregation measures enacted in the late nineteenth and early twentieth centuries compelled social separation of the races.[13] The legal system became in large measure a club to enforce these caste divisions. As the first Scottsboro trial of the 1930s demonstrated, even elementary considerations of due process could be abandoned in the clamor to maintain white control.[14]

After World War II both the executive branch of the federal government and the federal judiciary began to push for equal status between whites and blacks. This trend culminated with the historic 1954 decision in *Brown* v. *Board of Education*, which proscribed compulsory segregation in public schools as a violation of the equal protection clause.[15] Most southern states rallied to the banner of Massive Resistance and sought to use the legal system to obstruct implementation of racial desegregation. Statutes created a variety of school closing and pupil assignment schemes. Such legislation, although ultimately futile, helped southern states to limit drastically the amount of school integration between 1954 and 1964.[16] In the early 1960s many blacks grew impatient with the slow progress in achieving desegregation and increasingly resorted to direct forms of protest. There were sit-ins at segregated lunch counters and freedom rides, which challenged segregation in transportation facilities. Defenders of segregation resorted to arrests under state trespass or disorderly conduct measures.[17]

None of this is to suggest that other sections of the country escaped racial turmoil. Still, to an unequaled extent, the South's defense of slavery and racial caste lines influenced the behavior of judges and legislators. During much of southern history the need to support white domination dwarfed all legal concerns. Consequently, the legal history of the South was inevitably different from other sections of the country. Lawmakers were hostage to this issue. Before the Civil War, such able southern jurists as Thomas Ruffin[18] and John Belton O'Neall[19] devoted much of their talent to refining the law of slavery. Such a narrow focus was bound to take a toll on the national reputation of these judges.

This defensive attitude had important implications for developments in other areas of law as well. Since protection of slavery or racial segregation was paramount, legal experimentation was curtailed. Indeed, any change in the status quo was viewed with suspicion.[20] This may explain why, over time, southern law became a collection of archaic provisions and conservative rulings. In no area was this result more apparent than in the relationship between law and commerce.

2. Inhibition of Commercial Development

Most scholars agree that nineteenth-century jurisprudence encouraged commercial growth by revising common-law rules and modifying property relationships. However, there is sharp disagreement concerning the purpose and consequences of these legal developments.[21] The region surely participated in this national trend, and several scholars have stressed the emergence of a capitalist spirit in the South.[22] Yet it seems evident that southern lawmakers were less intent upon fostering commerce and industrial activity. Indeed, one may question whether the southern legal system, at least until the Civil War, did not operate to retard such development.

Before the twentieth century, land was the principal source of wealth and social status in the South. As a result, southern lawmakers had less incentive to devise new business techniques. On the contrary, in a capital-scarce economy, southern courts were more inclined to protect landed and slave-owning interests than to promote entrepreneurial energy. Hence, the region was generally sympathetic to debtors. From colonial stay laws to the bitter state debt controversies of the 1880s, southern lawmakers favored the debtor and were leery of creditors who often resided outside the region. For instance, South Carolina's notorious Pine Barren Act of 1785 permitted debtors to tender worthless or distant land in payment of their obligations.[23] A creditor's right to imprison debtors was modified extensively, and attachment laws protected a wide range of personal property from execution.[24] The homestead exemption, which originated in Texas in 1839 and spread rapidly to other southern states, was designed to protect the family home against seizure by owner's creditors.[25] As discussed earlier, there were also limits on the ability of creditors to reach slave property. Moreover, southerners showed hostility to local courts that functioned efficiently to collect debts or appeared to prefer commercial interests.[26]

The legal system inhibited economic development in other ways. Courts and legislatures strongly favored landlords over tenants and sharecroppers.[27] This encouraged a static, agricultural society in which a large class of tenant farmers sank into financial distress. Southern jurists were slow to adopt the doctrine of caveat emptor, a rule thought to benefit manufacturers and sellers.[28] While southern legislators certainly granted charters to business corporations, they never entered competition with other jurisdictions to lure corporate headquarters with hospitable laws. Distrust of corporations was often reflected in legal decisions. In 1809, for example, the Supreme Court of Virginia declared that acts of incorporation "ought never to be passed, but in consideration of services to be rendered to the public," and ruled that a corporate charter was alterable by later legislatures.[29] Moreover, judges and legislators frequently resisted the principle of limited liability for stockholders.[30]

Although suspicion of the business corporation moderated after the Civil War, it never entirely disappeared. Late nineteenth-century agrarian political movements attempted to restrict corporate power.[31] The Mississippi Constitution of 1890 provided that no charter of incorporation should be granted for longer than 99 years. Legislation restricted the amount of real property that a corporation could own, and in 1912 corporations were prohibited from acquiring any land for agricultural purposes.[32] As a result of such legal barriers, the South did not play a major role in the evolution of the modern business corporation. Among southern jurisdictions in the mid-twentieth century, only Maryland and Virginia were important states of incorporation, and they trailed far behind the leading corporate jurisdictions.[33]

There is some evidence that many judges in the South adhered to the vested rights doctrine in construing charters long after its abandonment in the North. For example, Arkansas courts rejected the *Charles River Bridge* opinion and ruled that ferry franchises were vested rights not subject to legislative interference.[34] Less willing to accept the competitive model as the path to economic growth, southern lawmakers were more intent upon protecting existing investments in an effort to create a stable business environment. This contributes to a picture of regional law that was not attuned to the facilitation of trade or the commercial need for improved transportation.

Law in the South was sympathetic to non-market concerns which muted attempts to order society through private business activity. Public health measures were an obvious example. Anxious to curtail the spread of disease, southern legislators imposed a program of medical inspection and quarantine for ships entering their ports. Yet the quarantine laws could disrupt trading patterns and cause financial loss to individuals.[35] Likewise, the relative absence of industrial development and a pervasive paternalism that is natural in hierarchical societies retarded the adoption of modern labor laws in the South. For example, the southern states were slow to enact workman's compensation. In 1948 Mississippi became the last state to establish such a system. If, as one commentator has suggested, "an entrepreneurial rather than a rentier spirit was favored" at the national level,[36] the opposite conclusion seems accurate for the South.

3. Personal Status

In a region devoted to tradition and deference, the law governing the status of persons assumed primary significance. Such laws were crucial in defining the social position of dependent classes. Foremost among these were the provisions governing marriage, the rights of married women, and the position of paupers.

Reflecting deep religious values, English law regarded marriage as indissoluble. There was no provision for divorce until the seventeenth century, and then such relief was available only by means of a private bill of divorce passed through Parliament. This effectively restricted absolute divorce to the wealthy or powerful. More limited remedies were available in the ecclesiastical courts, which had jurisdiction over matrimonial litigation. These church tribunals could grant an annulment or a divorce from bed and board. The divorce from bed and board was essentially a legal separation which did not permit either spouse to remarry. The southern colonies followed the English view on the dissolution of marriage. Thus, unlike the New England colonies, absolute divorce was not available in the South during the colonial era.[37]

Following the Revolution there was a gradual acceptance of absolute divorce under limited circumstances. Legislatures in Virginia, Georgia, and North Carolina began to grant some absolute divorces by private act. Petitions for divorce, however, soon occupied an undue amount of legislative time. By the start of the Civil War most states in the region had enacted general divorce statutes which empowered courts to terminate marriages on grounds of adultery, desertion, or cruelty. South Carolina, a solitary holdout, adhered to the traditional view and never granted a divorce.[38] Except for a brief experiment during Reconstruction, the Palmetto State made no provision for divorce, either legislative or judicial, until 1948. In that year the voters narrowly adopted a constitutional amendment authorizing absolute divorce.

The experience of Tennessee demonstrates that the newer states were somewhat more receptive to divorce. Tennessee legislators granted the first absolute divorce in 1797, only one year after statehood was achieved.[39] Two years later the lawmakers enacted a general divorce statute, authorizing the superior court to grant absolute divorce, divorce from bed and board, or annulment, with grounds for absolute divorce limited to bigamy, impotence, adultery, or desertion.[40] Despite the availability of judicial divorce, the Tennessee legislature exercised a concurrent jurisdiction to grant divorces until a new constitution in 1834 vested exclusive power over divorce matters in the courts. Although it has been asserted that southern lawmakers were more responsive to divorce applications from men than from women, the Tennessee legislature granted a large number of petitions submitted by wives. As was true in other southern states, subsequent legislation in the nineteenth century liberalized the grounds for absolute divorce.

The availability of divorce, of course, was only one part of the story. Further research is necessary, but it appears that southern judges looked with disfavor upon divorce and often gave conservative readings to general divorce statutes. For example, in 1858 the Tennessee Supreme Court conceived of its function as saving "families and society from the direful consequences of the indiscriminate dissolution of the bonds of matrimony."[41] The hold of the past was strong, and divorce was not readily obtainable until well into the twentieth century. In the 1930s, Florida and Arkansas reduced their residency requirements in an attempt to attract transient divorce applicants.[42] Such a move, coupled with South Carolina's belated recognition of divorce, heralded a fresh look at the problems of marriage and divorce.

Southerners accepted a patriarchal notion of marriage under which the wife's legal identity merged with that of her husband. William Blackstone, whose *Commentaries on the Laws of England* was so influential in shaping early American law, neatly summarized the situation:

> The very being or legal existence of the woman is suspended during the marriage, or at least is incorporated and consolidated into that of the husband; under whose wing, protection and cover, she performs everything; and is therefore called in our law-french a feme covert . . . and her condition during her marriage is called her coverture.[43]

One consequence of coverture was a significant limitation on the right of a wife to own or manage the property that she brought to the marriage. Personal property belonged to her husband absolutely and could be reached by his creditors. Title to land remained in the wife's name, but the husband was entitled to manage or rent her land during the marriage and could retain any profits. If there were any issue born alive of the marriage, the husband's interest was extended for his life under the doctrine of curtesy. The husband could alienate his wife's land to the extent of his interest, and it was subject to his creditors. Moreover, married women could not make independent contracts and had severely limited testamentary capacity. For her part, a wife was entitled to support and maintenance from her husband.[44]

Ironically, the conservative legal system of the southern states seemingly provided substantial protection for the economic position of married women. Since the common law left wives in a financially vulnerable situation, courts of equity had long eased the rigidity of the common law by recognizing a wife's separate estate in her property. By trust or antenuptial agreement a married woman's property could be managed, independent of her husband, for her benefit. Equity jurisdiction was well established in the South. Thus, southern judges recognized marriage settlements for women and vigorously supported a wife's separate estate in equity.[45]

In addition, jurists in the region protected dower rights for widows against the claims of creditors. During the post-Revolutionary era the South Carolina legislature enlarged a widow's right to dower and broadened her inheritance rights from an intestate husband.[46] Reflecting this concern for the status of married women, Judge Abraham Nott declared in 1819: "The progress of civilization has tended to ameliorate the condition of women, and to allow even to wives, something like personal identity. I never could see any good reason why they should not retain all their interest in personal as well as real estate."[47]

Southern interest in the property rights of married women was not restricted to protection of existing rights. In 1839 Mississippi initiated the movement among common-law jurisdictions to adopt married women's property acts.[48] Such legislation was usually enacted on a piecemeal basis, and the provisions of the statutes varied widely. In essence, these acts declared that the property of a married woman would continue as her separate estate. Modest in intent and scope, such legislation extended the earlier equity model to all wives. Six southern states granted such relief before the Civil War. Once again the newer states of the region were more open to change, while the seaboard jurisdictions only recognized such rights in women during the Reconstruction.[49] This is not to suggest that the primary motive for reform was to improve the position of women. On the contrary, the general demand for debtor relief was the overriding factor. Lawmakers sought to protect family property from the mismanagement of husbands and the claims of creditors.[50] Thus, if wives did not achieve equal legal status with their husbands, southern legislators and courts generally favored family needs and gave precedence to the rights of wives over the commercial interests of creditors.

Like married women, paupers constituted a dependent group at the fringe of the legal order. As might be expected, the poor laws of the South found their origin in those of the mother country.[51] This English background left important legacies with respect to both the substance and the administration of poor relief. There was a crucial distinction between paupers deserving of public assistance and vagrants. Able-bodied persons without suitable employment were subject to harsh penalties. Following the English practice, all southern states proscribed idleness and vagrancy. Thus, the North Carolina legislature declared in 1784 that "It becomes necessary for the Welfare of Community to suppress wandering, disorderly and idle Persons."[52] Lawmakers repeatedly sought to compel vagrants to find employment—by confinement in a workhouse, by a compulsory sale of their labor, or by imposing sanctions such as jail terms or military service.[53]

On the other hand, truly dependent persons, such as the elderly or infirm, had a legitimate claim for societal support. A pervasive localism characterized the administration of poor relief. Originally handled by the parish vestry, this duty was vested in county overseers of the poor following the Revolution.[54] Each unit of local government was responsible for the maintenance of its own paupers. The law of settlement, designed to deny relief to strangers, was the cornerstone of this policy. Persons likely to be charges on the poor fund could be removed to their place of settlement by the order of a justice of the peace. The locality of settlement was also responsible for relief expenses incurred pending removal. Southern states frequently set one year as the residence period required to gain a new settlement. Moreover, the poor laws underscored family and personal acountability for paupers. Family members were required to contribute toward the maintenance of poor relatives. Fathers of illegitimate children were liable for the expenses of such infants. These measures deflected some of the costs of poor relief, leaving public assistance as a last resort.[55]

The method of relief remained largely discretionary with the county overseers. Traditionally, overseers extended relief in the form of supplemental cash payments or gifts in kind. "Parishes," one historian declared, "preferred to allow the poor to continue to maintain their households and live independent lives whenever possible."[56] This was fully consistent with the view that paupers should simply be treated as unfortunate members of the community and not stigmatized. Following the Revolution, however, there was increased interest in establishing institutional settings for poor relief. Charleston had long maintained a poor house, and other localities experimented with this method of relief. Nonetheless, even where an almshouse existed, it seems apparent that many paupers continued to receive supplemental benefits while remaining at their homes.

The English poor laws had been devised for an agrarian society, and hence they may have worked relatively well in the plantation economy of the South. Furthermore, until the Civil War many potential objects of relief were encompassed within the bonds of slavery. The master was expected to furnish care for aged or ill slaves. At the same time, the poor laws may have operated to restrict labor mobility and, indirectly, to retard industrial growth. Urbanization, which ultimately undermined the poor laws, was not a major factor in the South until the early twentieth century. Lawmakers early recognized that southern cities, with their large population of transients, faced special problems in providing poor relief. Cities were given authority to care for the urban poor. In the late eighteenth century, South Carolina lawmakers began to make annual appropriations for the relief of transient poor in Charleston. This constituted a limited acknowledgement of state responsibility when local resources proved inadequate. Such a modest concession suggested the eventual appearance of state welfare boards at the start of the twentieth century.

4. The Judicial System

There is so little scholarship on the performance of the southern bench and bar that meaningful generalization is difficult. Historians have largely confined their attention to a handful of elite figures.[57] Literary images of southern lawyers cover a wide range, from Mr. Jekyl, a pompous defender of slavery in Harriet Beecher Stowe's *Dred: A Tale of the Great Dismal Swamp*[58] to Atticus Finch, the Jim Crow liberal in *To Kill a Mockingbird*.[59] Perhaps predominant is the notion of southern lawyers as amiable storytellers, long on rhetoric and short on legal acumen. Consider the description of the Virginia attorney Philpot Wart in John Pendleton Kennedy's *Swallow Barn*:

> His acquirements as a lawyer are held in high respect by the bar, although it is reported that he reads but little law of later date than Coke Littleton, to which book he manifests a remarkable affection, having perused it, as he boasts, some eight or ten times: but the truth is, he has not much time for other reading, being very much engrossed by written documents, in which he is painfully studious. He takes a great deal of authority upon himself, nevertheless, in regard to the Virginia decisions, inasmuch as he has been contemporary with most of the cases, and heard them, generally, from the courts themselves. Besides this, he practised in the times of Old Chancellor Wythe, and President Pendleton, and must necessarily have absorbed a great deal of that spirit of law-learning which has evaporated in the hands of the reporters. As Philly himself says, he understands the currents of the law; and knows where they must run; and therefore, has no need of looking into the cases.[60]

The unpopularity of the bar has been a recurrent theme in American legal history, and such hostility has occasionally appeared in the South. A resident of post-Revolutionary Charleston warned against electing attorneys in a municipal canvass: "Shun all lawyers, as they are more liable to corruption than other men; they being used to argue for Wrong, as well as Right, when paid for so doing."[61] Nonetheless, the practice of law has been regarded as an attractive profession throughout the history of the South. Widely viewed as a route to honor and distinction, a legal career frequently proved difficult to master and yielded a disappointing economic return.[62]

Recently the often unflattering portraits of the southern lawyer have been sharply challenged. Bertram Wyatt-Brown has observed that "the southern bar and bench would have been a credit to any state or national system."[63] Indeed, most of the existing studies indicate that southern lawyers performed credibly. Before the Revolution the South sent more lawyers to England for legal education than any other region.[64] Charles Warren maintained that South Carolina's colonial bar "was more highly educated than any Bar in America."[65] In 1779 the first American professorship of law was established at the College of William and Mary.[66] During the early national period Charleston, Richmond, and Baltimore were renowned for their prominent bars.[67] Many aspiring lawyers in nineteenth-century Virginia selected formal legal education rather than traditional apprenticeship training. Contrary to colorful but apocryphal tales of lawlessness, the southern frontier attracted able practitioners and adjusted early to settled legal norms.[68] Although the deepening sectional crisis over slavery stiffled antebellum interest in law reform, Thomas S. Grimké of South Carolina was an important proponent of the codification movement.[69] Edward Livingston prepared a famous civil code for Louisiana in 1825.

The second half of the nineteenth century presented new challenges to the southern bar. During the Civil War some lawyers served the Confederacy in often difficult legal positions.[70] Anxious to promote professional and ethical standards, southern attorneys formed bar associations. Thus, the Virginia State Bar Association was established in 1888, and the Mississippi State Bar in 1906.[71] These organizations worked to require formal legal education and a written bar examination for admission to practice.

The emerging picture of the southern judiciary is similarly positive. There was sustained opposition to equity jurisdiction in much of colonial America because chancery courts were associated with the royal prerogative and functioned without a jury. Yet southern colonies, with royal governors and under the strong influence of English law, accepted equity and established courts of chancery. Likewise, the newer states in the region vested equity jurisdiction early in their courts.[72] The nineteenth century saw considerable experimentation with the court structure of the region. States repeatedly altered their courts in an attempt to improve the administration of justice. The merger of law and equity and the nature of the appellate process were central problems.[73] Georgia, for example, did not establish a supreme court until 1846, foreshadowing the inability of the Confederate government to institute a high court.[74] More important, the South was at the forefront of the drive for the popular election of judges and the elimination of tenure during good behavior. As early as 1811 a South Carolina grand jury complained:

> That the tenure by which our Judges at Law and Equity hold their offices is incompatible with the principles of republicanism as well as detrimental to the real interests of the citizens. We would rather some [fixed] period should terminate every branch of public authority and that the elective principle should circulate through the whole system of our state jurisprudence. Let all power in our State be held by our simple and common tenure.[75]

In 1812, Georgia provided for the popular election of some judges, and in 1832 Mississippi became the first state to elect its entire bench.[76] Other states in the region quickly followed suit. Closely allied to this democratic impulse was a rich southern tradition of judicial impeachments directed against unpopular as well as incompetent judges.[77]

Judicial behavior is not easy to analyze. Among other things, assessments carry unspoken value assumptions about what judges ought to be doing. Southern judges have been viewed as supporters of the status quo, but such a conclusion may be skewed by the high visibility of race relations cases.[78] A study of southern jurists is further hampered by the glaring lack of appropriate judicial biographies. A host of important figures need scholarly attention: Spencer Roane and William Cabell of Virginia; John Overton, Nathan Green, John Catron, and Howell Jackson of Tennessee; Thomas Ruffin and William Gaston of North Carolina; and John F. Grimké, John Belton O'Neall, and Henry William Desaussure of South Carolina. Historians, however, must not restrict their focus to appellate judges. It is necessary to probe the routine working of trial courts. Certainly these tribunals had the most immediate impact on the lives of ordinary citizens.[79]

5. Violence and Crime

The South has a long-standing reputation for violence and criminal disorder. It also has an image as a region where violent white men went unpunished and where, until recently, citizens frequently resorted to vigilantism to maintain order. Certainly there is much evidence to support such conclusions. Reports of assaults, mayhem, and murder have filled southern newspapers from the early republic to the present. "Scenes of violence have become so frequent," conceded one antebellum editor in 1840, "[that they] often . . . go by without even a passing notice, until at last an appeal to brute force is acquiesced in as the only method of adjusting disagreements. . . ."[80] The lament was common: killings and assaults were epidemic; brutishness threatened the social order. Even more troublesome was the casualness with which southerners responded to the problem. After witnessing a deadly argument over property, a visitor to Georgia in 1838 wrote to her sister, "To us Northerners who have been unaccustomed to such scenes it is horrible beyond description—but to those who often witness such, it soon passes off with a few remarks or perhaps a jest."[81]

Whatever the causes of this violent behavior—and recent scholars have blamed the region's poverty, its racism, a pessimistic view of human nature, and even a debatable Celtic heritage[82]—historians have generally accepted the notion that an ineffective legal system intensified the combativeness of southern society. This conclusion is not new; it was a standard grievance of concerned citizens in both the Old and New South. "There is an utter inefficiency in the execution of our criminal jurisprudence," noted one antebellum editor. "Neither law officers nor citizens seem to care whether those who choose to violate the law . . . escape or not." The problem was not simply one of capture, but also of "great difficulty in conviction and punishment after detection."[83]

The themes of frontier individualism and the plantation system have served most frequently to explain the legal system's inability to deal with crime. No one has advanced these ideas with more assurance than Wilber J. Cash in his book, *The Mind of the South*. To Cash, an intense individualism, buttressed by a belief in white supremacy, blunted the development of law and government, while the growth of the plantation system kept the police power decentralized. An effective legal system was neither expected nor desired. When confronted by a threat to his security, the southerner demanded immediate satisfaction, not "some ponderous abstract justice in problematic tomorrow."[84]

Historians have done little to rebut Cash's interpretation. Charles Sydnor, for example, declared that just as geographical distance isolated the westerner from legal restraints, so "the social order diminished the force of law in the South."[85] For other scholars the private discipline enforced by masters over their slaves found its counterpart in extralegal or illegal means of resolving disputes between whites.

Although an ineffective legal response to crime may be yet another burden of southern history, there are reasons to doubt traditional interpretations of its causes. Students of the westward movement are no longer so certain that the frontier experience was excessively violent or individualistic. Much of the frontier, including the South, was a peaceful place where settlers tried to maintain order and recreate community.[86] The urban disorder of the nineteenth and twentieth centuries, especially in the North, makes it difficult to conclude that lawlessness was uniquely western or southern. Moreover, the idea that informal punishment of slaves diminished respect for legal process finds little support in recent scholarship. Several studies reveal a surprisingly high regard for due process in slave trials in the lower courts and upon appellate review. Thus, slavery may not have dulled the region's legal sensibilities as many scholars have supposed.[87]

Two other problems remain with older interpretations of southern criminal justice. Historians have rarely compared the southern experience with that of other states, even though such comparisons are essential to the argument that an inefficient criminal process was peculiarly southern.[88] A more fundamental weakness is that the literature on southern justice often has not examined the best evidence of the region's legal behavior, local court records.

Recent studies of the response of local courts to crime suggest the need to significantly revise standard themes advanced by historians, especially as they apply to the colonial and antebellum South. There is considerable evidence, for example, of the inability of local southern courts to complete prosecution in a large percentage of criminal cases. An examination of colonial courts in North Carolina revealed that only half of all bills of indictments brought before the General Court reached trial; almost one criminal action in three simply disappeared from the system. More dismal figures surfaced in a study of four counties in antebellum Georgia, where just one case in four reached a decision on the merits of the accusation. But in neither instance was the southern experience unique. Comparisons with local courts in colonial New York and antebellum Indiana revealed strikingly similar patterns of ineffective prosecution.[89] Southern law enforcement, in other words, was not atypical in its inability to secure judgments in criminal cases. The problem was endemic to rural, pre-bureaucratic communities in all regions.

Patterns of prosecution in southern jurisdictions parallel those found elsewhere. Most criminal actions involved petty offenses, although prosecutions for felonies consumed much of the time that courts devoted to criminal matters. Of the more serious crimes, theft and other property offenses appeared regularly on criminal dockets, with urbanizing areas devoting considerable prosecutorial energy to these cases. The available data suggest, moreover, that southern grand juries and prosecutors, like their northern counterparts, identified the propertyless as offenders in such cases.[90]

Crimes against morality also occupied the attention of local authorities. Although the incidence of prosecution was less than in the colonies and states of Puritan New England, gaming, liquor-related offenses, and sexual immorality were frequent crimes before southern trial courts. It was no accident that prohibition and other moral crusades found ready reception in the South; the region's legal system had a long heritage of attempting to regulate moral behavior. These findings suggest modification of traditional interpretations that emphasize southern laxity in crimes against morality and of recent arguments that post–1800 criminal process ignored such crimes in its attempt to protect the economic order. Perhaps crime as theft replaced crime as sin in the criminal codes and prosecution patterns of other states, but southern courts continued the effort to maintain a common morality.[91]

Of course, violent crime and not theft or moral disorder gave the South its image as a lawless region. Tales of duels, murder, and assault were stock items in scores of travel accounts, newspapers stories, and grand jury presentments. Historians also have credited southerners with a readiness to settle private disputes with fists, dirks, or pistols. Examinations of felony indictments appear to confirm this conclusion. Crimes against persons were constant items on court dockets; some studies have shown that almost four of every ten indictments involved either petty or serious acts of personal violence.[92] This pattern, present in the earliest records, continues to exist. In the mid-1970s the southern states led the nation in these crimes. Forty-two percent of all murders in 1975 were committed in the South; and the region's fastest growing urban area, Houston, had earned the sobriquet, "Murder City," for its large number of capital crimes.[93]

Yet the rate of indictments for violent behavior surpasses that for other regions, and it is inaccurate to claim that grand juries and circuit solicitors ignored violent crime or treated it casually. Instead, the figures suggest that prosecution of violent crime was a central concern of the legal system. In cases tried to a verdict, the violent offender stood little chance of acquittal, especially in jurisdictions within urbanizing areas. The success of courts in securing convictions in cases of violent crime underscores the social agreement that law rather than private vengeance provided the most acceptable method of resolving personal conflicts, at least between respectable white citizens. For most southerners, criminal justice remained a matter for the courts.[94]

Just as recent studies have challenged older interpretations of southern criminal process, so too have historians begun to examine more critically the region's practice of punishment. The accepted notion is that punition in the nineteenth-century South was synonymous with lynching and chain gangs. Therefore, it is surprising to discover that the penitentiary, usually associated with the commercial North, found a home in every antebellum slave state except the Carolinas and Florida. The lessons taught by Beccaria and Montesquieu were learned well by southern lawmakers, and the underlying principles of the penitentiary were clearly reformist. Within a short time after the establishment of these institutions, however, inmates became disproportionately urban and immigrant. With such a population, the impulse of redemption weakened significantly, and southern prisons followed a course parallel to their northern counterparts. Penitentiaries rapidly became overcrowded holding cells for social miscreants.[95]

Although the details remain sketchy, southern crime and justice underwent dramatic change in the immediate post–Civil War decades. The abolition of slavery removed the plantation system as a device for protecting white society, and the criminal justice system took its place. Former slaves, who had been prosecuted in separate courts and punished under separate codes, now filled local jails and state prisons. It is no accident that the penitentiary began to disappear during the 1860s and 1870s, with county road gangs and the convict–lease system emerging to take its place.

For especially menacing crimes attributed to blacks, lynching became a widespread alternative to the more uncertain process of trial. By the 1880s, lynching was an accepted part of the criminal justice system in many areas of the New South. From 1882 to 1903, at least 2,585 persons were lynched in the southern states; of these, 1,985 were blacks. Regardless of the causes of this extra-legal and illegal mob violence, its impact on the southern criminal justice system was striking, with a decline in established conceptions of due process and the disappearance of rehabilitation as a goal of punishment. Although many white southerners deplored the resort to lynching and worked for federal and state anti-lynching laws, the practice continued well into the twentieth century.[96]

No section of the United States has had a monopoly on violence or extra-legal activity. Yet the southerner's occasional acceptance of violence as a means of conflict resolution and social control remains a major theme in historical literature. The roots of this tradition run deep in the cultural values of the region and can be attributed only partly to the legal order. Still, southern lawmakers at times condoned, or showed indifference towards, the use of violence to maintain order, supplement law enforcement, or discipline individuals on the fringes of society. Much of the extra-legal activity exhibited a racial dimension and served as an informal technique to buttress the social order. The prevalence of dueling and regulator or vigilante movements, however, cannot be explained so simply.

Vigilantism may have originated in the South. Indeed, one authority characterized the South Carolina Regulators of the 1760s as "the prototype of American vigilance movements."[97] Vigilantes often assumed the law enforcement function of punishing both outlaws and immoral persons. Behind this phenomenon lay discontent with elite domination of local courts and a belief in the rightness of popular sovereignty. Thus, the desire for an equitable order often prevailed over respect for formal authority. Paradoxically, southern legal institutions co-existed well with this resort to extra-legal action. Since vigilantes acted to protect community values, southerners could extend support to both the judicial system and the practice of extra-legal redress.

Likewise, dueling was a legally forbidden but socially acceptable method of resolving personal disputes among "gentlemen of standing." Although the practice of dueling was not sectional, the Code Duello lingered longer in the South than elsewhere,[98] perhaps because of the region's well-defined and rigid class structure. Elite pressure dictated that gentlemen demonstrate courage and resolve their differences on the field of honor rather than resort to a court of law.[99]

Still other forms of violence demonstrate an occasional southern willingness to operate outside the constraints of formal legal institutions. Agricultural distress in the postbellum South caused small farmers to organize secret bands and use force in an effort to improve their economic lot. Night riders in Kentucky and Tennessee battled the power of the tobacco companies, headquartered outside the area, which threatened the livelihood of farmers and local citizenry. Whitecappers in Mississippi sought to break the stranglehold of local merchants over farmers. Finally, the region has long been associated with feuds, essentially revenge fights between families.[100] Unlike dueling and vigilantism, these examples of extra-legal activity reflect the frustration of disadvantaged elements in the society. Such violence ultimately produced only marginal changes in the social order but would be echoed in the ghetto riots of the 1960s and the 1980 Miami racial disturbances.

Conclusion

The themes of southern legal history leave the region and its scholars with an ambivalent legacy. While the South has claimed a distinctive heritage in matters of law and society, it has nonetheless remained part of the larger Union. The law of northern and western jurisdictions was never foreign to southern lawyers and judges, and southern lawmakers shared many of the same concerns, voiced the same rhetoric, and responded to many problems in the same manner as their counterparts in other regions. Yet it is difficult to escape the conclusion that the South was, and perhaps still is, different. All of the reasons assigned by historians as causes of the South's uniqueness also affected legal development in ways that kept the creators of southern law marching to a different drummer.

As legal history matures, the diversity that accompanied the development of American legal institutions will become apparent. Until recently, the New England experience dominated much of the literature and thus provided many of the themes that claim the attention of scholars. Southern legal history offers a measure of comparison, previously unexplored, for developments elsewhere in the nation. Too much research remains undone to predict how the area's legal heritage will modify our understanding of the evolution of American law. Yet the scholarship discussed above suggests that legal historians will discover what other historians of the region have long known: the South's past is filled with contradiction and irony, and its legacy in law, as in so much of southern society, is an uncertain one indeed.

NOTES

[1] C. Vann Woodward, "The Future of Southern History," in *The Future of History*, ed. Charles F. Delzell (Nashville, Tenn., 1977), 138.

[2] James Willard Hurst, *The Growth of American Law: The Law Makers*, (Boston, 1950), 18.

[3] James Willard Hurst, "The State of Legal History," *Reviews in American History*, X (Dec. 1982), 292.

[4] James Willard Hurst, *Law and Social Order in the United States* (Ithaca, N.Y., 1977), 57–63; Stephen B. Presser, "'Legal History' or the History of Law: A Primer on Bringing the Law's Past Into the Present," *Vanderbilt Law Review*, XXXV (May 1982), 849–90.

[5] Charles S. Sydnor, "The Southerner and the Laws," *Journal of Southern History*, VI (Feb. 1940), 12.

[6] A. E. Keir Nash, "Fairness and Formalism in the Trials of Blacks in the State Supreme Courts of the Old South," *Virginia Law Review*, LVI (Feb. 1970), 64–100; David Flanigan, "Criminal Procedure in Slave Trials in the Antebellum South," *Journal of Southern History*, XL (Aug. 1974), 537–64; Michael S. Hindus, "Black Justice Under White Law: Criminal Prosecutions of Blacks in Antebellum South Carolina," *Journal of American History*, LXIII (Dec. 1976), 575–99; A. E. Keir Nash, "Reason of Slavery: Understanding the Judicial Role in the Peculiar Institution," *Vanderbilt Law Review*, XXXII (Jan. 1979), 7–218; A. Leon Higginbotham, *In the Matter of Color: Race and the American Legal Process: The Colonial Period* (New York, 1978).

[7] John Edmund Stealey, III, "The Responsibilities and Liabilities of the Bailee of Slave Labor in Virginia," *American Journal of Legal History*, XII (Oct. 1968), 336–53; Arthur F. Howington, "'Not in the Condition of a Horse or an Ox': Ford v. Ford, The Law of Testamentary Manumission and the Tennessee Courts' Recognition of Slave Humanity," *Tennessee Historical Quarterly*, XXXIV (Fall 1975), 249–63; Thomas D. Morris, "'As If the Injury was Effected by the Natural Elements of Air, or Fire': Slave Wrongs and the Liability of Masters," *Law & Society Review*, XVI (1981–82), 569–99.

[8] Eugene D. Genovese, "Slavery in the Legal History of the South and the Nation," *Texas Law Review*, LIX (May 1981), 986–87; *Louisville and Nashville Railroad* v. *Yandell*, 56 Ky. 466 (1856).

[9] Nash, "Reason of Slavery," 123–84; Mark V. Tushnet, *The American Law of Slavery, 1810–1860* (Princeton, N.J., 1981), 191–228.

[10] The activities of the slave patrols, which included entering private property and punishing slaves, often resulted in litigation. *State* v. *Boyce*, 32 N.C. 536 (1849).

[11] Alan Frank January, "The First Nullification: The Negro Seamen Acts Controversy in South Carolina, 1822–1860" (Ph.D. dissertation, University of Iowa, 1976).

[12] Peter Daniel, *The Shadow of Slavery: Peonage in the South, 1901–1969* (Urbana, Ill., 1972); Daniel A. Novak, *The Wheel of Servitude: Black Forced Labor After Slavery* (Lexington, Ky., 1978).

[13] C. Vann Woodward, *The Strange Career of Jim Crow* (3rd rev. ed., New York, 1974); Roger L. Rice, "Residential Segregation by Law, 1910–1917," *Journal of Southern History*, XXXIV (May 1968), 179–99.

[14] Dan T. Carter, *Scottsboro: A Tragedy of the American South* (rev. ed., Baton Rouge, La., 1979). See also Charles H. Martin, *The Angelo Herndon Case and Southern Justice* (Baton Rouge, La., 1976).

[15] Richard Kluger, *Simple Justice: The History of Brown* v. *Board of Education and Black America's Struggle for Equality* (New York, 1976).

[16] Numan V. Bartley, *The Rise of Massive Resistance: Race and Politics in the South during the 1950s* (Baton Rouge, La., 1969); James W. Ely, Jr., *The Crisis of Conservative Virginia: The Byrd Organization and the Politics of Massive Resistance* (Knoxville, Tenn., 1976).

[17] William H. Chafe, *Civilities and Civil Rights: Greensboro, North Carolina, and the Black Struggle for Freedom* (New York, 1980); James W. Ely, Jr., "Negro Demonstrations and the Law: Danville as a Test Case," *Vanderbilt Law Review*, XXVII (Oct. 1974), 927–68.

[18] Patrick S. Brady, "Slavery, Race, and the Criminal Law in Antebellum North Carolina: A Reconsideration of the Thomas Ruffin Court," *North Carolina Central Law Journal*, X (Spring 1979), 248–60.

[19] A. E. Keir Nash, "Negro Rights, Unionism, and Greatness on the South Carolina Court

of Appeals: The Extraordinary Chief Justice John Belton O'Neall," *South Carolina Law Review*, XXI (1969), 141–90.

[20] See generally Michael S. Hindus, *Prison and Plantation: Crime, Justice, and Authority in Massachusetts and South Carolina, 1767–1878* (Chapel Hill, N.C., 1980).

[21] Compare James Willard Hurst, *Law and the Conditions of Freedom in the Nineteenth-Century United States* (Madison, Wisc., 1956), with Morton J. Horwitz, *The Transformation of American Law, 1780–1860* (Cambridge, Mass., 1977).

[22] James Oakes, *The Ruling Race: A History of American Slaveholders* (New York, 1982).

[23] James W. Ely, Jr., "American Independence and the Law: A Study of Post-Revolutionary South Carolina Legislation," *Vanderbilt Law Review*, XXVI (Oct. 1973), 939, 942–43.

[24] Peter J. Coleman, *Debtors and Creditors in America: Insolvency, Imprisonment for Debt, and Bankruptcy, 1607–1900* (Madison, Wisc., 1974), 159–246.

[25] Joseph W. McKnight, "Protection of the Family Home from Seizure by Creditors: The Sources and Evolution of a Legal Principle," *Southwestern Historical Quarterly*, LXXXVI (Jan. 1983), 369–99.

[26] James W. Ely, Jr., "Charleston's Court of Wardens, 1783–1800: A Post-Revolutionary Experiment in Municipal Justice," *South Carolina Law Review*, XXVI (Feb. 1976), 645–60.

[27] A. B. Book, "A Note on the Legal Status of Share-Tenants and Share-Croppers in the South," *Law and Contemporary Problems*, IV (Oct. 1937), 539–45. See *Harrison* v. *Ricks*, 71 N.C. 7 (1874); *State* v. *Austin*, 123 N.C. 749 (1898).

[28] *Barnard* v. *Yates*, 1 Nott & McCord (S.C.) 142 (1818); *Missroon and Timmons* v. *Waldo and Freeman*, 2 Nott & McCord (S.C.) 76 (1819).

[29] *Currie's Administrators* v. *Mutual Assurance Society*, 14 Va. 315, 347 (1809).

[30] *Hume* v. *Winyow and Wando Canal Co.*, 1 Carolina Law Journal 217 (1826), aff'd by Court of Appeals (1828).

[31] Albert D. Kirwan, *Revolt of the Rednecks: Mississippi Politics, 1876–1925* (Lexington, Ky., 1951), 166.

[32] Article 7, Sec. 178, Mississippi Constitution of 1890, in *The Federal and State Constitutions* (7 vols., Washington, 1909), IV, 2110; *Middleton* v. *Georgetown Mercantile Co.*, 117 Miss. 134, 77 So. 956 (1918).

[33] James Willard Hurst, *The Legitimacy of the Business Corporation in the Law of the United States, 1780–1970* (Charlottesville, Va., 1970), 149–50.

[34] Michael B. Dougan, "The Doctrine of Creative Destruction: Ferry and Bridge Law in Arkansas," *Arkansas Historical Quarterly*, XXXIX (Summer 1980), 136–58.

[35] James W. Ely, Jr., "Patterns of Statutory Enactment in South Carolina, 1720–1770," in *South Carolina Legal History*, ed. Herbert A. Johnson (Columbia, S.C., 1980), 73–75.

[36] Stanley I. Kutler, *Privilege and Creative Destruction: The Charles River Bridge Case* (Philadelphia, 1971), 5.

[37] Nelson M. Blake, *The Road to Reno: A History of Divorce in the United States* (Westport, Conn., 1962), 40–41; Note, "Early Statutory and Common Law of Divorce in North Carolina," *North Carolina Law Review*, XLI (1963), 604–21.

[38] Hindus, *Prison and Plantation*, 51–52; Blake, *Road to Reno*, 63, 234–35.

[39] Ch. 8, 1797 Tenn. Private Acts, *Acts Passed at the First Session of the Second General Assembly* (Knoxville, Tenn., 1797), 92.

[40] Ch. 19, 1799 Tenn. Public Acts, Edward Scott, *Laws of the State of Tennessee, 1715–1820* (2 vols., Knoxville, Tenn., 1821), I, 645; James W. Ely, Jr., "Andrew Jackson as Tennessee State Court Judge, 1798–1804," *Tennessee Historical Quarterly*, XL (Summer 1981), 147.

[41] *Rutledge* v. *Rutledge*, 37 Tenn. 554, 558 (1858).

[42] Blake, *Road to Reno*, 166–67.

[43] William Blackstone, *Commentaries on the Laws of England* (4 vols., Oxford, 1765), I, 430.

[44] George L. Haskins, "The Estate by the Martial Right," *University of Pennsylvania Law Review*, XCVII (Feb. 1949), 345–53.

⁴⁵ Marylynn Salmon, "Women and Property in South Carolina: The Evidence from Marriage Settlements," *William and Mary Quarterly*, 3rd ser., XXXIX (Oct. 1982), 655–85.
⁴⁶ Marylynn Salmon, "'Life, Liberty, and Dower': The Legal Status of Women After the American Revolution," in *Women, War, and Revolution*, eds. Carol R. Berkin and Clara M. Lovett (New York, 1980).
⁴⁷ *Sturgineger* v. *Hannal*, 2 Nott and McCord's Law and Equity Reports (S.C.) 147, 149 (1819).
⁴⁸ Comment, "Husband and Wife—Memorandum on the Mississippi Woman's Law of 1839," *Michigan Law Review*, XLII (April 1944), 1110–121; Lucie R. Bridgforth, "The Mississippi Married Woman's Property Act," paper delivered at Annual Meeting of American Society for Legal History, Washington, 1982.
⁴⁹ Suzanne D. Lebsock, "Radical Reconstruction and the Property Rights of Southern Women," *Journal of Southern History*, XLIII (May 1977), 195–216.
⁵⁰ Kay Ellen Thurman, "The Married Women's Property Acts" (M.A. thesis, University of Wisconsin, 1966).
⁵¹ Howard Mackey, "The Operation of the English Old Poor Law in Colonial Virginia," *Virginia Magazine of History and Biography*, LXXIII (Jan. 1965), 29–40; Stefan A. Riesenfeld, "The Formative Era of American Public Assistance Law," *California Law Review*, XLIII (May 1955), 175–233.
⁵² *State Records of North Carolina*, ed. Walter Clark (26 vols., Goldsboro, N.C., 1895–1914), XXIV, 597.
⁵³ For South Carolina's vagrancy act of 1787, see Ely, "American Independence and the Law," 966–67.
⁵⁴ Roy M. Brown, *Public Poor Relief in North Carolina* (Chapel Hill, N.C., 1928).
⁵⁵ John F. Grimké, *The South Carolina Justice of the Peace* (Philadelphia, 1788), 58.
⁵⁶ Alan D. Watson, "Public Poor Relief in Colonial North Carolina," *North Carolina Historical Review*, LIV (Oct. 1977), 347, 351.
⁵⁷ *The Papers of John Marshall, Vol. I, 1775–1788*, ed. Herbert A. Johnson (Williamsburg, Va., 1974); *The Papers of John Marshall, Vol. II, 1788–1795*, eds. Charles T. Cullen and Herbert A. Johnson (Williamsburg, Va., 1977); Clement Eaton, "A Mirror of the Southern Colonial Lawyer: The Fee Books of Patrick Henry, Thomas Jefferson, and Waightstill Avery," *William and Mary Quarterly*, 3rd series, VIII (Oct. 1951), 520–34; L. Lynn Hogue, "Nicholas Trott: Man of Law and Letters," *South Carolina Historical Magazine*, LXXVI (Jan. 1975), 25–34.
⁵⁸ Harriet Beecher Stowe, *Dred: A Tale of the Great Dismal Swamp* (2 vols., Boston, 1856).
⁵⁹ Thomas L. Shaffer, "The Moral Theology of Atticus Finch," *University of Pittsburgh Law Review*, XLII (Winter 1981), 181–224.
⁶⁰ John Pendleton Kennedy, *Swallow Barn, or A Sojourn in the Old Dominion* (2 vols., Philadelphia, 1832), I, 212.
⁶¹ Charleston, *Evening Gazette*, Aug. 25, 1786.
⁶² E. Lee Shepard, "Breaking Into the Profession: Establishing a Law Practice in Antebellum Virginia," *Journal of Southern History*, XLVIII (Aug. 1982), 393–410.
⁶³ Bertram Wyatt-Brown, *Southern Honor: Ethics and Behavior in the Old South* (New York, 1982), 263.
⁶⁴ J. G. de Roulhac Hamilton, "Southern Members of the Inns of Court," *North Carolina Historical Review*, X (Oct. 1933), 273–86.
⁶⁵ Charles Warren, *A History of the American Bar* (Boston 1911), 121. See also Hoyt P. Canady, "Legal Education in Colonial South Carolina," South Carolina Legal History, 99–118.
⁶⁶ *Legal Education in Virginia, 1779–1979*, ed. W. Hamilton Bryson (Charlottesville, Va., 1982), 22–23.
⁶⁷ Dennis R. Nolan, "The Effect of the Revolution on the Bar: The Maryland Experience," *Virginia Law Review*, LXII (June 1976), 969–97.
⁶⁸ James W. Ely, Jr., "The Legal Practice of Andrew Jackson," *Tennessee Historical Quar-*

terly, XXXVIII (Winter 1979), 421–35; Maxwell Bloomfield, "The Texas Bar in the Nineteenth Century," *Vanderbilt Law Review*, XXXII (Jan. 1979), 261–76; William B. Hamilton, *Anglo-American Law on the Frontier: Thomas Rodney and His Territorial Cases* (Durham, N.C., 1953).

[69] Charles M. Cook, *The American Codification Movement: A Study of Antebellum Legal Reform* (Westport, Conn., 1981), 128–30.

[70] Maxwell Bloomfield, *American Lawyers in a Changing Society, 1776–1876* (Cambridge, Mass., 1976), 271–301; Terry Calvani, "The Early Professional Career of Howell Jackson," *Vanderbilt Law Review*, XXX (Jan. 1977), 39–72.

[71] Michael de L. Landon, *The Honor and Dignity of the Profession: A History of the Mississippi State Bar, 1906–1976* (Jackson, Miss., 1979).

[72] Samuel C. Williams, "History of the Courts of Chancery of Tennessee," *Tennessee Law Review*, II (Nov. 1923), 6–23.

[73] Donald Senese, "Building the Pyramid: The Growth and Development of the State Court System in Antebellum South Carolina, 1800–1860," *South Carolina Law Review*, XXIV (1972), 357–79; Dunbar Rowland, *Courts, Judges, and Lawyers of Mississippi, 1798–1935* (Jackson, Miss., 1935).

[74] *A History of the Supreme Court of Georgia* (Macon, Ga., 1948), 1–18; William M. Robinson, *Justice in Grey: A History of the Judicial System of the Confederate States of America* (Cambridge, Mass., 1941).

[75] Presentments of the Grand Jury of Union District, October term 1811, Grand Jury Presentments, South Carolina Department of Archives and History.

[76] Lawrence M. Friedman, *A History of American Law* (New York, 1973), 111; Kermit L. Hall, "The Judiciary on Trial: State Constitutional Reform and the Rise of an Elected Judiciary," *The Historian*, XLV (May 1983), 337–54.

[77] James W. Ely, Jr., "'That no office whatever be held during life or good behavior': Judicial Impeachments and the Struggle for Democracy in South Carolina," *Vanderbilt Law Review*, XXX (March 1977), 167–208; Stephen A. Smith, "Impeachment, Address, and the Removal of Judges in Arkansas: An Historical Perspective," *Arkansas Law Review*, XXXII (Summer 1978), 253–68.

[78] Michael Meltsner, "Southern Appellate Courts: A Dead End," in *Southern Justice*, ed. Leon Friedman (New York, 1965), 136–54.

[79] Robert M. Ireland, *The County Courts in Antebellum Kentucky* (Lexington, Ky., 1972); Mary K. Bonsteel Tachau, *Federal Courts in the Early Republic: Kentucky, 1789–1816* (Princeton, N.J., 1978); Theodore Brown, Jr., "The Tennessee County Courts Under the North Carolina and Territorial Governments: The Davidson County Court of Pleas and Quarter Sessions, 1783–1796, as a Case Study," *Vanderbilt Law Review*, XXXII (Jan. 1979), 349–412; Paul M. McCain, *The County Court in North Carolina Before 1750* (Durham, N.C., 1954).

[80] Columbus (Ga.) *Weekly Enquirer*, April 8, 1840.

[81] Mary Ingraham to Susan Fisher, Dec. 9, 1838, in Susan Fisher Papers, Southern Historical Collection, University of North Carolina.

[82] These recent assessments of the origins of southern crime and violence are found in: Sheldon Hackney, "Southern Violence," *American Historical Review*, LXXIV (Feb. 1969), 906–25; Raymond D. Gastil, "Homicide and a Regional Culture of Violence," *American Sociological Review*, XXXVI (June 1971), 412–27; Dickson D. Bruce, Jr., *Violence and Culture in the Antebellum South* (Austin, Tex., 1979).

[83] Columbus (Ga.) *Enquirer*, April 9, 1846; Grand Jury Presentment, Bibb County (Ga.) Superior Court, *Minute Book V*, 175. See also Robert M. Ireland, "Law and Disorder in Nineteenth-Century Kentucky," *Vanderbilt Law Review*, XXXII (Jan. 1979), 281–300.

[84] Wilbur J. Cash, *The Mind of the South* (New York, 1941), 44–45.

[85] Sydnor, "The Southerner and the Laws," 12; John Hope Franklin, *The Militant South* (Cambridge, Mass., 1956), 14–32; Clement Eaton, "Mob Violence in the Old South,"

Mississippi Valley Historical Review, XXIX (Dec. 1942), 351–70; Michael S. Hindus, "The Contours of Crime and Justice in Massachusetts and South Carolina, 1767–1878," *American Journal of Legal History*, XXI (July 1977), 237.

86 Ray Allen Billington, *America's Frontier Heritage* (New York, 1966), 147; David J. Bodenhamer, "Law and Disorder on the Early Frontier: Marion County, Indiana, 1823–1850," *Western Historical Quarterly*, X (July 1979), 323–36.

87 A. E. Keir Nash, "The Texas Supreme Court and the Trial Rights of Blacks, 1845–1860," *Journal of American History*, LVIII (Dec. 1971), 622–42; Flanigan, "Criminal Procedures in Slave Trials in the Antebellum South;" Arthur Howington, "The Treatment of Slaves and Free Blacks in the State and Local Courts of Tennessee" (Ph.D. dissertation, Vanderbilt University, 1982).

88 An exception is Hindus, *Prison and Plantation*.

89 Donna J. Spindel and Stuart W. Thomas, Jr., "Crime and Society in North Carolina, 1663–1740," *Journal of Southern History*, XLIX (May 1983), 228; David J. Bodenhamer, "Law and Disorder in the Old South: The Situation in Georgia, 1830–1860," in Walter J. Fraser, Jr., and Winfred B. Moore, Jr., eds., *From the Old South to the New: Essays in the Transitional South* (Westport, Conn., 1981), 114.

90 David J. Bodenhamer, "The Efficiency of Criminal Justice in the Antebellum South," *Criminal Justice History*, III (1983); Spindel and Thomas, "Crime in North Carolina," 242.

91 Bradley Chapin, *Criminal Justice in Colonial America, 1606–1660* (Athens, Ga., 1983), 8–13; Spindel and Thomas, "Crime in North Carolina," 231; Bodenhamer, "Law and Disorder in the Old South," 113–14; also see Kathryn Preyer, "Crime, the Criminal Law and Reform in Post-Revolutionary Virginia," *Law and History Review*, I (1983), 53–85.

92 Edward Lynn Ayers, "Crime and Society in the Nineteenth-Century South," (Ph.D. dissertation, Yale University, 1980).

93 U.S. Department of Justice, *Uniform Crime Reports, 1975* (Washington, D.C., 1975).

94 David J. Bodenhamer, "Violence, Law, and Society in the Antebellum South," paper delivered at Annual Meeting of American Studies Association, Memphis, 1981.

95 The discussion of southern prisons and the convict-lease system draws heavily from Ayers, "Crime and Society in the Nineteenth-Century South," *passim*; Peter Daniel, "The Tennessee Convict War," *Tennessee Historical Quarterly*, XXXIV (Fall 1975), 273–92.

96 On lynching, see Jacquelyn Dowd Hall, *Revolt Against Chivalry: Jessie Daniel Ames and the Women's Campaign Against Chivalry* (New York, 1979), 129–57.

97 Richard Maxwell Brown, *The South Carolina Regulators* (Cambridge, Mass., 1963), 141.

98 James T. Moore, "The Death of the Duel: The Code Duello in Readjuster Virginia, 1879–1883," *Virginia Magazine of History and Biography*, LXXXIII (July 1975), 259–76.

99 Wyatt-Brown, *Southern Honor*, 350–61.

100 James O. Nall, *The Tobacco Night Riders of Kentucky and Tennessee, 1905–1909* (Louisville, Ky., 1939); Paul J. Vanderwood, *Night Riders of Reelfoot Lake* (Memphis, Tenn., 1969); William T. Holmes, "Whitecapping: Agrarian Violence in Mississippi, 1902–1906," *Journal of Southern History*, XXXV (May 1969); Virgil C. Jones, *The Hatfields and the McCoys* (Chapel Hill, N.C., 1948).

The Law Between the States:
Some Thoughts on
Southern Legal History

LAWRENCE M. FRIEDMAN

THERE IS SOMETHING rather alien about southern legal history, the subject of this essay. It is striking now how little the scholar from outside the region is likely to know about the special history of southern law—assuming there is such a thing—excepting a single subject, slavery and race relations, which has dominated the field almost to the exclusion of everything else.

There is, in a way, something paradoxical about the ignorance of outsiders. The paradox is that people recognize—or assume—that there is something special about the legal history of the South, that the usual principles and theories, such as they are, may lose their validity when we cross from North to South. There is no region quite like the South in this regard. Western legal history is also special, but special in a special way. Western legal history is "frontier" history basically, that is, not the history of a fixed region, but rather of a borderland, and a moving borderland at that. Western history, in other words, has stable elements: it is the location of the West that keeps moving. It starts in western New York or Connecticut and ends at the Pacific or even beyond. Indeed, California today is hardly "western" anymore because it is so big, so urban, so industrial.

If this point is correct, then it is only the South that has been a distinct American region in legal history (past the colonial period, at any rate). Yet, with the colossal exception of race relations, not much is known about what makes the region special—the exact differences between the South and the rest of the country, or how these differences in social life, economic structure, and the like reflect themselves in law.

This essay will begin with some observations about the neglect of southern legal history, then turn to a few guesses—one can hardly dignify them further—about the South as a legal region.

The neglect of southern legal history is partly, of course, an accident of location. A disproportionate amount of scholarly writing in American legal history deals with two states: Massachusetts, for the colonial period, and Wisconsin, for the nineteenth century. Whatever one can say about these states, they were not selected on scientific grounds. If Willard Hurst had lived in Kentucky, Kentucky not Wisconsin would dominate the nineteenth century. Legal history, though definitely on the upswing, is an underdeveloped field. Most topics are unwritten about, most sources untouched, most localities unchronicled. There is a study here, a study there. Two interesting books deal with criminal justice in nineteenth-century South Carolina;[1] no books, as far as I know, do the same for North Carolina.

But it is not only scholars who have neglected the South: the South has been ignored by the jural community as well. The South was always a legal backwater, at least in the sense that northern courts, and northern treatise writers, paid little attention to southern authorities. Let me mention two striking instances. The first is the fellow-servant rule. The rule was first hatched in England, in *Priestley* v. *Fowler*.[2] That was in 1837. The leading American decision, of course, is the *Farwell* case (1842); the opinion was written by the chief justice of Massachusetts, Lemuel Shaw.[3]

It is the "leading case," not "first case," because *Farwell* was, in point of fact, *not* the first American fellow-servant case. That was *Murray* v. *South Carolina Rr.*,[4] decided in South Carolina in 1841. Like *Farwell*, it was a railroad case. The plaintiff, James Murray, a man of "intemperate habits" and a "tailor by trade," had gotten himself a job as "second fireman" on the railroad line. He lost a leg in an accident. Some of the judges doubted whether Murray really proved any negligence, but the jury nevertheless awarded him $1,500. There were four separate opinions (two were dissents).

Yet, the southern case was ignored then and is ignored now; however, everybody knows and cites *Farwell* and considers it the leading case. The reasons do not lie in the merits. *Farwell* was an extraordinary document. But this, one suspects, had little to do with its fame. *Priestley* v. *Fowler* was poorly reasoned and socially obtuse, which did not affect its place in legal history. *Murray* was in fact far more perceptive than *Priestley* v. *Fowler*, and it discussed policy issues in an articulate, intelligent way. But a Massachusetts case in the nineteenth century simply had citation power than a South Carolina case was bound to lack.

This point could be documented in studies of citation patterns. Peter Harris measured cites *by* twenty state supreme courts (including Alabama, Tennessee, and North Carolina) *of* cases from other state supreme courts, for the period 1870–1970. His figures suggest a persistent lack of citation power. Southern states did better than certain others (*nobody* seemed to cite Delaware or South Dakota), but no southern state was a citation "star." New York was cited eleven times as often as Tennessee.[5] Of course, citation is not the same as influence. But it is a rough indicator of prestige, as the nineteenth century understood this. Massachusetts and New York were great luminaries, frequently cited by other states. Alabama and Mississippi, most definitely, were not.[6]

The same point can be illustrated in the history of family law. The first general adoption law, we are told, was the Massachusetts law of 1851.[7] Before this, there was no general mechanism for adopting children. The Massachusetts law, sure enough, served as a pattern for adoption laws in the other states.

But, once more, Massachusetts was *not* the first; once more, there was a southern predecessor. This time it was Alabama, which scooped Massachusetts; Alabama passed an adoption law one year earlier, in 1850.[8]

Why are these southern instances ignored? Why did northern courts fail to cite courts in the South? Perhaps to northern courts, southern law was regional—local, not mainstream. Not that Iowa or Vermont did better. But in the nineteenth century, by common consent, there was a *core* to the legal system, a cutting edge, and it was not in the South. This is probably still true, though to a lesser degree, and there has been some redefinition of the core. (Today, the courts of California are cited much more than those of Massachusetts.)

The nineteenth-century attitude can of course serve as an alibi for northern historians. They can ignore the South in good conscience, slavery and race excepted, because nobody worked up the data, and because the past itself treated the South as a lesser light.

But the South does not deserve its obscurity. The lack of research hurts legal history generally. Our theories are based on material drawn from other parts of the country. Whether the theories hold true if we add southern data is, in most cases, unknown. To take one simple example: there has been a good deal of interest lately on the legal status of women. Two books have appeared on the subject of married women's property laws.[9] Both books deal with New York and stress the politics of New York and the women's movements in that state. But the first such law was enacted, not in New York, but in Mississippi (1839).[10] Nobody has written a book about Mississippi, at least not yet.

On the other hand, a lively, fresh, and important group of scholars, mostly young, have taken it on themselves to do something about the neglect of the South. A number of books and symposia have appeared.[11] This is the other side of the coin: it comes from the South's consciousness of itself as a region, as a special place with a special history. Other sections of the country have no sense of themselves as entities. It is an asset the South can well exploit.

What is distinctive about the South? There is, of course, much literature on this point. Characteristics claimed as special for the region are of course also relevant to the legal system. One characteristic, for example, is "the prevalence and acceptance of violence as a means of conflict resolution within the region."[12] The evidence for this comes from figures on southern homicide rates, and the like. A couple of points are worth noting: most special southern traits (identified by southerners themselves, mind you) are rather uncomplimentary. Also, the violence mentioned is not violence *per se*, but violence as a method of resolving conflicts. Nobody claims that mugging in New York is conflict-resolution. Southern violence is supposed to be different. Violence in the South is not the *enemy* of law and order, but a substitute for it: the orthodox legal regime was either imperfectly organized or was rejected by southern society for one reason or another.

Southern violence, then, ties in to another theme: the patriarchal South, that is, the South as pre-bureaucratic, pre-rational, or downright anti-rational (using *rational* in a Weberian sense). This is the notion that leading southerners—the men who set the intellectual, moral, and political tone of southern society—were not really democrats, not believers in popular government. They were not rational capitalists either, but rather semi-feudal in thought, archaic, bound to an ancient type of social order. The planter elite ruled with tough but fatherly grace—love cocooned in a system of manly rectitude. This was of course the basis on which the South defended its "peculiar institution"; the notion comes through strongly in the writings of people like George Fitzhugh.[13] And it was certainly part of the self-perception, or self-delusion, of leading planters.

For example, in her recent, masterful biography of James Henry Hammond, Drew Faust describes her man as "torn . . . between . . . notions of patriarchal dominance and an undeniable need to be not just feared but loved." Hammond wanted his wife to be "both vassal and companion." He had a similar attitude toward his slaves. The ideology of slavery "offered him legitimation in his never-ending quest for despotic sway at the same time it promised that as paternalist he would be both revered and loved."[14]

Take Hammond for the moment as an archetype, standing for the whole class of planters—not the majority of southern voters, but a most influential group. If we want to use terms like "ruling class," or "elite," men like Hammond certainly fill the bill. The desire to be both feared and loved is neither strange nor unusual. In fact, it is arguably quite functional, since a ruler who is feared and loved may be more secure in his position than somebody who is feared and not loved, or loved but not feared. As Douglas Hay suggested in his brilliant essay on eighteenth-century British criminal justice, a regime of terror mixed with mercy can be extraordinarily effective—much more so than a regime of mercy alone, or terror alone.[15]

This "paternalism" comes out most clearly in the relationship of master and slave; but Faust mentions it also in connection with family matters: the wife as both "vassal and companion." What kind of legal order guarantees this sort of paternalism? We have already suggested an answer. The legal system is much better at the vassal part than the companion part. Legal rules can create a framework for *subjugating* wife, child, slave, worker, or subordinate; this leaves to the discretion of the ruler the mercy, the loving-kindness aspect of paternal rule.

This then may be the way to a whole cluster of traits that some scholars claim they see in the South. Southern law is archaic, antirational, nonbureaucratic. It is prone to outbursts of lawlessness, not because southern society is old-fashioned (whatever that would mean) or pre-capitalist, but because the peculiar form of rule that benefitted a landed elite, and especially owners of slaves, implied this kind of legal order.

This general point is the thrust of Michael Hindus' study of Massachusetts and South Carolina, or at any rate, the portion on South Carolina.[16] In South Carolina, rational reform of the legal system was resisted in the name of "absolute preservation of existing authority relationships at all costs." The aim was "to restore a pattern of deference and unchallenged authority." Thus, South Carolina never granted its legal system the Weberian "monopoly of violence." It left plenty of violence in the hands of the planters; regulators, slave patrols, and dueling were also signs of a profound legal privatism. Simply to label all of this as "archaic" explains nothing. Rather, there are solutions here to a particular set of social problems, at least as defined by the planters and their allies.

South Carolina had other legal peculiarities. It was the only state in the Union that, throughout the nineteenth century, allowed no absolute divorce whatsoever. The South was, in general, retrograde on this score. Southern states hung on much longer than northern states to legislative divorce. Divorce was therefore rarer in the South than in the North. Of course, there was marital disharmony in the South, and marriages must have collapsed, just as in the North. But the South was reluctant to rationalize legal status. It is interesting to note, too, that the proportion of men who were plaintiffs in divorce actions was higher in the South than in the North in the late nineteenth century.[17] Divorce was, thus, still a male way to punish a "vassal and companion" who strayed at a time when northern states had already moved to a different stage: mass-produced, collusive divorce.

Much of this is speculative—guesswork, in other words. Hindus' study is a rare example of actually digging into southern records. Other work of this kind has been going on in recent years. Scholars have been busily combing through court records and case reports to find out more about slavery in action, and this is good.[18] But the rest of southern life needs to be explored as well.

Hammond, the planter, died during the Civil War. The last half of the century was not a happy time for the South. Research on this period has also been dominated by race relations, and in many ways none the worse for it. When the northern troops withdrew, a period of white supremacy began with one-party government. The legal traits that scholars saw in the antebellum South lingered on: the same mixture of structure and discretion. The abolition of slavery meant a certain degree of formalism in labor relations, in arrangements between white landowners and black workers; but these were always supplemented by informal arrangements, and a rather substantial, chilling literature describes in some detail the labor system in operation.[19]

One example will illustrate once more the special character of southern legal process—and its ambiguities. I once did a tiny bit of research on criminal records of the circuit court of Leon County, Florida. In this court, up to six complete "trials" were often held on a single day before a single jury. Yet this was not just a criminal court; it did other business too. A best guess is that the typical "trial" took about half an hour. The charge, testimony on both sides, jury instructions, and verdict—all this took place in dazzling speed.

The proceedings are much like those that John Langbein has described for England in the eighteenth century.[20] They are, however, different in some regards from proceedings Robert Percival and I examined in Alameda County, California, for the period 1870–1910.[21] In Alameda County, less than half the felony cases actually went to the jury. The rest were dismissed or ended with a guilty plea. In something like twelve percent or more of the cases, it was plain that the guilty plea was part of a system of plea-bargaining.[22]

There was, as far as one could tell, little or no plea-bargaining in Florida in 1890. The system in Leon County was "pre-professional." In general, criminal justice in this country has traveled a long but steady journey from a system controlled by laymen to a system controlled by professionals. At the outset, laymen dominated the process entirely. Neither party had a lawyer; and the main decisions were all made by laymen—justices of the peace, grand jurymen, petty jurymen, and so on.

Today the system is highly professionalized. The jury has shrunk to a shadow of itself. The grand jury has lost most of its function in many states. Professionals dominate the system: professional police, full-time prosecutors, public defenders, not to mention probation officers, parole officials, detectives, experts in forensic medicine, psychiatrists. The list is endless.

Plea-bargaining is the professional's way of handling routine cases in our system. It is essentially a kind of administrative process. It replaces an earlier (more amateur) method: trial by jury. But before plea-bargaining, there never was a golden age of trials. The trials in the days before plea-bargaining, in routine cases, were of the English sort, the sort described by Langbein, the sort found in Leon County, Florida.

This is worth bringing up because it makes a point about southern legal history, or rather two points that look in opposite directions. The first is the familiar one about southern backwardness. Compared to Alameda County, California, Leon County seems primitive—in professionalism, organization, degree of rationalization. It fits the picture, or the stereotype, that Hindus and others use to describe the Old South.

But we must not exaggerate the importance of these findings, and that is the second point. The mode of trial in Leon County—assuming it is typical[23]—is different in form from modes in Alameda County, but is in many ways its functional equivalent. How different are the *results* of trials in the two counties? Both methods dealt rapidly and efficiently with ordinary crimes. In both jurisdictions, full due process treatment was reserved only for important cases—murder trials, for example. To give such treatment to the theft of a hog, a shoplifting episode, an assault in the barroom, would be a waste of resources (or so the system felt).[24]

Another aspect of southern legal history that stands out is the mode of dealing with conventional morality. On the surface, the Old South and the not-so-old South are in rather marked contrast. Hindus thought he saw a clear distinction between "state supervision of morals" in Massachusetts, though it had calmed down considerably since the furious snoopiness of the seventeenth century, when Massachusetts still carried on its books laws against fornication and adultery, and there were always at least a few prosecutions. South Carolina did not punish fornication at all. The attitude in South Carolina toward adultery and prostitution was rather relaxed, according to Hindus. Not that the state approved of "extramarital sexual activity," but the prevailing attitude was that "these areas were not appropriate to the exercise of state jurisdiction." They were not for "formal authority" to deal with; they were to be handled, if at all, by those who wielded informal power.[25]

There is some reason to be suspicious of this picture. Massachusetts and South Carolina were perhaps more alike than Hindus leads us to think. In the first half of the nineteenth century, concern with fornication and adultery seemed to diminish, except insofar as this behavior was an issue of *public* morality. This point is neatly illustrated by an old Alabama case, *Collins* v. *State*, decided in 1848.[26] Collins was indicted and convicted for living in adultery with a certain Polly Williams. Collins was married, but he also spent one night a week at Polly's house, half a mile from his home. He carried on in this way for seven months.

The high court affirmed the conviction, but the case was admittedly close. The statute spoke of "living together" in fornication or adultery. Fornication and adultery were not crimes in themselves; isolated acts did not constitute crimes: there had to be a definite pattern. Once a week was enough to satisfy the statute.

In other states, statutes were even more explicit: the crime was "open and notorious" adultery.[27] In Virginia, for example, in the Code of 1887, adultery and fornication *were* crimes, but a separate (and more serious crime) was committed if "any persons, not married to each other, lewdly and lasciviously associate and cohabit together, or, whether married or not," carry on "open and gross lewdness and lasciviousness."[28]

Whether we accept Hindus' picture or not, there is no question that there was, all over the country, a rebirth of interest in victimless crime at the very end of the nineteenth century and on into the twentieth,[29] and Massachusetts, with its book-snooping, its Watch and Ward Society, marched along with the nation, if not at the head of the parade. But the South perhaps outdid the North in purity. The heart of prohibition was in the South. The South was the stronghold of traditional values. The Bible Belt is southern, and the Scopes trial took place in the South.

To be sure, the crusade against red-light districts was a national movement, and its great document was the Chicago Vice Commission Report of 1911, which exposed the "social evil" in that city. But the campaign had its southern phase as well, which closed down Storyville in New Orleans and drove prostitution underground, at least for a while. The influence of this movement lingered longer in the South than elsewhere. And, as far as I know, no northern state ever tried to ban cigarettes completely, as Arkansas did for a while in the early twentieth century.[30] The *legal* battle against sin, sodomy, and pornography is fought, apparently, more tirelessly, consistently, and openly in the South than elsewhere in the country.

This is another theme well worth exploring. What it illustrates, perhaps, is the fragility of southern society—or at any rate, its *sense* of fragility. Southern intolerance of other ways of life reflects some deep sense of threat, some prodding insecurity. We punish people who have different codes of morals, different styles of life, only when we feel that heresy, if left unchecked, can destroy our society utterly.

Both the attitude of live-and-let-live, which Hindus thought he saw in the antebellum South, and the Puritanism (if we can call it that) of the later period may reflect, paradoxically, a single, basic idea: traditional morals must be preserved at all costs. Disagreement went only to the question of method. In James Hammond's South, planters held on to moral hegemony the same way they ruled in general, preferring informal means to formal law. In the late nineteenth century, for whatever reasons, different (and more formal) tactics seemed in order. The *ideas* underlying crackdown campaigns were older than the campaigns themselves. Similarly, the Jim Crow laws of the 1890s do not tell us when segregation and white supremacy began. Quite the contrary.[31] The morals laws of the period have to be read the same way. They were a new tactic, not a change in ideology.

Why was the tactic considered necessary? Why more so in the South than elsewhere? These are difficult, complicated questions with no satisfying answers. The sense of vulnerability is crucial. Persecution is an index of fear. This is not a southern generalization, but a national one. The witch hunts of the 1920s, the crusades against the Mormons in Utah, book-bannings and book-burnings, the McCarthy era—these illustrate the same simple point.

But fear of what? The morals crusades presuppose that society cannot, will not, survive, if it abandons *official* commitments to old-time morality. Stress the word *official* because everybody knows that the flesh is, has been, and always will be weak. Nothing will alter its weakness. But many people are convinced that, to keep society stable, they must fight for the old moral code, that people will turn totally to sin and debauchery if sin is not outlawed, and kept outlawed. Laws do not prevent sin altogether, but people sin less often, less openly, and with more guilt when sin is illegal.

We often hear about "unenforceable laws." Prohibition is cited as a prime example. The phrase is misleading. No law is unenforceable if enough effort and muscle go into enforcement. It is also wrong to say, as some careless writers do, that "nobody" obeyed prohibition, except those who were dry to begin with. Some people did stop drinking, and those that drank at least changed their forms and habits of drinking, if not the amount.[32] This is true of other laws as well. Maybe nobody obeys the speed limit, but everyone slows down when a patrol car goes by, to give only one example.

This discussion may appear far afield, at least in regard to southern legal history. The point is this: there seems to be, on the surface at least, a consistent set of attitudes that southern law reflects and that contrasts at least in details with legal culture and behavior in other parts of the country. And the traits seem to hang together, in ways not always easy to explain; they seem to fit other aspects of southern history and the character of southern society. Certainly there is much here that deserves new research.

What underlies these traits? As far as the fear just mentioned is concerned, the obvious candidate is once again, and inescapably, race. The white South was always more homogeneous than the white North, but the white South sat on top of a mass of suppressed blacks, a population the South did not and could not trust, a constant enemy within. Where a dominant population had the same sort of fear—the Chinese in California come to mind—we tend to find similar intolerance. But race was special in the South, and the sheer numbers of blacks produced a unique social structure. California was anxious to drive out its Chinese, who were only a tiny minority; the South hated but needed its millions of blacks. This brute demographic fact may support a whole cluster of attitudes, which affected in turn the shape of the law and of legal process. At least this is somewhere to start.

This essay has said little or nothing about economic regulation. Here again, there is a received wisdom—the recalcitrant, conservative South: southern reluctance to join the parade to regulate industry, reluctance to ban child labor, reluctance to enact welfare laws, to tax and control and to spend. Mississippi was the last state to pass a workmen's compensation law (1948). All other states passed theirs between 1913 and 1920.[33] The Keating-Owen Bill (1916), designed to ban the products of child labor from interstate commerce, passed the United States Senate by a vote of 56 to 12; 10 out of the 12 no's were from Southern textile states, and the test case, *Hammer* v. *Dagenhart*, came from North Carolina.[34] In this as in other regards, including, of course, civil rights, the impulse to nationalize or federalize issues grew out of regional jealousies, and the South was the odd region out.

Of course, the story is not that simple. There was strong support in the South for child labor laws, along with the opposition. And many southerners saw such laws as another attempt by northern capital to keep the South in its place. Textile manufacturing moved from North to South, and then out completely, to places like South Korea and Taiwan. Whether this is good or bad for the country, or the world, is not for legal historians to say. But economic currents color the struggle over child labor. Almost everybody could agree that young children do not belong in coal mines; but the child labor issue was inextricably tied to a larger debate and a larger struggle over labor relations, unionization, and the best way to boost the economy.

Differences among regions tended to be differences in timing, pace, and manner, not differences in fundamentals. If one compares the typical southern statute book of, say, 1910 with its northern or western equivalent, the overwhelming impression is one of similarity, not difference. Take, for example, Arkansas, which I have labeled, possibly wrongly, as a stronghold of southern legal puritanism. In 1906 (Act 69), the Arkansas legislature abolished the fellow servant rule for railroad companies, coal mine companies, and corporations in general. A 1911 statute (Act 88) strengthened this law in regard to railroads. Interestingly, this statute had a comparative negligence clause: "the fact that an employee may have been guilty of contributory negligence shall not bar a recovery" if the negligence was of "lesser degree" than the negligence of the common carrier.

Of course, these too are surface perceptions, and close research on underlying realities might reveal a vast, unbridgeable gulf between the living law of New Hampshire or Oregon and that of Alabama or Tennessee. It is by no means clear whether this is so or not. Here I must stress, once more, how much we need southern history, not just for the sake of the South, but for the sake of all legal historians. We need the South—to test ideas, to check out hypotheses, to prove by comparison.

Return to an earlier example: the law of adoption. The statute that gets the credit was passed in Massachusetts in 1851. In fact, Alabama came first. Aside from possible wounded feelings in Alabama, who cares? In one sense, nobody. But *theories* about adoption law might depend on the sequencing here. Lately, there has been a good deal of interest in the history of family law; a number of scholars are at work in this field.[35] Some of these scholars have tried to explain the rise of adoption law at this time in terms of changing family structure. They discuss a decline in the power of fathers and a rise in the authority of judges.

Another theory, which is in some ways more compelling, stresses something quite different: mass ownership of land. Changes in family law are seen as attempts to provide easy, orderly, and standard methods of selling, giving, and devising land. Without this factor to worry about, who would care whether a child was adopted or simply living with foster parents?

Perhaps neither theory is right; perhaps both of them are. The point is that the speculation is based on Massachusetts data, not data from Alabama. The Alabama statute casts doubt on both theories! Alabama land was less widely held than land in Massachusetts, and families were presumably more patriarchal. By rights then, Massachusetts should have been first with its law; Alabama should have lagged years behind. At the very least, the Alabama statute invites us to reexamine our premises, with special reference to southern conditions.

One final point, about the possible convergence of North and South. The South had a unique identity in the nineteenth century. Is it possible that all this has ended? Can it be that southern legal history (and southern history in general) concerns a culture that no longer survives, that there is, in short, no longer any South? It may have been swallowed up in something else, the so-called Sun Belt, which includes such exotic places as New Mexico and, heaven help us, California.

The convergence thesis is not specifically about the South; it is about the country as a whole. The notion is that the United States is now an economic, political, and cultural unit. What was distinctive about South or North is now widely diffused. The one-party South has vanished. Black culture is no longer southern. More blacks live in northern cities than in southern ones. The South has given us its peculiar institution, and the result is a society neither peculiar nor southern any more. Even warm weather is no longer a unique southern property. The lower Southwest is even warmer, and so is Hawaii. Important parts of the South are not especially southern, if they ever were: southern Florida, for example.

Convergence is inevitable because of modern technology, mass communication, and the American habit of mobility. Business is interstate; so is the workforce. The junior executive transfers from Philadelphia to Atlanta, then back to Denver. Workers drift from Detroit to Houston, and from Birmingham to Phoenix. Television and the movies spread the national uni-culture; even "local" news on TV is cut from a uniform pattern, so strikingly similar that only the weather map tells you what city you are in. There is no regional architecture to speak of: office buildings, like airports, are the same in every city, for example. Indeed, the line between city and country is not what it used to be. Television is as pervasive in Keokuk, Iowa, as it is in New York City. The isolation of small town life has disappeared.

All this should imply convergence in legal systems, and there is evidence that this has happened.[36] If the social order has converged or melted down in some sort of melting pot, then one must expect the same thing in the legal order, too. I will not belabor the point. Southern historians will document this notion—or disprove it; the last word will be theirs. They will let us know if their field is part of a continuing *special* story; whether it is an island, or a river lost now in the great American sea.

NOTES

[1] Jack K. Williams, *Vogues in Villany, Crime and Retribution in Ante-Bellum South Carolina* (Columbia, S.C., 1959); Michael S. Hindus, *Prison and Plantation: Crime, Justice and Authority in Massachusetts and South Carolina, 1767–1878* (Chapel Hill, N.C., 1980).

² 150 Eng. R. 1030 (Ex. 1837).

³ *Farwell* v. *Boston & Worcester Railroad Corp.*, 45 Mass. (4 Met.) 49 (1842); Lawrence M. Friedman and Jack Ladinsky, "Social Change and the Law of Industrial Accidents," *Columbia Law Review*, LXVII (1967), 50.

⁴ 25 S.C.L. (1 McMul.) 385 (1941).

⁵ Peter Harris, *The Communication of Precedent Among State Supreme Courts* (Ph.D. dissertation, Yale University, 1980), cited in Lawrence M. Friedman, *et al.*, "State Supreme Courts: A Century of Style and Citation," *Stanford Law Review*, XXXIII (1981), 773. For a comprehensive set of measures of prestige and influence confirming the generally low ranking of southern high courts, see Rodney L. Mott, "Judicial Influence" in *American Political Science Review*, XXX (1936), 295.

⁶ Another quick exercise in empiricism would be to thumb through Christopher Langdell's *Cases on Contracts* (Boston, 1870), the Gutenberg Bible of the case-method, and other early case-books. In Langdell, the vast majority of the cases were English. The American cases were from New York and Massachusetts, with only a few exceptions. Not a single contracts case worthy of notice, or which first or best illustrates some principle of law, ever came out of the states of the old Confederacy, as far as Langdell was concerned.

⁷ Massachusetts, *Laws* (1851), ch. 324. See Joseph Ben-Or, "The Law of Adoption in the United States: Its Massachusetts Origins and the Statute of 1851," *New England Historical & Genealogical Register*, CXXX (1976), 259.

⁸ See Alabama, *Statutes* (1849–50), Act 79, on procedures to be followed "whenever any person or persons shall desire to alter or change the name of any child or children adopted by him or her, or shall desire to adopt any child or children without such change of name, so as to enable such child or children to inherit his or her estate."

⁹ Peggy A. Rabkin, *Fathers to Daughters: The Legal Foundations of Female Emancipation* (Westport, Conn., 1980); Norma Basch, *In the Eyes of the Law: Women, Marriage and Property in Nineteenth-Century New York* (New York, 1982).

¹⁰ Mississippi, *Laws* (1839), ch. 48.

¹¹ A noteworthy example is the Symposium on the Legal History of the South in the *Vanderbilt Law Review*, XXXII (1979).

¹² James W. Ely, Jr. and Terry Calvani, "Foreward," *ibid.*, 3.

¹³ *Sociology for the South; or the Failure of Free Society* (Richmond, Va., 1854), is the classic apology for the southern social order.

¹⁴ Drew G. Faust, *James Henry Hammond and the Old South: A Design for Mastery* (Chapel Hill, N.C., 1982), 381.

¹⁵ Douglas Hay, "Property, Authority and the Criminal Law" in Hay, *et al.*, *Albion's Fatal Tree: Crime and Society in Eighteenth-Century England* (New York, 1975), 17–64.

¹⁶ Hindus, *Prison and Plantation*, 249.

¹⁷ Lawrence M. Friedman and Robert V. Percival, "Who Sues for Divorce? From Fault through Fiction to Freedom," *Journal of Legal Studies*, V (1976), 61, 72, 74.

¹⁸ See, for example, Daniel J. Flanigan, "Criminal Procedure in Slave Trials in the Antebellum South, *Journal of Southern History*, XL (1974), 537–64; A. E. Keir Nash, "Reason of Slavery: Understanding the Judicial Role in the Peculiar Institution," *Vanderbilt Law Review*, XXXII (1979), 7–218.

¹⁹ William Cohen, "Negro Involuntary Servitude in the South, 1863–1940: A Preliminary Analysis," *Journal of Southern History*, XLII (1976), 31–60; Pete Daniel, *The Shadow of Slavery: Peonage in the South, 1901–1969* (New York, 1972).

²⁰ John H. Langbein, "The Criminal Trial Before the Lawyers," *University of Chicago Law Review*, XLV (1978), 263–317.

²¹ Lawrence M. Friedman and Robert V. Percival, *The Roots of Justice: Crime and Punishment in Alameda County, California* (Chapel Hill, N.C., 1981).

²² Lawrence M. Friedman, "Plea Bargaining in Historical Perspective," *Law and Society Review*, XIII (1979), 247–60.

²³ David Bodenhamer has found plea-bargaining in Georgia in the nineteenth century, and

thus it is clear that the Leon County pattern is not universal and may even be unusual. David J. Bodenhamer, "Patterns of Criminal Sentencing in Antebellum America: A North-South Comparison," unpublished paper, Academy of Criminal Justice Sciences, Louisville, Ky., March 1982.

[24] It is possible that there are in fact important differences in outcome, too, but research to show this is lacking so far.

[25] Hindus, *Prison and Plantation*, 49.

[26] 14 Ala. 608 (1848).

[27] Illinois, *Revised Statutes* (1845), ch. 30, Sec. 123; California, *Laws* (1871–72), 380 ("open and notorious cohabitation and adultery").

[28] This carried a fine of $50 to $100; for a second offense one could be jailed for six months to a year. Fornication and adultery, on the other hand, were to be fined "not less than twenty dollars." Virginia, *Code of 1887*, secs. 3786, 3787.

[29] See Lawrence M. Friedman, "Notes toward a History of American Justice," *Buffalo Law Review*, XXIV (1974), 111.

[30] Arkansas, *Laws* (1907), No. 280.

[31] C. Vann Woodward, *The Strange Career of Jim Crow* (2nd ed., New York, 1966).

[32] See J. C. Burnham, "New Perspectives on the Prohibition 'Experiment' of the 1920's," *Journal of Social History*, II (1968), 51.

[33] See Friedman and Ladinsky, "Social Change and the Law of Industrial Accidents," 50.

[34] See Stephen B. Wood, *Constitutional Politics in the Progressive Era: Child Labor and the Law* (Chicago, 1968).

[35] See, for example, Jamil S. Zainaldin, "The Emergence of a Modern American Family Law: Child Custody, Adoption, and the Courts, 1796–1851," *Northwestern Law Review*, LXXIII (1979), 1038; Stephen B. Presser, "The Historical Background of the American Law of Adoption," *Journal of Family Law*, XI (1971), 443. A book on the history of family law by Michael Grossberg is in press.

[36] When Robert Percival and I compared the flow of cases through courts in two counties in California—one urban, one rural—for the period 1870 and 1970, we expected to find enormous differences in culture; we found, instead, enormous convergence. The rural county, San Benito, still has a small population—18,000—but it is part of the general culture. Friedman and Percival, "A Tale of Two Courts: Litigation in Alameda and San Benito Counties," *Law and Society Review*, X (1978), 267. We should have suspected, during our field research when we found bagels and cream cheese for sale in the county seat, that something was happening to small-town America. The something was convergence.

Part II
Law and the Southern Economy

Law and the Antebellum Southern Economy: An Interpretation

TONY A. FREYER

THE HISTORY OF law and the antebellum southern economy has yet to be written. There are, of course, many studies of slavery, but as important as the peculiar institution was, it represented only one dimension of the southern legal and economic order. Any attempt to consider that order as part of a wider social system necessarily confronts two basic questions. The first involves the degree to which "slaveocracy interests" and democratic politics influenced governmental policies; the second concerns the extent to which these policies differed from those fashioned outside the South.[1]

Historians who have addressed these questions have not agreed. Marxists have argued that, despite the triumph of Jacksonian democracy in the 1830s, slaveholders exercised a hegemony through which government policies reflected the interests of the slaveholding class. To the extent that Marxists have considered the question of southern distinctiveness in legal-economic relations beyond criminal and slave law, they seem to have suggested that, but for a few significant exceptions, policy outcomes were similar in the North and South.[2] Non-Marxists have contended that democracy fostered a political culture in which slaveholders, in spite of their superior economic power, were forced to bargain with and concede to the interests of the great majority of nonslaveholders. Ironically, in so far as non-Marxists have addressed the question of policy distinctiveness, they agree with the Marxists that North and South pursued a similar course, even though, in the end, the South's development was retarded.[3]

This essay attempts neither to present a definitive history of law and the southern economy nor to resolve the Marxist–non-Marxist debate. The purpose is rather to consider salient features of the antebellum South's political economy in terms of an analytical framework that might be useful in further considerations of the subject. The study will approach the legal process as a device for maintaining social order in a society characterized by a great disparity of wealth and power existing alongside democratic institutions.[4] In such a democratic society the law may be understood as a means by which resources were allocated among social classes.[5] The argument is that southern courts and legislatures helped preserve social equilibrium through a proportionate distribution of goods and services from large propertied classes to small or nonpropertied classes. While this distribution was rarely if ever equitable, it nonetheless helped to weaken social-class solidarity and could even foster a basis for interclass association.[6]

Attention to the distributive character of law places the issue of policy distinctiveness in a new light. The formal, legal means of resource allocation may have been similar in the North and South. What distinguished the policy results in the two regions, however, were the groups whose interests the legal process enforced. Although there were certainly social class differences in both the North and South and the small and middling propertied classes constituted a majority in both regions, the basis of wealth in the South was, of course, slavery. If the law served a distributive purpose, how did it affect the power of the large slaveholding class versus other groups in southern society? The answer to this question is that differences in policy outcomes between North and South grew out of conflicts between large and small or nonslaveholding interests, which resulted in the perpetuation of the large slaveholder's power. In the resolution of these conflicts, policies emerged that limited the South's economic development compared to the North's, as was evident in the areas of transportation, credit, and property.

Government aid to railroads had a distributive impact.[7] Like the rest of the nation, railroad construction in the South confronted a chronic scarcity of capital, which created the necessity for government finance and taxation. There were four sources of government aid—federal, state, municipal, and county—but it was state and local governments that provided most of the tax support.[8]

Diverse motivations underlay southerners' acceptance of the tax burden that made this support possible. In *The Southern Banner* of 1840, "Neckar" exclaimed that "Great Profits" could be "undoubtedly anticipated" from building a railroad line.[9] Intense local rivalries, leading to political logrolling, revealed additional interests at stake in legislative battles over railroad charters. The Columbus (Ga.) *Enquirer* exclaimed that the "great object" in getting a certain charter from the Georgia assembly was to give that community "the power to control and prevent the construction of a railroad by way of West Point to Montgomery." The obstruction effort was essential for the town's property owners, for "if those owning property here do not make it, then it cannot be expected that others, having but little interest involved, will do it for them."[10]

The multiplicity of local interests resulted in trade-offs, which in turn sustained demands for equalization of opportunity. "[W]hen government purposes to extend aid to private enterprise," one commentator noted, "it is duty bound to do this in such a manner as to benefit the greatest number possible."[11] Such logic could appeal to small farmers on the fringes of the worldwide staple economy. One such promoter in Hart County, Georgia, located on the northern edge of Augusta, called for a railroad link to Augusta at a public meeting in 1858 in the town of Hartwell. A railroad would, he exclaimed, "be a link in the iron chain that would girdle the world—that the electric wire would follow the line, and that the pulses of Europe and the British Isles might be felt to throb in the quiet town of Hartwell. . . . And the lack of transportation would no longer confine our home products to home consumption."[12]

Other interests looked to the railroad as a means to diversify their business beyond cotton. Merchants in cotton growing areas looked to the up-country as a new market where, as one newspaper pointed out, a "new, and an essentially different trade" existed. Prior to the construction of the railroad, "our trade has been almost exclusively connected with the cotton business; hereafter it will embrace an illimitable field of production," from the "rich valleys of Tennessee" to the "teeming bosom of . . . the Mississippi."[13] Merchants' desire to improve the economic status of the local community could override concern for the cotton planter's interests. A report criticized a road in Georgia that permitted a line with railroads in South Carolina. *"It is true that equal facilities are afforded the planter* [by the road]," it read, "but . . . it threatened a constant drain from the state of Georgia, for the benefit of South Carolina."[14]

In battles over construction of particular routes, planters and their critics resorted to arguments based on class. A North Carolina government report charged that several charters being sought in the legislature were "only calculated to benefit the rich, at the expense of the poor."[15] A New Orleans booster, in an effort to get support of a local property tax that would aid railroad construction, condemned the planters (who would pay the bulk of the tax and therefore opposed it in the legislature) as an owner class who "live on the princely revenues of their estate and . . . inheritances while the toiling, diligent merchants . . . labor the whole year round . . . supporting themselves and adding to the wealth of the community." These landlords, he exclaimed, "produce nothing in reality and enjoy the wealth of the community." For these views, he was castigated as an agent of socialism and agrarianism by "levying a tax on one portion of citizens and making them contribute against their will to promote the interests of another class of society."[16] In Mississippi, planters who lived in the cotton growing counties along the River resorted to class-conflict appeals when they opposed railroads for the northern and eastern portions of the state. There were similar attacks arising from railroad controversies in South Carolina, Alabama, and elsewhere.[17]

Inseparable from these considerations was a concern about loss of population. Population, of course, was the basis of political representation in the U.S. House of Representatives and the Electoral College, as well as state legislatures. Because of this connection, relative population decline within the South as a whole was a continuous source of tension between North and South and between tidewater and up-country sections within states.[18] But a community's economic well-being (whether conceived as local, state, or regional) also was considered ultimately to be dependent upon population. Although rural and urban population was increasing in the antebellum South, growth as compared to the rest of the nation was slower and more uneven.

Many southern communities also encountered a marked difficulty in holding population. A persistent population shift fostered a sense of threat, which in turn stimulated the intense local rivalry that was such a significant factor behind the demand for railroads.[19] That population loss, community well-being, and railroads were interrelated was frequently noted in the southern press.[20] A report from the Alabama legislature urging state aid for railroads queried whether the people's representatives would "stand still and behold unmoved . . . the emigration of her citizens; and yield without a struggle the profits of her remnant agriculture and commence to enrich other states and build up foreign cities that add nothing to her strength and pay no tribute for her protection."[21]

What was the ultimate consequence of these varied motivations and clashes of interest? Unlike the North, the antebellum South never developed an integrated rail system based on trunk lines; but neither did the region construct a system that was subject to the control of the planter class.[22] Although some planters certainly supported railroads, others, particularly those served by water transportation, opposed them. And perhaps more significantly, pressure also came from merchants and even small farmers in towns and up-country counties whose economies were undergoing, had already achieved, or had potential to attain, a degree of economic diversification. These considerations suggest that the social origins of railroad promotion derived from a multiplicity of groups seeking to achieve, maintain, or strengthen the position of a particular local interest.

There were of course winners and losers in these local struggles. And planters, merchants, and other groups resorted to class arguments whether they supported or opposed railroads. But local rivalries more than class divisions were the bases of conflict, which meant that railroad-building in the South was conceived in terms that accommodated as many interests as possible. As a Texas legislative report explained, "Construction of one of these roads would afford little advantage to the people or property on the line of another. To apply State bounty to one, to the exclusion of another, would be unjust and a fruitful source of discontent." Thus, the only "scheme" that could "command public unanimity" was one satisfying a wide range of interests across the state."[23]

Localism, of course, influenced the construction of railroads throughout the nation. But, until the Civil War, considerable regional diversity characterized the antebellum railroad network. Roads in New England and New York established managerial structures that were the basis of the great systems Alfred Chandler describes for the late nineteenth century. The triumph of the systems meant that centralized, private managerial power had displaced the influence of local interest prior to 1860. In the South, however, there was no such victory until after the War.[24] The failure to consolidate the region's roads into unified systems thus represented a significant difference between North and South.

Large planters supported railroads, primarily in an effort to strengthen staple growing areas.[25] Small farmers, storekeepers, even certain merchants wanted railroads, however, in order to bring about economic development through increased population and commercial and agricultural diversification. The failure to construct the trunk lines may have, as Eugene D. Genovese has noted, benefited planters at the expense of this development.[26] But the possibility of such a result should not obscure the extent to which local up-country interests were able to get tax support from planters to pay for railroads that benefited small farmers and storekeepers. At least in the short run, the law supported a distribution of resources from large- to small-propertied classes before the Civil War.

Legal rules governing credit transactions also helped to distribute the benefits and risks of business exchanges. As in the rest of the United States, credit was essential to the economic order of the antebellum South. The large planter's participation in the world market depended upon credit channeled through the factor.[27] The smaller, middle-class farmer's place in the staple economy depended upon credit supplied by the storekeeper. And others of this small-farmer class, whose market orientation may have been marginal, also relied upon credit provided by the country store.[28] Interestingly, even those engaged in subsistence economic activities apparently perceived at times the necessity for exchanges using credit as indicated by the regular appearance of temporary wagon yards that storekeepers erected throughout remote areas of the South to carry on trade through the extension of small loans.[29] To some degree, banks played a role in credit distribution, primarily in cotton or sugar production, urban commerce, and construction of internal improvements. Essentially adjuncts to the factor's business however, banks provided little of the credit used by the great majority of southerners engaged in farming and economic subsistence.[30]

Dependency upon credit fostered a high degree of social interdependency. One Elizabeth Akins wrote Alexander Stephens, future Vice President of the Confederacy, concerning the hardships resulting from the arrest and month-long imprisonment of her husband. His business was "neglected at home," she wrote Stephens, and "without his planning for a crop I do not know how I will be able to make bread for my children . . . I make the appeal to your ever readiness to relieve the distress & I promise you that if you will aid me with a few dollars at this time it shall always be remembered by a grateful heart."[31] An artisan named John Belk made a similar appeal for $25 to the prominent lawyer: "If you will condescend to assist me that much this one time I will be under the greatest obligation to you all times."[32]

The personal interdependence implicit in these exchanges was not unique, in part because they reflected significant political realities. Country storekeepers extended generous loans to their customers, often without interest for long periods. Estate inventories copied into county probate records reveal a similar pattern whereby wealthy planters lent money or sold goods on credit to small farmers, artisans, and the poor.[33] Perhaps as much as twenty percent of such loans, however, were never paid back. Yet, this

did not mean that the well-off creditor gained nothing, for while
a poor debtor might not ever make financial payment, he would
likely feel beholden at election time to vote in a manner favorable
to his benefactor's interest.[34]

The force of personal relationships was also strong among merchants. Merchants' resistance to business incorporation and the
principle of limited liability underlying it suggests the strength of
these bonds. Most mercantile firms in the antebellum South, as
in the nation, were individual enterprises or partnerships. The
social status and economic strength of a firm depended in large
part upon the personal liability of its members. Thus, the limited
liability gained through incorporation was not particularly attractive to southern merchants because it undermined traditional
bonds of individual accountability.[35] Merchants and other southerners transferred their distrust of corporate forms to banks. This
distrust, as one commentator has noted, grew in part out of the
"fear" that "quasi-political delegations" implicit in the economic
terms of credit transactions "would give way to more impersonal,
distant, and invulnerable ways of conducting business."[36] Although banks were clearly vital to the southern economy, and certain of the region's planters and businessmen had even supported
the Bank of the United States, most southerners preferred to deal
personally with merchants rather than "heartless" corporations.[37]

In other ways, law sustained personal relationships. The law of
agency governing the status of factors and planters in disputes that
arose from the marketing of the cotton crop attempted to balance
the interests of both groups without favoring one over the other.[38]
But perhaps the single most important example of the law's influence involved debt default and recovery. The law of insolvency
or bankruptcy—the difference between the two was unclear during the antebellum period—governed debtor-creditor rights.[39]
Because the law never established an unqualified distinction between insolvency and bankruptcy, the ultimate beneficiaries were
debtors—and virtually every property holding southerner was a
debtor.[40] As one Alabama lawyer explained, "They [the proper-
tied] all run in debt . . . never pay cash, and are always one year
behind hand. They wait for a sale of their crops. The roads are

bad, the prices low. They cannot pay. They all wait to be sued. A suit is brought—no defense is made—an execution is taken out and is paid with all the costs and they even think it is a good bargain. The rate of interest allowed is but 8 pr. cent. So much is this below real value that a man will let his debts go unpaid, pay interest and costs and buy negroes for making cotton or land and think it even then profitable and will be much obliged to his plaintiff if he will wait for the due course of law and not personally fall out with him."[41] The case files of insolvents in the federal district courts of the District of Columbia suggest a similar record of debt among those whose businesses failed in nearby Virginia communities.[42]

A significant instance of the laws enforcing social reciprocity was its sanction of the practice of using preferential creditors. According to this practice, a bankrupt debtor could choose to pay off one or several creditors while giving little or nothing to the rest. Such a debtor would transfer his assets to the preferred creditor by endorsement of a bill or note. Through a personal agreement—or accommodation—the preferred creditor, upon receiving the bill or note, would take only a small part of what was owed him, or perhaps nothing at all. This left the debtor with a stake to start over after he was formally declared bankrupt. The forms of accommodation represented by the practice of preferring creditors could become quite complex. The sort of loans recorded in estate inventories between wealthy planters and the poor and storekeeper loans made without interest to small farmers represented forms of accommodation.[43] Many loans made by factors and banks to large planters were also consistent with these forms.[44] But even though the law sanctioned the social bonds underlying debtor-creditor relations, it did so within limits. On occasion merchants attempted to push measures through their legislatures that would benefit them at the expense of other debtor interests. Sometimes the pressure for such legislation reached the point in which merchants ignored states' rights and called for a national bankruptcy law. But state legislatures and Congress gave in to such pressures only rarely, and the measures passed did not stay in force long.[45] On the whole then, law in the South favored debtors, but not to the point of singling out merchants at the expense of either poor whites or planters.

Sustaining the social reciprocity and interdependency of debtor-creditor relations was the legal principle of negotiability. Negotiability was the principle by which bills and notes were legally transferred from one person to another. Given the nation's persistent scarcity of specie and its confused currency, the credit represented by innumerable transactions of negotiable paper was crucial to economic life. And such practices as the preference of creditors—which depended upon transfer of assets through the assignment of bills or notes—would have been considerably more difficult if not for the legal guarantees inherent in the negotiability principle.[46] The U.S. Supreme Court's decision of *Swift* v. *Tyson* in 1842 significantly encouraged state courts to adopt the rule of negotiability; by the 1850s, high courts in Alabama, North Carolina, Arkansas, and Tennessee followed the *Swift* rule. In doing so, southern courts supported a legal principle that made possible certain business practices that benefited debtors of all classes.[47]

Though the role of debtor-creditor law in the South was complex, its distributive impact was nonetheless significant. Negotiability, *Swift* v. *Tyson*, and the preference of creditors aided the interests of southern debtors as a whole. But where disputes arose between planters and factors, as occurred in cases of agent versus principal, the result involved *intra*-class rather than *inter*-class interests and hence were not distributive in character. Evidence of one class-interest giving up something to another class was apparent, except in cases in which creditors—planters, storekeepers, merchants—extended loans to the poor or those possessing little property. As noted above, as much as twenty percent of these loans were never paid back. Although addressing this issue in another context, *Hunt's Merchants' Magazine* captured the essence of the situation in 1856. Creditors were making a "sort of gratuitous contribution" to debtors, concluded *Hunt's*, and suggested that a more appropriate means of providing this aid might be the Home Missionary Society.[48]

Peter Coleman noted that, throughout the nation's early history, "the laws of debtor and creditor in the South developed along paths broadly similar to the ones followed in the Middle Atlantic and New England regions."[49] But while the forms of the law were similar, the social relations it maintained differed fundamentally in one sense: in the South while certain small or nonpropertied classes received economic assistance as debtors, they nonetheless felt beholden politically as citizens and voters to the slaveholding planters and mercantile classes. Thus, social bonds and legal rules reenforced Jacksonian democracy, which in turn meant that debtor-creditor law gave even nonslaveholders a stake in the slaveholder's world. Again, southern society felt in a profound way the reach of distributive justice.

The law governing property rights also may be understood in distributive terms.[50] In both northern and southern states the law recognized two distinct approaches to the rights and interests of herdsmen. One common law doctrine held that stock owners were obligated to fence *in* their animals; the other legal principle required a farmer to construct fences around his fields to keep wandering stock *out*.[51] In antebellum Mississippi (as in the rest of the South) the open range prevailed, as one early settler noted. Without "owning a rood of land" a stock raiser could "graze 5000 sheep, . . . from the eastern bank of the Pearl your flock may roam from county to county, till it reaches the margin of the Mobile River, and never be put off the public domain."[52] This largess did not meet with the approval of everyone however. A Mississippi planter complained about the property damage caused by another grazer, the "'old, pirating, fence-breaking, corn-destroying, long-snouted, big-boned and leather-bellied' Land Pike hog."[53]

Mississippi, Georgia, and Alabama courts required even the railroads to recognize the herdsmen's interest.[54] In a typical case from Mississippi, *Vicksburg & Jackson R.R. Co* v. *Patton* (1856), a train hit and killed several horses and a mule grazing on a company's tracks. At the trial the owner admitted that the value of the property lost amounted to between $500 and $600. The jury, however, after hearing a witness testify that the engineer was running the train the "fastest ever," awarded more than $1,200. Because the judgment seemed "vindictive," the railroad appealed, arguing that, under English common law doctrine, stock had to be enclosed. According to the English rule it followed that the company was not liable for damage done to animals on its tracks because they should have been fenced. The state supreme court rejected the argument, holding that the "common law is not adapted to the circumstances and conditions of the people of this State, where the population is not dense, and where there are large tracks of uncultivated and unenclosed lands fit for pasturage of cattle." From the "earliest settlements" of Mississippi, the court continued, people had "permitted their domestic animals to run at large in the 'range,' and to pasture on unenclosed lands; and hence the English rule is not in force here."[55]

Certain southern agricultural reformers did not agree with such sentiments. During the first half of the nineteenth century, John Taylor of Caroline, Edmund Ruffin, and others called for the passage of stock laws that would close the open range. To some, the stock-law issue represented simply a struggle between "haves" and "have nots."[56] A writer in Ruffin's *Farmer's Register* no doubt articulated the editor's views: "Those frequently have the largest stock who have the least land to graze . . . . I understand in the northern states where the rights of property have always been better understood, . . . men are expected and compelled to support their stock at their own expense."[57]

Perhaps in response to such sentiment, some state legislatures and courts did sanction a limited restriction of the open range. In Virginia, North Carolina, and elsewhere, counties or individual towns could, through a majority vote of local citizens, make the stock law optional within their jurisdictions.[58] It is unclear whether battles over local option laws represented, as Ruffin and others contended, a struggle between powerful planter interests and landless or small-farmer livestock raisers. It was suggestive, however, that in Virginia, Ruffin was exasperated with planters in his neighborhood who were too preoccupied with other matters to support his campaign for a stock-law option. And in states like Mississippi, Alabama, and Georgia where many of the South's largest plantations existed, no limitations on wandering livestock were imposed at all.[59] Such a law would, held a Georgia judge in

1860 in another context, "require a revolution in our people's habits of thought and action."[60] It does seem apparent, then, that lawmakers fashioned policy that spread the benefits and costs of the open range throughout classes, though in this case herdsmen seem to have come out ahead.

In other ways the law's treatment had a distributive impact. In an eminent domain case a Georgia appellant court did not hesitate to shift the cost of establishing a right-of-way from the property holder to the railroad. In sanctioning the property holder's interest, the judge admitted the need to protect "all the *vested* rights" granted in the company's charter "in a most sacred manner." At the same time, however, the court was "bound to guard with great care and vigilance, the rights of citizens against all unauthorized encroachment."[61] Another area in which law was shaped to protect one interest at the expense of another was women's property rights. In South Carolina, Mississippi, Alabama, and elsewhere, these rights received legal protection, though not so much out of a concern for women's own legal status as because of a felt need to protect family assets from the claims of creditors.[62]

But perhaps the single most prominent category of property rights involved the law of race relations. Historians have long debated the extent to which the southern legal order condoned a paternalistic relationship between master and slave.[63] Antebellum southerners also addressed this problem. An essay written in 1858 by Associate Justice of the U.S. Supreme Court John A. Campbell, an Alabamian and future citizen of the Confederacy, noted that, among other things, the "connection of husband and wife, and parent and child, are sacred in a Christian State." Yet, Campbell admitted, practical business considerations limited the law's effectiveness in maintaining either Christian or paternalistic master-slave relations. "The liability of the slave to change his relation on the bankruptcy of his master, and the frequency with which occurs," Campbell observed, "has . . . deprived the relation of some of its patriarchical nature." The justice argued that the "great end of society . . . would surely be promoted by withdrawing slaves, in some measure, from the market, as a basis of credit." That such attitudes were acceptable to many southerners was indicated by the fact that Campbell's propositions were in-corporated into the formal resolutions of the Nashville Conven-tion during the debates over the Compromise of 1850.[64]

Whatever position one takes concerning the legal status of slav-ery, the interplay of the institution, the market, and credit re-quire emphasis. Ultimately, the law's overriding purpose was to enable whites to compete in the market. Even the closest human bond was subject to market pressures, and in the end the law did little or nothing to ameliorate this grim reality. But within these market realities there were significant variations, as Mark Tush-net and A. E. Keir Nash have shown (though from quite different ideological perspectives). In numerous cases appellate judges could place considerations of "humanity" over those of "interest." In such cases the law in effect sustained the welfare of the dispossessed against the propertied and thus could be understood in distribu-tive terms.

The law might also sustain the rights of free blacks. In the trial courts of Alabama, whites sued blacks in 29 percent of cases for debt, but in fully 71 percent, free men sought recovery *from* whites because of the latter's nonpayment. A provision of the Alabama code limited free blacks' testimony against whites to cases where the amount at issue was $20 or less. In reality, however, only one case came within that limit, while some 56 percent of the suits against whites involved sums greater than $100, and in 26 per-cent, the amounts involved more than $1,000. Thus, despite the statute, free blacks initiated complaints and made defenses. But perhaps of most significance, blacks *won* in 66 percent of those suits for which existing records permit a determination of the verdict. Further, where a free black creditor sued a white debtor, the courts ruled for the black in 89 percent of the cases.[65] Appellate decisions in debt suits in other states suggest that the Alabama lower courts' treatment of free blacks was not unique.[66] Since free blacks were recognized under the law as second-class citizens in most re-spects, any significant affirmation of their property rights over whites represented a distributive result.

But the distributive implications of property law were not con-fined to slaves and free blacks. The law of eminent domain and women's property rights, at least to some degree, encouraged large propertied interests—railroad corporations and male slaveholders—to turn over a proportion of their property to smaller-propertied or weaker classes. Perhaps the most significant instance of the law's function, however, was the stock law. Courts and legislatures sustained the interests of small or nonslaveholding herdsmen against the strongest and most powerful planters, such as Ruffin.

These policy outcomes did not undermine the planter's power as much as they represented a frank acknowledgement that such power—in order to be preserved—needed to accommodate diverse class interests. Thus, the married women's property laws protected family assets (especially slaves) from creditors; eminent domain protected all property holders from corporate power; and the stock law, even though it challenged large planters' interests, nonetheless did not threaten the value of slavery itself, but rather sustained an economic activity that was vital to small slaveholders who constituted a majority of all those southerners who held slaves in the first place. Why, however, slaveholders countenanced property rights that recognized the humanity of slaves and free blacks raises a question outside the limits of this discussion. But it may be that the answer lies in the southerners' particularist racial attitude, as identified by Gary Mills, Joel Williamson, and Bertram Wyatt-Brown.[67]

Thus the South accommodated divergent class interests through its property law. One fundamental result of this accommodation was that, in return for policies that protected their property rights, small property holders ultimately acquiesced to a slave regime upon which depended the planter's and the merchant's wealth and influence. Another result was that the law sanctioned forms of property rights that, in comparison with the North, retarded economic development. Women's property laws, property-holder implementation of eminent domain, and even stock laws existed in the North, but by 1860 the corporate power increasingly threatened the social interests upon which such policies rested. In the South, by contrast, these policies—in conjunction with those governing transportation and credit—reflected an economic system in which considerations involving the preservation of social and political stability were given priority over developmental efficiencies associated with corporations.

In the antebellum South, as in the North, law allocated resources. Social-class interests certainly shaped and were shaped by this allocation in both regions; the political economy of slavery, however, fostered policy outcomes that ultimately weakened the South's competitive advantage. Contributing to the South's developmental lag was the distributive character of southern law. Law served a distributive function when state taxation made possible railroads for small-propertied classes in up-country and isolated areas; when planters and merchants extended generous loans to the poor or less fortunate regardless of the likelihood that they would ever be paid back; and when planters accommodated the interests of herdsmen and treated free blacks and slaves with a measure of humanity. The weight of small or nonslaveholding voting majorities, of course, influenced such results, but also at work, at least in certain instances, were pressures arising from bonds of social reciprocity that bridged class distinctions. In other cases social interdependency was either weak or nonexistent, but large-propertied classes nevertheless accepted a distribution of resources that favored small-propertied holders. Ultimately such concessions did not diminish the slaveholders' power as much as it sustained it by containing social-class conflict, by fostering acceptance of the value of slavery as the basis of wealth, and by encouraging interclass, socio-political association. Thus southern law served to maintain social equilibrium at the expense of economic development, which in no small measure helped bring about a tragic Civil War.

NOTES

[1] The basic question is discussed in Harry N. Scheiber, "Government and the Economy: Studies of the 'Commonwealth' Policy in Nineteenth-Century America," *Journal of Interdisciplinary History*, III (Summer 1972), 135–151, especially pp. 150–51. The author gratefully acknowledges the assistance of the Charles Warren Center, Harvard University, the Earhart Foundation, the Eleutherian Mills-Hagley Foundation, National Endowment for the Humanities, and the University of Alabama School of Law. For suggestions I also thank

Lawrence M. Friedman, Eugene Genovese, Forrest McDonald, and Grady McWhiney. Rick Sawyer, Alabama Law School Class of '83, was helpful in many ways also.
² Eugene D. Genovese, *The Political Economy of Slavery: Studies in the Economy and Society of the Slave South* (New York, 1967), 163; Eugene D. Genovese and Elizabeth Fox-Genovese, "The Slave Economies in Political Perspective," *The Journal of American History*, LXVI (June 1979), 16; and Morton J. Horwitz, *The Transformation of American Law, 1780–1860* (Cambridge, 1977), *passim*. Although this important work by Horwitz generally ignores the South, where examples *are* drawn from the region they are considered with those from the North, suggesting there was little or no significant difference between the two sections. The major exception (ignored by Horwitz) is the stock law issue examined by Steve Hahn, "The Yeomanry of the Non-Plantation South: Upper Piedmont Georgia, 1850–1860," in Robert C. McMath, Jr. and Vernon Burton, eds., *Class, Conflict and Consensus: Antebellum Southern Community Studies* (Westport, Conn., 1982); and Hahn, "Hunting, Fishing, and Foraging: Common Rights and Class Relations in the Postbellum South," *Radical History Review*, XXVI (1982), 38–43. See also Harold D. Woodman, *King Cotton & His Retainers: Financing & Marketing the Cotton Crop of the South, 1800–1925* (Lexington, Ky., 1968).
³ J. Mills Thornton, *Politics and Power in a Slave Society: Alabama, 1800–1860* (Baton Rouge, La., 1978) and James Oakes, *The Ruling Race: A History of American Slaveholders* (New York, 1982), support this conclusion especially when taken in context with the references to railroads cited in the section on railroads below. For the influence of Jacksonian democracy on internal improvements, see Milton S. Heath, "Public Co-Operation in Railroad Construction in the Southern States to 1861," (Ph.D. dissertation, Harvard University, 1937), and other familiar works by Carter Goodrich and Fletcher M. Green. See also Lewis C. Gray, *History of Agriculture in the Southern United States to 1860* (2 vols., Washington, 1958), II, 933–36; and Fred Bateman and Thomas Weiss, *A Deplorable Scarcity: The Failure of Industrialization in the Slave Economy* (Chapel Hill, N.C., 1981).
⁴ Although resting principally upon criminal justice, Bertram Wyatt-Brown, *Southern Honor: Ethics and Behavior in the Old South* (New York, 1982) develops an analytical framework that I find helpful in the areas of transportation, credit, and property.
⁵ The pioneering study of law as a means for resource allocation is of course J. Willard Hurst, *Law and the Conditions of Freedom in the Nineteenth Century United States* (Madison, Wisc., 1956). Historians who consider the analytical importance of social class in this connection typically stress the degree to which corporate and other large propertied interests are subsidized at the expense of small or nonpropertied groups: see especially Genovese and Horwitz cited at note 2. Gary T. Schwartz, "Tort Law and the Economy in Nineteenth-Century America: A Reinterpretation," *Yale Law Journal*, IX (July 1981), 1717–75; Tony Freyer "Antebellum Commercial Law: Common Law Approaches to Secured Transactions," *Kentucky Law Journal*, LXX (1981–1982), 593–608; and Freyer, "Reassessing the Impact of Eminent Domain in Early American Economic Development," *Wisconsin Law Review*, (1981), 1263–86, explore the *inter*-class social impact of these policies, which did not exploit large property interests solely at the expense of small or nonpropertied interests.
⁶ My definition of "distribution" is taken from John T. Noonan, Jr., *Persons & Masks of the Law* (New York, 1976), 136.
⁷ Ulrich B. Phillips, *A History of Transportation in the Eastern Cotton Belt to 1860* (New York, 1908), is useful, but Milton Sydney Heath's research is of larger scope and by far the best on government-business relations: Heath, "Public Railroad Construction and the Development of Private Enterprise in the South Before 1861," *Journal of Economic History*, X (Supplement, 1950), 40–53; Heath, *Constructive Liberalism: The Role of the State in Economic Development in Georgia to 1860* (Cambridge, 1954), 254–92. See also Carter Goodrich, *Government Promotion of American Canals and Railroads, 1800–1890* (New York, 1960), 4, 46f, 104, 171, 181f, 108f; and R. S. Cotterill, "Southern Railroads and Western Trade, 1840–

66   *Law and Antebellum Southern Economy*

1850," *The Mississippi Valley Historical Review*, III (March 1917), 436; Cotterhill, "The Beginnings of Railroads in the Southwest," *The Mississippi Valley Historical Review*, VIII (March 1922), 318–26.

[8] For figures, see Heath, "Public Co-Operation," 1–33, 229, 252–53. For more general discussion and comparison with rest of U.S., see Goodrich, *Government Promotion*, cited below. For separate states see: MacGill and Meyer, *History of Transportation*, 414–86. Cecil Kenneth Brown, *A State Movement in Railroad Development* (Chapel Hill, N.C., 1928); Merl E. Reed, *New Orleans and the Railroads: The Struggle for Commercial Empire, 1830–1860* (Baton Rouge, La., 1966); Samuel Melancthon Derrick, *Centennial History of South Carolina Railroads* (Columbia, S.C., 1930); Charles Clinton Weaver, "Internal Improvements in North Carolina Previous to 1860," in *Johns Hopkins University Studies in Historical and Political Science*, XXI (March-April 1903), 76–94; William Elejius Martin, "Internal Improvement in Alabama," *Johns Hopkins University Studies in Historical and Political Science*, XX (April 1902), 64–78; Heath, *Constructive Liberalism*, 254–92; and Lewis Cecil Gray, *History of Agriculture in the Southern United States to 1860* (2 vols., Esdhinhyon, 1958), II, 933–36.

[9] *American Railroad Journal*, XI (Oct. 1840), 216 (hereafter cited *ARJ*).

[10] "*Enquirer* of Muscogee," *ARJ*, XIX (July 1846), 439, 440.

[11] "Tehuantepec Railroad," *ARJ*, XXIV (Dec. 1851), 769.

[12] As quoted, Harris, 28–30; for fuller reference to Harris, see note 33.

[13] *ARJ*, XIX (July 1846), 427, 428. See also *ARJ*, XXIV (Jan. 1852), 6; "Camden, S.C. Branch Railroad," *ARJ*, XIX (June 1846), 411; *ARJ*, VIII (April 1839), 206.

[14] "Muscogee Railroad Meeting," *ARJ*, XIX (Sept. 1846), 587 (italics in original). See also *ARJ*, XVI (April 1843), 126; ARJ, XIX (Oct. 1846), 669; Brown, *A State Movement*, 19–20, 22, 26, 28, 63–66, 155, 278, 282; Ambler, *Sectionalism in Virginia*, 124, 175, 180–81, 241–43, 302, 313.

[15] *ARJ*, XVI (April 1843), 125.

[16] As quoted in Reed, *New Orleans*, 89, 90.

[17] Heath, "Public Co-Operation," 45–46, 178–79; Phillips, *Cotton Belt*, 96–97; Martin, "Internal Improvements in Alabama," 75–76.

[18] Fletcher M. Green, *Constitutional Development in the South Atlantic States, 1776–1860* (Chapel Hill, N.C., 1930), 162–64.

[19] Allan Pred, *Urban Growth and City-Systems in the United States, 1840–1860* (Cambridge, Mass., 1980), 38–59, 109–17. Gray, *Southern Agriculture*, II, 929, 936; Heath, "Public Co-Operation," 25–27; Thornton, *Politics and Power*, 292–93; Paul K. Conkin, *Prophets of Prosperity: America's First Political Economists* (Bloomington, Ind., 1980), 27–34, 90, 106–07, 138–39, 153–59, 161, 265, 299–300.

[20] *ARJ*, XVI (April 1843), 124; *ARJ*, I (Oct. 1832), 658; *ARJ*, XVI (Oct. 1843), 300; *ARJ*, XVIII (Sept. 1845), 580; *ARJ*, XVIII (Oct. 1845), 659, 660; *ARJ*, XVIII (Nov. 1845), 759; *ARJ*, XIX (April 1846), 251; *ARJ*, XXIV (Dec. 1851), 789; *ARJ*, XXIV (Jan. 1852), 20, 35; *ARJ*, XXV (Feb. 1852), 86; *ARJ*, XXV (May 1852), 346; *ARJ*, XXV (June 1852), 406.

[21] *ARJ*, XXIV (Jan. 1852), 21.

[22] George Rogers Taylor and Irene D. Neu, *The American Railroad Network, 1861–1890* (Cambridge, Mass., 1956), 41–48, and Heath, "Public Co-Operation," *passim*. But see Eugene D. Genovese, *Political Economy of Slavery*, 164.

[23] "Texas Internal Improvement Convention," *ARJ*, XVI (Sept. 1852), 580.

[24] Alfred D. Chandler, Jr., *The Visible Hand: The Managerial Revolution in America* (Cambridge, Mass., 1977), 81–121; George Rogers Taylor and Irene D. Neu, *The American Railroad Network, 1861–1890* (Cambridge, Mass., 1956), 41–48; and especially Heath, "Public Co-Operation," *passim*.

[25] Genovese and Fox-Genovese, "Slave Economies," 16.

[26] *Ibid*.

[27] Woodman, *King Cotton*, 3–199.

[28] Lewis E. Atherton, *The Southern Country Store, 1800–1860* (Baton Rouge, La., 1949).

[29] *Ibid.*, 48–49, 92–95; Hahn, "Yeomanry of the Non-Plantation South."

[30] George D. Green, *Finance and Economic Development in the Old South: Louisiana Banking, 1804–1861* (Stanford, Calif., 1972), 174; Woodman, *King Cotton*, 93–126.

[31] J. William Harris (Clark University) gave me these examples from his excellent study now in progress on antebellum Augusta, Georgia.

[32] *Ibid.*, as quoted, 288.

[33] *Ibid.*; Atherton, 113–14, 116–20.

[34] *Ibid.*, 281–91. Atherton, *Southern Country Store*, 123.

[35] Kilbourne, *Louisiana Commercial Law*, 116; Atherton, *Southern Country Store*, 158–63.

[36] Wyatt-Brown, *Southern Honor*, 345–46.

[37] James R. Sharp, *The Jacksonians versus the Banks: Politics in the States After the Panic of 1837* (New York, 1970), 55–122, 215–84; Thomas P. Govan, *Nicholas Biddle: Nationalists and Public Banker, 1786–1844* (Chicago, 1959), 217. For southern businessmen's support of the BUS, see John M. McFaul, *The Politics of Jacksonian Finance*, 19.

[38] Woodman, *King Cotton*, 60–72; Ralph W. Haskins, "Planter and Cotton Factor in the Old South: Some Areas of Friction," *Agricultural History*, XXIX (Jan. 1955), 1–14.

[39] Peter J. Coleman, *Debtors and Creditors in America: Insolvency, Imprisonment for Debt, and Bankruptcy, 1607–1900* (Madison, Wisc., 1974), 9–12, 188.

[40] Wyatt-Brown, *Southern Honor*, 345–46.

[41] James B. Oakes, *The Ruling Race*, as quoted, 61–62.

[42] Freyer, "Antebellum Commercial Law," 606–07.

[43] *Ibid.*; and Tony Allan Freyer, *Forums of Order: The Federal Courts and Business in American History* (Greenwich, Conn., 1979), 59.

[44] Woodman, *King Cotton*, 71, 98–126.

[45] Charles Warren, *Bankruptcy in U.S. History* (Cambridge, Mass., 1935), 3–94. Anonymous author of essay in *Southern Review*, cited Kilbourne, *Louisiana Commercial Law*, 9.

[46] Freyer, *Forums of Order*, 36.

[47] *Ibid.*, 53–98; see also Freyer, "Antebellum Commercial Law," 605–08; Richard Kilbourne, "Securing Commercial Transactions in the Antebellum Legal System of Louisiana," *Kentucky Law Journal*, LXX (1981–82), 616–20; Harold R. Weinberg, "Commercial Paper in Economic Theory and Legal History," *ibid.*, 587–92; Woodman, *King Cotton*, 116–19; Freyer, *Forums of Order*, 1–19, 36–52. But see Horwitz, *Transformation of American Law*, 211–12; *Bank of Mobile* v. *Hall*, 6 Ala. *639 (1844)*; *Fenouille* v. *Hamilton*, 35 Ala. 319 (1859); *Reddick* v. *Jones*, 28 N.C. (6 Ired.) 107 (1845); *Bertrand* v. *Barkman*, 13 Ark. 150 (1852); *Nichol, Hill & Co.* v. *Bate*, 10 Yerger 429 (1837). See also cases and discussion in Tony Freyer, *Harmony & Dissonance: The Swift & Erie Cases in American Federalism* (New York, 1981), 46–47.

[48] "Some suggestions on Southern Trade," *Hunt's Merchants' Magazine* XXXIV (1856), 522.

[49] Coleman, *Debtors and Creditors*, 242.

[50] J. Crawford King, Jr., "The Closing of the Southern Range: An Exploratory Study," *Journal of Southern History*, XLVIII (Feb. 1982), 53–70. Forrest McDonald and Grady McWhiney, "The Antebellum Southern Herdsman: A Reinterpretation," *Journal of Southern History*, XLI (May 1975), 147–66; McDonald and McWhiney, "The South from Self-Sufficiency to Peonage: A Interpretation," *American Historical Review*, LXXXV (Dec. 1980), 1095–1118. See also Steven Hahn's work cited in note 2.

[51] King, "Southern Range," 53.

[52] Wyatt-Brown, *Southern Honor*, as quoted, 36–37.

[53] King, "Southern Range," as quoted, 68.

[54] *Vicksburg and Jackson R.R. Co.* v. *Patton*, 31 Miss. 156 (1856); *Macon & Western R.R. Co.* v. *Lester*, 30 Geo. Rep. 911 (1860); *Nashville & Chattanooga R. R. Co.* v. *Peacock*, 25 Ala. 229 (1854). I am grateful to Steven Hahn for these references.

[55] 31 Miss. 156.

[56] King, "Southern Range," 55–56.

68 _Law and Antebellum Southern Economy_

[57] _Ibid._, as quoted 55.

[58] _Hellen_ v. _Noe_, 3 Ire. 493 (1843); _Whitefield_ v. _Longest_, 6 Ire. 268 (1846). William Kauffman Scarborough, _The Diary of Edmund Ruffin_ (2 vols., Baton Rouge, La., 1972–1976), II, 452–53. King, "Southern Range," 55.

[59] King, "Southern Range," 55–56.

[60] _Macon & Western R. R. Co._ v. _Lester_, 30 Geo. Rep. 911.

[61] _Doe exdem Carr_ v. _The Georgia R.R., & Banking Co._, 1 Geo. Rep. 524 (1846). This holding is consistent with the argument for upper-South and mid-Atlantic states; see Tony Freyer, "Reassessing the Impact of Eminent Domain," 1263–68.

[62] Marylynn Salmon, "Trust Estates and Marriage Settlements," unpublished paper, 1979; Lucie R. Bridgeforth, "The Mississippi Woman's Property Act," paper delivered at the 1982 meeting of the American Society for Legal History; Elizabeth Gaspar Brown, "Husband and Wife—Memorandum on the Mississippi Woman's Law of 1839," _Michigan Law Review_, XLII (1943–1944), 1110–1121; Wyatt-Brown, _Southern Honor_, 254–71.

[63] For legal historians' treatment, compare A. E. Keir Nash, "Reasons of Slavery: Understanding the Judicial Role in the Peculiar Institution," _Vanderbilt Law Review_, XXXII (Jan. 1979), 7–218, and Mark V. Tushnet, _The American Law of Slavery, 1810–1860: Considerations of Humanity and Interest_ (Princeton, N.J., 1981).

[64] Henry G. Connor, _John Archibald Campbell: Associate Justice of the United States Supreme Court, 1853–1861_ (New York, 1961), 106–07, 108. For good interpretive overviews of issues implicit here, see Wyatt-Brown, _Southern Honor_, 57–58, 362–65, 378–79; Oakes, _Ruling Race_, 169–79.

[65] These figures are those of Gary B. Mills (to whom I am grateful for the use of his work), "Free Blacks and the Courts of Law in Antebellum 'Anglo' Alabama" (unpublished paper).

[66] See, for example, _Roger_ v. _Norton_, 5 Hayn 6 (1823).

[67] Joel Williamson, _New People: Miscegenation and Mullattoes in the United States_ (New York, 1980); and Gary B. Mills, "Miscegenation and the Free Negro in Antebellum 'Anglo' Alabama: A Reexamination of Southern Race Relations," _Journal of American History_, LXVIII (June 1981), 16–34. But see Wyatt-Brown, _Southern Honor_, 522, whence comes my use of the term "particularism."

Federalism, the Southern Regional Economy, and Public Policy Since 1865

HARRY N. SCHEIBER
with assistance of Greg Schultz

HISTORIANS AND SOCIAL analysts have long been intrigued with the problem of the "colonial South"—that is, the long-persistent southern regional dependence upon the industrial and commercial North, together with the political responses that this colonialism evoked and the impact of persistent dependency upon the southern mentality.[1] Still, scholars remain captive, in some important ways, to the way in which proponents of postbellum "New South" industrialization and regional economic independence conceptualized the problem of dependency in an era long past. We often rely upon inherited analytical perspectives and even upon New South rhetoric; and so, despite some excellent scholarly work on the problem, we tend to deal with southern regional economic development in terms that permit only a partial understanding of the issues. In particular, the legal and constitutional dimensions of the problem in the course of southern history since 1865 have been insufficiently explored. It is the purpose of this essay to approach the history of the southern regional economy and public policy from the perspective of constitutional and legal history; it will suggest a way of looking at the "colonial South" rather different from views that have dominated much of the historical literature.

This study examines in particular some aspects of legal process from the Reconstruction era to modern times that illustrate the interplay of (1) regional economic interests of the South, (2) public policymaking by the southern states, and (3) the framework and

69

dynamics of the federal system as it became progressively more centralized over the past 100 years. How southern regional and local interest groups, and also how the states "as states,"[2] pursued their economic goals will be kept at the fore. In counterpoint with that concern is another, portraying how the lines of influence ran in the other direction—that is, how the doctrines, structures, and dynamics of American federalism affected southern regional policy and legal process in the states and how the South's role as an actor in the federal system has changed over time, especially since 1933. It is in the nature of this inquiry that central elements of southern social and political development—regionalism, states' rights, and the race question—appear frequently but not always in their most familiar modes. For as happens so often when we pull aside the historical curtain to look again at the southern past, sorting out social realities from political rhetoric and the misty images of regional pride is not an easy matter.

I

Despite its prevailing agrarian orientation and the notorious domination of planter elites, the antebellum South produced a record of considerable diversity in the state governments' uses of public power and resources in pursuit of economic interests. The South had shared, before 1861, in the pattern of economic rivalries among the states, rivalries that found expression in a variety of policies, although governmental activism in the South was tempered and constrained by concern to maintain systematic structures of slavery and planter hegemony, as well as by the effects of "agrarian bias" in southern thought. Despite constraints, however, southern policy had been marked by rivalistic state mercantilism; this was true especially in the 1850s, but to some degree it had prevailed in state policy much earlier—for example, in Virginia's adoption of a public works program as early as 1819.[3]

In the antebellum period in the United States generally, the pursuit of self-interested measures by state governments had been given broad play because dual federalism was a reality and not just a constitutional theory.[4] That is to say, the states enjoyed a large measure of autonomy in ordering economic relationships and setting policy within their respective jurisdictions. The dominance of dual federalism in law and in practice assured the vitality of such autonomy for the states. Slavery, of course, was the most important measure of that autonomy. Other aspects of state authority included their extensive range of control—largely unhampered by assertions of Congressional authority or by restraints imposed by the Supreme Court—over commercial law, property law, transportation policy and development, banking (and even currency to a large degree), tort law, the relations of free labor and management, and the disposition and regulation (such as it was) of natural resources.[5]

Rivalry was an important part of this picture in the pre–Civil War period; indeed, it was an all-consuming concern of state leadership. The states saw themselves as rivals with one another in the quest for labor, capital, and enterprise. This sense of rivalry in some instances energized government and fostered the kind of state activity usually termed "state mercantilism." This was the positive side of such rivalry. In other instances, however, a more negative mode of policy formulation and state action was evident. It was defensive, parochial, narrow, and jealous; it could even verge on the paranoid. This negative side of the dynamics of state rivalry found expression in parochialism—a sort of xenophobia—that became a constant, sometimes prominent or even controlling, element of the legal process.

This parochialism found expression in various ways, especially in exclusionist efforts in law. State measures, for example, placed out-of-state producers and shippers of goods at a distinct disadvantage in comparison to their in-state competitors.[6] In political dialogue, it took the form of exhortations to home-state capitalists to free their state economies from reliance upon outside sources of investment and outside control of local economic institutions. Examples of such antebellum parochialism abound in the legislative debates and popular press of the period. DeBow, for example, published a plea by a Georgia spokesman for his state to cease being "only a great plantation for the benefit of Charleston banks"; the writer urged diversification of Georgia's economy and home-owned manufacturing and promoted the idea of a railroad system (such as Georgia actually undertook prior to the Civil War) that would allow the state to "appropriate her own improvements to the building up and enriching of her own people" instead of outsiders.[7] Similarly, the Virginia board of public works called upon the people of their state to seek "freedom from commercial vassalage" by building up their own urban entrepôts for organizing, controlling, and garnering the profits of the state's trade in agricultural goods.[8]

Just as the strident defense of parochial interests—and its common corollary, a call for mobilization of public resources to maximize economic autonomy and advantage—was commonplace, so did it have serious consequences for policy and law. Thus the governor of South Carolina in 1853 championed state aid to railroads in order to protect the state's trade from control by "foreign" interests, that it might be managed "for our benefit" instead.[9] In a particularly vivid expression of rivalistic sentiment, a Georgia legislator in 1847 denounced the idea of chartering a railroad that would allow Charleston to tap by rail into Georgia's state-supported central railway line. He pointed out that Georgia had promoted its central line with its own state resources and for Georgia's own interests; the last thing in the world that he wanted was for Charleston to benefit from it. He declared that he "hoped to live long enough to see an impassable gulf or Chinese Wall between Georgia and South Carolina, that we may be forever separated from her arrogant meddlers."[10]

In the South, as elsewhere in the antebellum United States, the term "foreign" was employed commonly to refer to out-of-state and not merely nondomestic (non-American) interests. Thus "antiforeignism" as a general expression of parochialism was a factor of no small importance in the making of economic policy. It had a palpable effect on interregional investment: there was resistance to plans (as in Georgia noted above) that would give charters or approve routes threatening to draw off trade to "foreign" ports; and there was resistance to permitting outside interests to obtain charters for banks or other enterprises. Whenever the spectre of "foreign" interests entered a debate, at the least it offered an opportunity to latch onto parochialism as a rhetorical device.

The Civil War and Reconstruction period introduced a new

phase of federalism and recast in fundamental ways the context of
both southern regionalism and parochial state mercantilism in the
South. No longer was dual federalism dominant, as it had been
prior to 1861, either in the formal law or the actual workings of
the national governmental system. The Thirteenth, Fourteenth,
and Fifteenth Amendments were of such scope that the revised
Constitution amounted to a second, quite different charter of
powers—one that provided for undisputed national authority in
ways previously unacceptable or ambiguous. We are warranted
in accepting Professor Tribe's terming it "The Constitution,
Model II."[11] Moreover, there occurred in the 1860s a dramatic
centralization of policy responsibilities, with the consequent reduction—though certainly not the elimination—of state autonomy in vital areas of policy.[12]

Coinciding with this new centralizing of power, in the federal
system, dual problems emerged in the southern regional economy—problems that persisted down to the mid-twentieth century. First was the problem of lagging southern regional incomes
and economic development. Contrary to the economic pattern
elsewhere in the United States (with the exception of a few areas
of the North dependent on a single staple or deficient generally in
natural resources), in the South the regions that had been settled
longest experienced a *decline* in relative income; outside the South,
the pattern was one of *rising* relative income of the oldest-settled
regions as they either diversified or industrialized. Second was the
problem of economic colonialism—the economic regime by which
outside interests exercised an exploitative type of control over the
regional economy. The plight of poor whites and the black population in the South, over the course of the ensuing decades, was
a tragic and vivid indicator of the depth of these dual problems.[13]

It is against the background of centralizing trends in the federal
system and these economic patterns that one must explore the legal and constitutional history for perspectives upon the interplay
of regionalism, public policy, and economic colonialism.

II

The most notable aspect of the South's response to centralizing
federalism was, of course, the classic constitutional resort to state

rights' doctrines and the apologia put forward for continuing oppression of the region's black population.[14] This was not, however, the regional leadership's only response either to centralization or to the constitutional doctrines that supported the concentration of powers in the national government. Another southern response focused upon a set of narrower, more technical issues that related to federalism—its doctrines and its operation—in the late nineteenth century.

The first such issue concerned the judiciary bills enacted and considered by Congress during Reconstruction and afterward, especially with regard to the jurisdiction of federal courts. At the center of attention was the matter of federal diversity jurisdiction, the legal mechanism whereby a corporation domiciled in one jurisdiction could remove suit initiated in another one into federal courts. Also at issue was the organization of the federal judicial system itself.[15] What kind of position did the southern leadership take on these issues? And what does the southern role—illuminated by conventional analysis of debates and votes in Congress, as well as other sources—indicate about regionalism and the position of the South with regard to the new federalism?

In reviewing the Congressional debates, one finds that there was very strong—almost uniform—southern support for efforts to curb the jurisdiction of federal courts, especially their diversity jurisdiction. Southern representatives, including border state leaders from Kentucky, Arkansas, and Missouri, were in the vanguard of resistance to expansions of federal judicial authority. In 1880, for example, there was a well-organized effort in Congress to reverse the effect of two recent Supreme Court decisions, *Insurance Company* v. *Morse* and the *Pensacola Telegraph Company Case*,[16] in which the courts struck down state regulation of important economic interests. This congressional effort was nothing less than an attempt to redefine corporate citizenship altogether, so as to preclude the sort of diversity removal that had brought such cases into the federal courts for trial.[17] The author of the revision bill, Rep. David Culberson of Texas, explained that his bill was designed "simply to place such corporations upon the same plane with citizens of the State in which they carry on business."[18] Although he was sensitive to the charge that he was fostering mindless anti-corporation sentiment, Culberson insisted that the 1875 Judiciary Act, which had enlarged the federal courts' jurisdiction and, in his view, upset the balance of state and federal power that the Founders had intended to prevail, should be amended so that it would severely restrict the grounds on which a corporation might remove a cause from the state courts to the federal.[19]

Southern support for the Culberson bill, organized in coalition with western representatives, was strong;[20] and nearly all from the South who spoke out in debate agreed with the sentiments of Rep. John Philips of Missouri, who declared:

> Step by step has the jurisdiction of the Federal courts been extended by positive statutory enactment and the construction of the judges on the bench, until these courts have in large measure taken to themselves the control and trial of cases which in the opinion of the statesmen and jurists of the best epoch of the Republic belonged exclusively to the domestic courts of the States.[21]

The aggrandizement of federal judicial power, Philips contended, amounted to "an insidious process, silent in its operations, stealthy in its approach, and most dangerous in its tendency," leading to the undermining of self-government. "A more effectual instrumentality of despoiling the weak and timid, and oppressing the poor man, could scarcely suggest itself to the most selfish of governments."[22] Similarly, Rep. Benton McMillin of Tennessee complained that the expansion of federal courts' jurisdiction left the states "mere skeletons of what they were . . . and of what it was intended by those who framed [the Constitution] they should be."[23]

With southern support, the House passed the Culberson bill on four occasions from 1880 to 1887; but it failed in the Senate, and diversity jurisdiction continued to be a source of contention and bitterness in the South. To the demands of those who wanted the courts curbed, northern representatives responded that with local prejudice and sectional tensions so notorious it was impossible to expect northern-based corporations to obtain even-handed justice in the southern states. Capital investment would not be risked in the South if the federal courts could not be relied upon to protect it.[24]

The southern position on court reorganization also revealed regional attitudes and objectives. As the result of Reconstruction-era legislation reforming jurisdiction, the federal court dockets had become congested; and from the legal profession, from the bench itself, and particularly from southern and midwestern Congressmen came proposals for expanding the number of district judges and establishing new intermediate appellate tribunals.[25] Some southern representatives spoke in favor of creating new circuit courts, as proposed in 1882 by Senator David Davis of Illinois, formerly a Justice of the Supreme Court. They found in the Davis bill an opportunity to have new judges appointed who would not be so fiercely partisan as those named to the bench during Reconstruction.[26] Augustus Garland of Arkansas, for example, an undeviating critic of the federal courts' diversity jurisdiction and removal rules, saw a possibility that newly created appeals courts, "held to a particular locality" and most likely staffed by people from the regions in which the judges sat, would mean "courts would be localized and brought home to the bosom and to the business of the people."[27] Southerners spoke angrily of "very unworthy judges" sitting in their region, of "disgraceful" performances by the district courts, and of rule-making and decisions prejudicial to southern interests.[28] Southern critics also perceived judicial megalomania: "The United States courts in my State," contended a Louisiana Senator, Benjamin Jonas, "never relax their grip upon jurisdiction when they once get hold of it, or when a suit has been once begun."[29]

Ineluctably, the southern representatives' contributions to the debate turned away fom organizational reform to deal with substantive complaints. Thus Jonas denounced removal of causes under the Reconstruction judiciary acts. Never to his knowledge he said, had a case been removed from the Louisiana state courts to the federal courts "because truthfully of local prejudices"; rather, there had been instances of transfers [that is, removals] of suits . . . which were a complete fraud," and such fraud and deception were the real reason why the federal dockets were congested.[30] Jonas' views were echoed by Senator James George of Mississippi, who similarly attributed the backlog of cases in federal courts to the removal and diversity rules. These rules, he declared, were "but another step in the direction of centralization —centralization of power in the Federal Government, centralization of the money power, centralization of business and professional power."[31] Return to a federalism that the Founders of 1787 could have understood, George argued, and no expansion of the federal judiciary would be necessary. Throughout the debates of the Davis bill, moreover, southern representatives expressed their fears that creation of new judgeships would simply lead to the addition of judges "of the same political faith" (that is, Republican) as subscribed to by nearly all then sitting on the federal bench.[32] In the same vein, Senator Wilkinson Call of Florida, a vitriolic opponent of civil rights for blacks, denounced partisanship in federal judicial appointments; he asserted further that to allow the increase in jurisdictional authority to continue unchecked would endanger the basic institutions of self-government.[33]

Whether they ended by supporting the Davis bill's reforms or voting against them, the southerners who spoke in the debates resorted to strong rhetoric in criticism of the federal courts. They declared repeatedly that outsiders' appointments to the courts fastened political and economic vassalage on the South. Invariably Republicans, the federal judges were hostile to the South, hostile to the Democratic party, and solicitous of the interests of northern corporations and other business interests that faced suits eligible for removal to federal courts. The southern Congressional spokesmen thereby made an explicit linkage between federal jurisdictional issues and economic colonialism. They contended, in other words, that outsider control of the southern economy was being maintained by manipulation of the legal process: northern commercial litigants and Republican judges employed the diversity lever to take important cases out of the southern state courts, to advance northern interests, and to vitiate the autonomous power of the states. They generalized from the technical jurisdiction question to argue—in terms that Charles Beard would have found entirely congenial[34]—that the centralization of political power, under the new federalism reinforced by the Reconstruction judiciary acts, was intimately linked with economic hegemony and the pursuit of northern corporate interests in the South. Although they did not contend that curbing the federal courts was in itself an entire solution to the colonialism problem, southern spokesmen saw the extension of federal judicial power as a central part of the problem. They viewed judicial reform as an important, perhaps indispensable, part of the solution.

By the 1890s the closely related issue of federal receiverships in railroad bankruptcy cases had captured the attention of southern regional spokesmen. A significant proportion of southern railroads—more than twenty companies, owning in excess of 4,000 miles of line—went into receivership in the mid–1870s, many of them remaining under receivers' control well into the next decade.[35] In the 1893 panic and the general business depression of 1893–1897, the southern railroad lines were again badly hit. Some 33 southern railroad corporations, operating nearly half the South's overall mileage, went into receivership in that decade.[36] All these lines filed for receivership in the federal courts, and in the absence of specific statutory authority, federal judges interpreted their equity powers as adequate to establish receiverships.[37] The railroad receivership issue therefore immediately became a highly visible and controversial one in southern politics. It too served to link the issues of economic colonialism and federal judicial power. The fact that many of the bankrupt railroads remained under receivers' control for very extended periods of time increased the visibility of these interrelated issues. Although the attack upon the courts came most strongly from emergent Populist elements in southern politics, more conservative voices were also heard in what became an important expression of southern regionalism.[38]

During his governorship in South Carolina, Bell Tillman, for example, ardently attacked receiverships, making them a major political issue. The equitable powers of federal courts in railroad receivership administration had "no basis in law or justice," Tillman declared,

> and could only spring from that perpetual grasping after more power which characterized the judges of the United States Circuit and District courts. One by one the reserved rights of the States are being absorbed by the Federal judiciary. . . .[39]

Tillman called upon Congress to "restrain the unlicensed and iniquitous powers exercised" by the federal courts in these cases by imposing statutory limitations on the judiciary.[40] The South Carolina legislature in 1894 petitioned Congress in the strongest terms, demanding an end to the receivership control—which already had been in effect for four years—of the South Carolina Railroad. In light of the extensive discretion that the federal court in South Carolina had given this railroad's appointed receiver, the legislature contended, it was "a ludicrous misnomer to call him a receiver of the court of equity."[41] In fact, the receivership established the basis for an arbitrary and unfettered control of the line, to the detriment of South Carolina's economy and, because the court blocked the enforcement of state laws against the road in receivership, the state government itself. Hence, the receiver became, *de facto*,

> a railroad president, with the chancellor as his chief counsel; without a board of directors to trouble or restrain him; without responsibility to mortgage creditors; with a docile, facile court to pass at his behest orders in advance to justify whatsoever he may desire to do. Call him rather a Federal pro-consul, lording it over a subject province.[42]

By authorizing the receiver to resist payment of state taxes and enforcement of the state's dispensary (liquor) law, the legislators charged, "a Federal judge . . . encourages others to be law breakers, and becomes himself an apostle of anarchy."[43]

The real issue, of course, was states' rights and enmity toward northern creditors of the line, not "anarchy." Similarly, in Texas, Governor James Stephen Hogg led an attack on federal courts involving a series of colorful (if not to say lurid) wrangles with two federal circuit court judges and in response to federal injunctions that eventually would issue in the case of *Reagan* v. *Farmers Loan and Trust*.[44] Hogg charged that the state had been rendered impotent by malefactors on the federal bench. As was true of the South Carolina situation, the one in Texas involved some extraordinary manipulation of power and of railroad assets.[45] Neither Hogg nor Tillman was railing against imaginary evils. Yet Hogg, too, generalized the matter to make it one of states' rights. "Has the State reached that condition of retrogression and imbecility that it must remain a helpless witness?" he asked. "Must she admit that her autonomy has at last been destroyed by the Federal circuit judges?"[46] He therefore proposed legislation prohibiting railroad officials from using company property to advance their own private interests in other enterprises—a reasonable enough idea. Hogg also asked the state legislature, however, to require forfeiture of the property of any railroad in receivership for more than three years (whether under federal equity jurisdiction or not) and to appropriate funds for state prosecution of federal officials "when they violate State laws or wilfully infringe on State's rights."[47] The second proposal was disingenuous at best; and the last was clearly demagogic, being a crude, patently unconstitutional tactic to translate political and legal issues into confrontations that could easily lead to use of force.

III

The southern leadership's use of the judiciary issues—diversity jurisdiction and removal, as well as the equity receivership power—raises some interesting questions about what lay behind the tactics. It was plausible enough to argue that outside interests used the federal courts as a lever to control major institutions in the southern regional economy. The issue was a popular one, too, appealing to a warranted outrage over some dramatic abuses of power in the case of receiverships, and, above all, appealing to states' rights sentiment. It cannot be said, however, that these were more than fairly superficial issues so far as the economic colonialism problem was concerned. The attack on federal judicial rules and jurisdiction did not address effectively the real problems of southern economic retardation or dependency. The critics of the federal courts, directing their attack in a way that dovetailed well with racist views, were setting up a smoke screen. With all the noise about this "federalism issue," they tended to obscure the fact that they were doing little at home to correct the fundamental problems that underlay stagnation and dependency.

To a lesser degree, perhaps, the same may be said of the notorious, protracted controversy over the region's railroad freight rates.[48] Years of scholarly analysis, following upon decades of intense political activity regarding discriminatory freight rates alleged to have fastened dependency to the North on major southern economic interests, have failed to produce a definitive judgment as to whether or not rate discrimination was in fact more than a surface issue. That is to say, it is still fair to ask whether the discriminatory rates cut very deeply as a cause of fundamental economic problems in the South.[49] Without denying the symbolic importance of the issue, especially its significance in fostering sectional political collaboration, one can still contend plausibly that the railroad rate issue was only window dressing in comparison with the crop-lien system, public education, racial segregation, and legally condoned discrimination, public health policy, and a host of other issues in law and policy that shaped southern social institutions and economic welfare. Indeed, the enormous political effort poured into the rates question may be seen as another diversionary or obscurantist episode—whether by design, by lack of vision, or by honest misunderstanding—that absorbed reformist energies which might have been devoted more profitably to correction of the region's real problems.

That "the embargo [sic] laid on the Southern States by the extortionate charges for transportation is the chief factor in retarding its growth" was a proposition argued by such knowledgeable southern leaders as Walter Clark, who advanced this view to the annual railroad commissioners' national meeting in 1899.[50] Like others in southern politics who inveighed against federal judicial power and against outsiders controlling southern railroads, Clark resorted to the rhetoric of xenophobia and antiforeignism. By dint of railroad control in the South, he charged, New York and London financiers had become "the real owners of the soil."[51] These concerns led Clark to conclude that the popular election of federal judges was not only a wise but an "indispensable" measure, if the South were ever to get justice from the national courts.[52] To the modern observer, however, it is hard to believe that popular judicial election was potentially a major weapon for dealing with the deeply rooted economic problems of the South.

A similar evidence of political energies turned to matters of federalism that were hardly a core problem of the southern economy was the southern position on anti-drummer legislation. Virginia, Tennessee, Texas, North Carolina, and Louisiana were among the states which imposed license taxes or special taxes upon travelling commercial salesmen who operated on behalf of out-of-state firms.[53] From 1868 on, the annual meetings of the national Board of Trade frequently debated the anti-drummer laws; and southern spokesmen, including representatives from Baltimore, Nashville, New Orleans, Mobile, Charleston, and Richmond, generally spoke in favor of the laws not only on states' rights grounds but also on the grounds that the laws were essential as a weapon the South could wield against economic domination from outside.[54] Unless such laws were permitted to stand, as W.S. Hastie of the Charleston Board of Trade stated in the 1871 meeting, "New York, Boston and Philadelphia will absorb the whole business of the country."[55] Another argument that southern delegates sometimes made was that the war–devastated southern states were "very poor, and have heavy taxes to pay"; they said that licensing and other duties imposed on out-of-state-based commercial travellers helped relieve somewhat the tax burdens carried by home-state citizens.[56] The South did not present a united front on anti-drummer laws in the 1880s. Atlanta and New Orleans were among the cities whose merchants lent some support to the idea of national regulation of drummers.[57] But the southerners who did support the laws traded heavily on antiforeign, xenophobic rhetoric mixed with states' rights doctrines.

The parochial and exclusionist style of legislation represented by anti-drummer laws also included such regulations as the attempts by several states to restrict incursions by boats from neighboring states into their oyster and shrimp fisheries.[58] There was also an interest in anti-alien landholding legislation (not peculiar to the South, to be sure, but given great prominence by Gov. Hogg of Texas and some other Populist types), intended as a response to economic colonialism of a different sort from that represented by commercial travellers or railroad interests.[59] After the turn of the century, moreover, Texas undertook by the Robertson Law of 1907 to force out-of-state ("foreign") insurance companies to invest within Texas all income from premiums collected in the state. This would stop the companies, the author of the 1907 law declared, from "taking from Texas money belonging to Texas people and hoarding it in New York to be there used by the officials of the great insurance companies."[60] Following enactment of the Robertson Law, the Texas legislature adopted still other measures strongly biased against out-of-state insurance firms. Throughout the South, politicians resorted to antiforeignism and the associated rhetoric of opposition to economic colonialism, as they espoused similar legislation in the insurance field.[61]

If the "federalism issues" such as diversity jurisdiction and receivership rules were shadowboxing, insofar as solving southern economic problems was concerned, then certainly the best that one can say about anti-alien landholding laws, anti-drummer laws, and similar legislation is that they represented policy that was defensive, fragmentary, and certainly ineffectual in dealing with either economic stagnation or the economic colonialism problem. Even if such laws had withstood constitutional challenge and had been enforced aggressively, it seems unlikely they would have made a great difference in southern economic development. Moreover, the southern states retained sufficient autonomy and formal authority to attack the basic economic problems they confronted, yet they chose not to use that authority, a fact that goes farther than generalizations about aggressive northern capitalists or about centralizing federalism toward explaining why the South's economic problems were so intractable.

An impressive range of autonomous powers remained with the states, even in a centralizing federalism.[62] For example, the terms on which "foreign" capital came into a state (especially when corporate powers or the routes of railroad lines were involved) were defined by the legislatures without substantial interference from the national government. The states set their own policies with regard to eminent domain, taxation and tax exemption, labor relations, and the regulation of factory conditions. Also among the policies that were formulated and enforced by the states, with practical immunity after 1877 from outside interference, were those pertaining to agricultural labor. As important studies by

Frenice Logan, Pete Daniel, Harold Woodman, and other scholars have demonstrated, the southern state governments were left
with a very free hand in regard to crop liens, share wages, and even
peonage. For example, a combination of "federal [official] apathy,
local custom, and community acquiescence" permitted inhumane
practices in southern peonage to continue for literally decades after nominally successful legal challenge.[63] By dint of the authority
they exercised, the southern state governments harshly limited the
possibility of black emigration; they invited corporate capital on
the most generous and liberal terms (at great cost to tax revenues
and to the potential, at least in the short term, of improving public
services); they bolstered a highly coercive regime of labor-own-
ership relations in agriculture with the effect of keeping the freed
blacks in poverty and a condition of subjugation; and they maintained, through common law decisions and legislation, a policy on
tort and nuisance that gave industry broad license to pollute and
otherwise externalize the costs of manufacturing and mining at the
expense of the public weal.[64] Notoriously, the education and social welfare policies of the southern states in the late nineteenth
century revealed the depths not only of racism but also of a willingness by the people in control to sacrifice learning, public health,
and other humane concerns for the higher considerations that
prevailed: profit and white supremacy.[65]

    The tragedy of such policies, as C. Vann Woodward has writ-
ten, is that they institutionalized irresponsible social attitudes.[66]
Neglect of education and other social services, together with a
willingness to see the cheap labor of the South used as a lure for
investment, became embedded in public and private law alike. The
complicity of southern white elite and middle-class elements in this
process was notorious—an "evil companionship," as Woodward
called it, that linked industrialization with a starved public sector
and exploited workers.[67] Moreover, this complicity sometimes took
violent forms, as in the Virginia and Western Virginia coal regions where the new coal barons recruited local lawyers, bankers,
merchants, and others in support of their blatant use of armed force
to take control of local governmental structures and law enforcement.[68] Moreover, the wave of "reform" in suffrage and voting that

disenfranchised the South's black population sometimes also resulted in the virtual disenfranchisement of mountaineer and other poorer white elements of the population.[69]

Insofar as state and local governments took advantage of the autonomy afforded them by federalism, they exercised power in ways that invited and deepened the effects of economic exploitation. There was an almost incredible absence of positive, coherent, effectual policy directed at the upgrading of human resources. Instead, both the region's natural resources and its labor were offered up on terms highly destructive to southern welfare in the long run.[70] In the minds of some analysts, the economic domination of the South by outsiders in the late nineteenth century was nothing more than the second wave of the Civil War, an economic conquest set up by the success of military conquest.[71] To portray it so oversimplifies the realities. The process by which southern governments and private-sector leadership bartered away the region's resources, environment, and labor, while binding the poorest agricultural workers to the land—and to the region—on harsh terms enforced by criminal-law sanctions,[72] was a process in which the southern elite was making conscious, costly, and by no means inevitable choices.

The southern states in the half century following the Civil War were still setting their own agendas; they controlled for themselves key areas of policy that could have been geared to positive, effective improvement of social welfare and a controlled industrialization.[73] One rough measure of the choices that could have been made were the reform laws enacted during Hoke Smith's governorship in Georgia, in 1906–1907, especially the Railroad Commission Act. Whether Hoke Smith–style progressivism should be termed "radical" or not is a value-laden question that could be debated forever. But there is no denying that the reform measures enacted in Georgia represented a large-scale shift toward public responsibility over key elements of the private sector and that they established a basis for a different kind of economic development in Georgia.[74] How quickly the effect of those reforms was vitiated—partly by capture of the public utilities commission, partly by the succumbing of the Georgia progressives to the lure of an intractable racism, partly by the naked economic power of the interests as they fought back—is a vivid indication of how tragic was the dilemma of the South in that day.

The proponents of New South industrialization varied in their styles of exhortation and celebration of economic transformation. Some stressed reconciliation with the North as a goal and result of industrial growth and investment; others portrayed the New South movement as one that would permit the region to achieve economic independence and, in the long run, enable the South to achieve an ultimate "victory over the hated Yankee."[75] By the turn of the century, however, not only the more radical critics of the new industrial order in the South—leaders such as Hogg, Clark, and Tillman, who led the attack on the federal judicial power—but also some of the South's own industrialists had begun to dwell regularly on the proposition that control of their economic destiny had slipped out of southerners' hands.[76] Historians have accepted such reasoning and contentions as a reality, and, in this sense, have been captured by the rhetoric of southern political dialogue. In reality, the South controlled enough of the policy agenda and commanded enough resources to have set the region on a very different course. To have done so successfully, of course, would have required a transformation also in attitudes toward race, toward the social reponsibilities of state government, and toward the purposes of the active state with regard to economic development and industrialization. That such sweeping transformations—running entirely counter to the prevailing social and cultural realities of the South—did not occur ought not obscure the fact that federalism of the late nineteenth century left ample room for the autonomous government of the states to take a very different course.[77] The legal process and the constitutional framework were not the sources of the problem. Neither, for all the power and influence of northern capital, did the source lie alone in the dynamics of interregional investment. The core of the problem lay in legal and political culture, and in political will.

IV

The nationalization of major reform issues in the 1890s and the Progressive era established a new political and constitutional framework for southern regionalism. The definition and pursuit of interests or goals self-consciously defined by southern leaders and reformers as "regional" now had to be responsive to some basic changes in the national political scene. The establishment of federal regulation of railroads in 1887, the enactment of a national industrial policy (however ambiguous) with the Sherman Act of 1890, the inauguration of conservation programs in the nineties, and the movements that culminated in reforms in tariff and banking policy—all imposed a national orientation on southerners' consideration of such questions and their importance for their region. On the other hand, the same broad trend toward what Dewey Grantham has termed "the nationalization of reform,"[78] elicited great concern in the South that two new dangers were looming. The first concern was that the acceptance of reform initiatives from Washington would lead to a wholesale reception of anti-states' rights, nationalistic constitutionalism that could be the death knell of white supremacy and the dominant southern variant of constitutionalism. The second concern was that by pulling the levers of national power and by pursuing policy goals through federal legislation, the northern economic interests that were seen as exploiters of (or competitors with) the South would find new ways of subordinating southern interests to their own quest for profit and power.

Consequently there were two distinct southern responses to innovations in national policy and to the new claims for national constitutional authority. The first was the well-known Populist-Progressive "reform" response, in which southern reform forces—including the radical reformers of the 1890s and the centrist, respectable reformers of the Progressive era—joined on a number of issues with like-minded political leaders elsewhere in the country. They endorsed railroad regulation, stronger corporate regulation, banking reform, and tariff reductions with proper solicitude, of course, for such interests as Louisiana sugar growers. This support focused on what legislation in Washington could do for the South.[79] Linked with these new concerns were those expressed by the "voices of protest from the New South,"[80] individual reformers who pressed for social-justice measures and educational reform at the state level, whether with the sort of radical bent exemplified by the early-phase Tom Watson of Georgia or, instead, with the conservatively colored style that would spawn the "business progressivism" of the post–World War I era.[81] The second southern response was very different, for it embodied a negative variant of sectionalism on the well-known model of white supremacy and states' rights: it represented the region's capacity for organizing on a sectional basis to fight off reforms that threatened what were seen as vital southern interests.[82] Specific examples of each style of response will illustrate how a changing federal system and shifts toward nationalism in public policy led to distinctive southern responses.

Mobilization of southern support for national banking reform, culminating in strong bloc support by the South for the Federal Reserve Act of 1913,[83] exemplified both the strength and the limitations of the positive southern response to nationalization of reform. The Congressional debate took place, of course, in the wake of the Pujo Committee's celebrated inquiry into the "Money Trust" and against the background of the committee's charges that a clique of major banking firms in the Northeast, mainly on Wall Street, controlled credit and finance throughout the national economy. Moreover, the discipline of White House–led policymaking and party loyalty did much, as Richard Abrams has reminded us, to keep the southern caucus in line.[84] Nonetheless, a close analysis of the debates reveals a rhetoric of sectional animosity and concern to liberate southern regional interests from the stranglehold of northeastern banks; there is little evidence that runs against a contention that the Federal Reserve measure, despite the shift toward national power that it represented, captured the imagination of southern leadership as an issue that was right for the South. In fact, Carter Glass of Virginia, principal architect of the bill, and other southern spokesmen stressed the prospect that creation of regionally defined Federal Reserve districts would accomplish a practical *decentralization* of real economic power even though it was under direction of the federal government. Rep. Percy Quin of Mississippi, for example, contended that "the oppression of special privilege, greed, and graft" was attributable to the concentration of real power in a few privately controlled giant banking firms.[85] In place of monopoly of the money power on Wall Street, he and his southern colleagues argued, the reform bill would give influence and control over credit to district boards representative of their respective regions and on which sat members from banks in those regions.[86] Once the Democratic caucus had successfully incorporated into the bill the hotly debated provision for short-term agricultural credit, there was no question that even in the most radical wing of the southern group full support was forthcoming. "For the first time," Rep. Thomas Heflin of Alabama declared, "a President of the United States . . . has stood between the great cotton producers of the South and those who have so long robbed and plundered them."[87]

Resorting to the expansion of federal power—with all its implications for constitutional practice and the theory of federalism and states' rights—was justified by southerners in Congress on two grounds. The special sectional concern for agrarian interests was, of course, the first. The second was a qualified but nonetheless explicit endorsement of the positive state. Rep. Rufus Hardy of Texas expressed the latter view when he admitted that the Federal Reserve idea "violates many ancient precepts of supposed wisdom" and embraced to some degree the concept of governmental "paternalism."[88] The times, and the magnitude of the evils that were confronted, Hardy went on, absolutely required this sort of departure:

> If this bill be paternalistic, the English-speaking peoples have never refused to adopt just such paternalistic laws when self-preservation or even the undoubted general welfare demanded; their wise purpose always being to preserve the greatest amount of individualism consistent with the highest good for the whole people. . . .[89]

Moreover, the Federal Reserve system itself was modelled upon—and would embody the best results of—the federal system itself: "The success of our various State governments has clearly proven that this diversity [among the nation's regions] renders necessary separate governments to take care of peculiar local conditions."[90]

In the final vote on the bill, the South lined up almost solidly in favor. In the House the southern votes went 106–6 for the bill

(136–13 including border states); and in the Senate the regional vote was 19–0 (26–4 including border-state votes).[91] Illustrative of the perils of pursuing regional interests through national legislation, however, was the debate that ensued once the special commission appointed to select the locations and number of Federal Reserve districts had reported. Intra-regional jealousy and parochialism immediately surfaced, none of it more bitter than the split within the South itself, especially over the naming of two Federal Reserve cities in Missouri, the overlooking of Baltimore and New Orleans in favor of Atlanta and Dallas, and the commission's decision to create the maximum number of districts allowed by the law (twelve) instead of leaving room for new ones to be created in the future.[92] This sort of squabbling and rivalry *within* sectional blocs, once a policy decision had been agreed upon and when distinct local advantages and disadvantages were ineluctably to result from the actual uses of newly granted governmental powers, was to reappear in many other situations in subsequent years. Once set in motion, the political forces born of particularism and localized self-interest do not often attain equilibrium or disappear once a regional interest is defined and pursued; the more purely local, more narrowly focused interests typically demand their due, and it is impossible to satisfy all of them.

There were a few—but only a few—other instances in the early twentieth century when the South coalesced on reform measures that required energizing national government, even if at the expense of state authority. One particularly interesting example was the proposal for establishment of a federal bureau of markets, debated in Congress in 1911–12. Inspired by the Populist demands for government intervention in the agricultural sector, this proposal—even more than the Federal Reserve Act—would have introduced "paternalism" and federal influence in the marketplace on an unprecedented scale.[93] Nearly all the principal sponsors of the idea, embodied in four different legislative versions in the 1911–12 session of Congress, were southerners.[94]

The range of such measures to win strong sympathy from southern leadership or rank and file, however, was small indeed. Most of what did appeal to the South was oriented toward the pressing needs of a beleaguered agricultural sector in international markets.[95] Good roads, vocational and agricultural education, the marketing and banking reform proposals, general anti-trust legislation, the income tax, and rising interest in exercising regional influence on railroad regulatory policy pretty much exhausted the list. Little wonder, in fact, that historians have rather neglected (as a recent analyst complains) the social-justice reform movement in the South, the movement for "franchises, services, and regulations" of business in the states, and other "areas of social concern and commitment" that required "an expanded concept of governmental responsibilities."[96] For, in fact, such reform elements and social commitments in the South had little in the way of broad-based support, sustained elite commitment, or actual accomplishment. Southern progressivism came to a focus on prohibition—another reform that required a new role for the central government, albeit based on a formal constitutional amendment—and the limited aims of "good government" administrative reforms. The eloquent voices of social justice in the New South are honored properly, but not for their legislative or political successes—only for their courage and vision.[97]

The negative variant of the southern regional response to proposals for nationalization of reform is best illustrated by the notorious southern opposition to national child labor regulation. The South had its own proponents of child labor reform, to be sure, but their achievements were minimal in terms of getting legislation or achieving effective enforcement of what little was forthcoming from their state legislatures.[98] The real focus of attention was in Congress and the federal courts, that is to say, on the merits of national legislation regulating child labor and on the litigation challenging the constitutionality of laws whose practical effect was to clamp down on the southern states and their textile industry and coal mines, with their blatant exploitation of children. As had been true of the late-nineteenth-century campaigns against federal equity receiverships and diversity jurisdiction of federal courts, there was a negative, parochial resort to the principles of dual federalism for regional and local purposes in the southern campaign against effective national control of child labor. It was regionalism often cast in constitutional rhetoric, but in a negative mode.

At the essence of the struggle against national reform in this instance—and what must be kept at the center of the analysis if one is to understand the significance of the fight—is the irony that the South was contending for states' rights, continued state autonomy in labor policy, and a limitation upon national power for the express purpose of maintaining a regional wage differential that militated against the southern working class and its welfare! That northern textile manufacturers wished to resort to minimum national standards on child labor for the same reasons that the South had sought banking reform—as a way of pursuing regional advantage—was, of course, itself indisputable.[99] The southern textile industry's response, however, illustrated an old dilemma for the region: to adopt reform legislation or to admit federal minimum standards would force the South to find some other basis than wage competition on which to seek and hold industrial investment.[100]

What followed was an unremitting attack by the southern manufacturers and their political allies against the constitutionality of a federal police power, against the policy itself and the premises regarding southern exploitation of labor, and against the northern textile interests that were their rivals for investment and markets.[101] As Stephen Wood has shown in his study of this episode in American legal and political history, the southern manufacturers were also defending a system of milltown paternalism that transcended the immediate issues of wages and national competition.[102] In Congress, moreover, the fight over child labor regulation brought to the surface the notorious connection in the southern mind between dual federalism and race: once the federal government has been given control over labor conditions, said the minority report (written by three southern representatives) on the 1916 Child Labor Act, it would "regulate the daily lives of the people in the grave *social, racial and economic problems* which confront them—[and] what function will there remain for the States to perform in our dual system; what will be left of local self-government—that birthright of our race come down to us all the way from Runnymede to Yorktown?"[103] Neither equal-protection ideals nor the arguments favoring paternalism when conditions absolutely required it, heard in the bank-reform debate, played a visible part in southern opposition to the child labor act.

In the face of a gradually centralizing federalism, then, the regionalism expressed by the South on important matters of state *versus* federal authority continued to be cast largely in terms that were defensive and contended for the autonomy of the states in determining the legal environment of business enterprise, labor, and race relations among other matters. "Leave it to the States. Have faith in the States."[104] This contention remained a rallying cry of unique effectiveness in a region that feared how a principled position on law or a pragmatic position on policy could easily lead to large-scale federal interference in the peculiar "domestic affairs," including race relations, of their states.

Thus any fundamental change in the South's role in the federal system, and in the manner in which the changing dynamics of federalism and national politics affected the South's economy and society, had to await the crisis environment and policy initiatives of the New Deal era.

V

The New Deal years brought a series of changes in national governance and constitutional law so far-reaching as to alter fundamentally the relationship between the South and the rest of the nation. There was in the first place a constitutional "revolution," as it is usually termed,[105] as the result of the Supreme Court's belated but wholesale acceptance after 1935 of the commerce clause as a charter for unprecedented national measures. By 1938 the general welfare clause had been reinvigorated, the contract clause sharply reduced as a barrier to state action, and emergency powers sweepingly redefined by the Court: state mortgage relief laws, national intervention in agriculture for crop and price controls, the imposition of federal administrative regulation of labor relations, production and sale of hydroelectric power by an agency of the federal government, and enforcement of national minimum wage and hours regulations had been upheld in landmark cases.[106] As the Civil War had inaugurated a distinct era of constitutional history on new principles, so too did the New Deal in the 1930s.[107] The New Deal policies and their confirmation in the transformation of constitutional law read like a litany of the worst fears of southern champions of states' rights from the Republic's beginnings to that day. Ineluctably, this transformation of the constitutional order changed at its foundations the premises of any southern definition and defense of regional interests.

A second, vitally related, feature of the New Deal era was the fundamental change in policy—along with the drastic centralization of real power that accompanied it—that resulted from the Hundred Days of 1933 and from the legislation of the ensuing years. (This was, of course, the focus of litigation on multiple fronts that produced the revolution in constitutional law that validated the New Deal's programs.) At the outset of the Great Depression, the South was still heavily agricultural in its economic orientation and in the distribution of population and workforce. The New Deal measures making agriculture a nationally managed sector therefore had deep effects in southern society and economic life—effects all the more profound because of related legislation that followed, undertaking resettlement of impoverished farmers, aid to displaced or economically distressed farm tenants, farm-mortgage aid, soil conservation and reclamation projects, and the like.[108]

One of the most radical measures of the New Deal, the Tennessee Valley Authority project, was another source of social and economic transformation in a major region of the South. As Philip Selznick's classic study of the Authority has demonstrated, TVA also had a transforming effect on southern political institutions and the structure of both public administration and local politics.[109] As a region that lagged badly behind the rest of the nation in average income, the South was especially affected too by the New Deal programs of relief and federally sponsored public works.[110] Moreover, the federal grant-in-aid programs for road construction, education, maternity care, and veterans' aid all had massive—and in some instances disproportionate—regional impact in the South. Like TVA and the Rural Electrification Administration pro-

grams, some of the other New Deal initiatives were aimed specifically at southern regional programs, were skewed in favor of
the southern states as recipients of aid, or had a general redistrib-
utive basis and objective that naturally worked most to the relative advantage of the South as the poorest region.[111]

These two basic developments, which fundamentally changed
the nation's political economy and its federal system, meant that
agenda-setting passed from the state capitals to Washington. The
decisions and policies that could truly make a difference in the regional political economy of the South, in other words, were those
which came from the center. That the South was largely left alone
on the matter of civil rights constituted an exception to what happened more generally in the thirties, although segregation was an
exception of no small magnitude. The autonomy of the southern
state governments—their formal constitutional authority as well
as the extent to which the realities of politics left them autonomous in setting policies that mattered—was not given up easily.
In fact, as is well known, the South's conservative elements pushed
back against the extensions of national governmental power; and
at a superficial level, at least, they managed to temper or fend off
some of the New Deal measures that had truly radical potential
and that threatened the southern *status quo* (especially in the realm
of machine politics) most overtly.[112] Even taking into account the
political skirmishes and conservative, states' rights backlash in the
South, it is hard to quarrel with Professor Tindall's conclusion that
"state politics . . . in the South became a kind of shadow-boxing
with issues that were determined elsewhere."[113]

The intractability of Depression problems, the continuing relationship between race and poverty in the region, the sometimes
ineffectual and often-designedly mild reforming effects of New
Deal measures (especially in agriculture), and the heavy burdens
of a long history of exploiting human as well as material resources
meant that the South emerged from the 1930s still well behind the
rest of the nation economically.[114] Because of the dual revolution
in political economy and constitutional law, however, the ability
of its state governments permanently to fix the *status quo* or to
maintain an essentially irrational posture on economic and social

policy was now undermined. Above all, the enormous scope and the reach of New Deal policies that established national minimum standards in the area of social welfare no less than in wages and hours or in factory safety meant that trading on cheap labor could no longer serve to the same degree as it had done in the past in the quest for regional industrialization. The stage was set, then, for a new pattern of economic development, for a new southern role in the dynamics of the federal system, and for the transformation of both legal process and political structure in the South. World War II and Cold War defense expenditures, federal research and development programs culminating in the modern-day aerospace efforts, and a newly fashioned grant-in-aid program on a vastly expanded scale from the mid-1960s to the present, combined to speed social, political, and economic change in the South.[115] Residual elements of dual federalism and parochialism, even of interregional rivalry conducted by giving away resources or exemptions, continued to operate and do so today—witness the tax exemption and energy subsidy programs that are offered by southern state and local governments.[116] But the older established patterns that prevailed from the Civil War down to the New Deal no longer prevail, either in the configuration of southern state law or in the role of the South in the federal system. The revolution in civil rights of the last thirty years is a political counterpoint to the transformations of law and political economy that were wrought as the legacy of the New Deal and subsequent developments in American politics and federalism.

There is great irony in the emergence of the Sun Belt, with its seemingly favored status in relation to the distribution of federal largesse, for it reflects the political and economic realities of a transformed federal system. In this transformed, post–New Deal system, the South has obtained enormous economic advantages from the very giant federal government whose emergence and power the states' righters had fought for so long. In pre–New Deal days, positive federal programs and federal spending patterns had only a marginal impact upon the configuration of regional (or state) advantage or disadvantage in the distribution of economic power; the flow of federal funds was but a marginal factor in aggregative regional income, employment, and distributive patterns. The

South generally opposed any change in that regime—a regime that was also a bulwark of white supremacy—amd therefore foresook the championing of a potentially effective approach to the solution of regional economic problems that could have complemented the uses of autonomous state power to help break out of economic colonialism. Since the New Deal, however, the giantism of national government and the high proportion of overall GNP represented by federal activities have meant that the geographical targeting of federal funds and the location of federal employment and activities can be of truly decisive significance in determining the structure of regional economic advantage. The great beneficiary of this change has been the South. The southern urban centers have enjoyed a surge in federal bureaucratic growth; a large portion of the military and aerospace spending of the last two decades has been in the Sun Belt, including the Old South and Texas; and these larger effects of federal governmental policies and spending have converged with the effects of grant-in-aid and other national programs to help create the conditions for industrialization, diversification, and urbanization in the South.[117]

To be sure, state autonomy—not only in the South, but elsewhere in the country as well—remains a potentially decisive element in shaping economic welfare and particularly the distribution of income. For proof of this, we need look no further than the notorious historic lag in southern educational expenditures and commitments, the state-to-state disparities in unemployment and disability benefits, and the continuing differences that derive from the "right-to-work" legislation of states that leapt at the opening afforded by the Taft-Hartley Act to place organized labor on a different footing than in the majority of states.[118] Nonetheless, in the current day, the South has come to rest its development strategies[119] and much of its prosperity upon the effects of a transformed, centralized federalism representative of its worst fears of an earlier era.

NOTES

[1] The classic treatment is C. Vann Woodward, *Origins of the New South, 1877–1913* (Baton Rouge, La., 1951). The much-visited colonialism theme is also treated extensively in George

B. Tindall, *The Emergence of the New South, 1913–1945* (Baton Rouge, La., 1967); David R. Goldfield, *Cotton Fields and Skyscrapers: Southern City and Region, 1607–1980* at 118–32 *et passim* (Baton Rouge, La., 1982); and, most recently, Patrick J. Hearden, *Independence and Empire: The New South's Cotton Mill Campaign, 1865–1901* (DeKalb, Ill., 1982). See also the classic study by William H. Nicholls, *Southern Tradition and Regional Progress* (Chapel Hill, N.C., 1960).

² A phrase given a new lease on life in constitutional law by the majority opinion in *National League of Cities* v. *Usery*, 426 U.S. 833 (1979). That the states would pursue their individual interests but also be wary against any aggrandizement of national power that threatened the scope of their jurisdictional authority was one of the main arguments, of course, mobilized by authors of *The Federalist* essays during the debates over ratification. See *The Federalist*, No. 45, for example.

³ See Carter Goodrich, "Internal Improvements Reconsidered," *Journal of Economic History*, XXX (1970), 289–311; Goodrich, *Government Promotion of American Canals and Railroads, 1800–1890* (New York, 1960); Milton Heath, *Constructive Liberalism: The Role of the State in the Economic Development of Georgia to 1860* (Cambridge, Mass., 1954); Merle Reed, *New Orleans and the Railroads: The Struggle for Commercial Empire, 1830–1860* (Baton Rouge, La., 1966).

⁴ The basic maxims of dual federalism, as formulated by Professor Corwin, were as follows: "1. The national government is one of enumerated powers only; 2. Also, the purposes which it may constitutionally promote are few; 3. Within their respective spheres the two centers of government are 'sovereign' and hence 'equal.' 4. The relation of the two centers with each other is one of tension rather than collaboration." Corwin, "The Passing of Dual Federalism," *Virginia Law Review*, XXXVI (1950), 5. I have made the argument, *in extenso*, that the period 1789–1861 is one of dual federalism in action as well as in constitutional theory, in Scheiber, "Federalism and the American Economic Order, 1789–1910," *Law and Society Review*, X (Fall 1975), 57–100. For an historical overview, see David Walker, *Toward a Functioning Federalism* (Boston, 1981), 19–131. See also Robert Lively, "The American System: A Review Article," *Business History Review*, XXIX (1955), 81.

⁵ Scheiber, "Federalism and the American Economic Order," at 72–96.

⁶ See George Rogers Taylor, *The Transportation Revolution, 1815–1860* (New York, 1951). The present article is a companion piece, in a sense, to a study recently published that dealt mainly with the West and explored legal process in the states: Scheiber, "Xenophobia and Parochialism in the History of American Legal Process: From the Jacksonian Era to the Sagebrush Rebellion," *William and Mary Law Review*, XXIII (1982), 625. The present work, unlike that one, deals with controversies surrounding federal policy and lawmaking; and it deals with the South and its peculiar regional problems (especially economic colonialism), topics not considered in the scope of the earlier article.

⁷ J. D. B. De Bow, *Industrial Resources of the Southern and Western States* (3 vols., New Orleans, 1857), I, 359.

⁸ Report of 1853, quoted in David R. Goldfield, *Urban Growth in the Age of Sectionalism: Virginia, 1847–61* (Baton Rouge, La., 1977), 23–24.

⁹ Message on the Blue Ridge Railroad, quoted in *Railroad Record*, I (1853), 693.

¹⁰ Quoted in Richard Shryock, *Georgia and the Union in 1850* (Durham, N.C., 1926), 60.

¹¹ Laurence Tribe, *American Constitutional Law* (Mineola, N.Y., 1978), 4–7, 427–55.

¹² The classic case for the Civil War as introducing a new political economy is Louis Hacker, *The Triumph of American Capitalism* (New York, 1946). See also Scheiber, "Economic Change in the Civil War Era," *Civil War History*, XI (1965), 407–09; J. G. Randall and David Donald, *The Civil War and Reconstruction* (2nd ed., Boston, 1961), 274–91; and Harold Hyman, *A More Perfect Union: The Impact of the Civil War and Reconstruction on the Constitution* (New York, 1973).

¹³ See works cited in note 1, above, and also: *Regionalism and the South: Selected Papers of Rupert Vance*, John Shelton Reed and Daniel Joseph Singal, eds., (Chapel Hill, N.C., 1982);

John C. McKinney and Edgar T. Thompson, eds., *The South in Continuity and Change* (Durham, N.C., 1965); Alfred J. Watkins and David C. Perry, "Regional Change and the Impact of Uneven Urban Development," *The Rise of the Sunbelt Cities*, in Perry and Watkins, eds., (Beverly Hills and London, 1977).

[14] The record is laid out fully in Woodward, *Origins of the New South*; see also William Gillette, *Retreat from Reconstruction, 1869–1879* (Baton Rouge, La., 1979).

[15] The diversity issue is treated historically in Gerald Henderson, *The Position of Foreign Corporations in American Constitutional Law* (Cambridge, Mass., 1918). A full modern analysis of the history, stressing western regionalism and the constitutional questions, is Tony Freyer, *Forums of Order: The Federal Courts and Business in American History* (Greenwich, Conn., 1979). On southern voting behavior and rhetoric in Congress on rivers and harbors, the tariff, monetary issues, and railroad regulation, see Terry L. Seip, *The South Returns to Congress: Men, Economic Measures, and Intersectional Relationships, 1868–1879* (Baton Rouge, La., 1983); and Carl V. Harris, "Right Fork or Left Fork? The Section-Party Alignments of Southern Democrats in Congress, 1873–1897," *Journal of Southern History*, XLII (1976), 471–506.

[16] *Insurance Co.* v. *Morse*, 20 Wall. 445 (U.S. 1874); *Pensacola Telegraph Co.* v. *Western Union*, 96 U.S. 1 (1877). See F. D. G. Ribble, *State and National Power over Commerce* (New York, 1937).

[17] For provisions of the bill, see 10 *Congressional Record* 701 (1880).

[18] *Ibid.*

[19] In a later debate, in 1883, over his bill (then reintroduced), Culberson explicitly dissociated himself from "the senseless clamor" against corporations in general. 14 *Congressional Record* 1248 (1883).

[20] The southern and western coalition is treated by Tony Freyer, both in *Forums of Order* and "Federal Courts, Localism, and the National Economy, 1865–1900," *Business History Review*, LIII (1979), 344–63.

[21] 10 *Congressional Record* 816 (1880).

[22] *Ibid.* at 816.

[23] *Ibid.* at 817.

[24] *Ibid.* at 850 (speech of Rep. George D. Robinson of Massachusetts). To this contention Rep. Hilary Herbert of Alabama replied that the South and West needed capital so that their courts could not afford to—and would not—discriminate against corporations domiciled in the Northeast. *Ibid.* at 1014. For scholarly accounts of legislation concerning the extension of jurisdiction of the federal courts, see the classic study by Felix Frankfurter and James M. Landis, *The Business of the Supreme Court: A Study in the Federal Judicial System* (New York, 1927); William Wiecek, "The Reconstruction of Federal Judicial Power," *American Journal of Legal History*, XIII (1969), 333; and Stanley Kutler, *Judicial Power and Reconstruction Politics* (Chicago, 1968).

[25] Frankfurter and Landis, *Business of the Supreme Court*, 64–85.

[26] See, for example, 13 *Congressional Record* 3544 (1882). Southerners mobilized in criticism of another reorganization bill, in 1890, on the same grounds, warning that it would simply mean another wave of new Republican appointees hostile to the South. See 21 *Congressional Record* 3407, 10285, 10288 (1890).

[27] 13 *Congressional Record* 3546 (1882).

[28] *Ibid.* at 3546 (speeches of Butler, Ingalls); *ibid.* at 3598 (Call), at 2790 (Wilkerson).

[29] *Ibid.* at 3602.

[30] *Ibid.* at 3603.

[31] *Ibid.* at 3829.

[32] *Ibid.* at 3598.

[33] *Ibid.* at 3787.

[34] That is, given Beard's view that industrial capitalism of the North triumphed in the Civil War and dictated the terms of Reconstruction measures for purposes of advancing

its economic interests. See his *The Rise of American Civilization*, with co-author Mary Beard (New York, 1935).

[35] John F. Stover, *The Railroads of the South, 1865–1900: A Study in Finance and Control* (Chapel Hill, N.C., 1955), 122–24.

[36] *Ibid.*, 257–58.

[37] Henry Clay Caldwell, "Railroad Receiverships in the Federal Courts," *American Law Review*, XXX (1896), 161; Albro Martin, "Railroads and the Equity Receivership: An Essay on Institutional Change," *Journal of Economic History*, XXXIV (1974), 685.

[38] See Seymour D. Thompson, "The Court Management of Railroads," *American Law Review*, XXVII (1893), 481.

[39] Quoted in "Memorial of the General Assembly of the State of South Carolina . . . in the Matter of Receivers of Railroad Corporations and the Equity Jurisdiction of the Courts of the United States," *American Law Review*, XXIX (1894), 161, 172.

[40] *Ibid.*, 172.

[41] *Ibid.*, 183.

[42] *Ibid.*

[43] *Ibid.*, 171.

[44] 154 U.S. 362 (1894).

[45] See Robert C. Cotner, *James Stephen Hogg: A Biography* (Austin, Tex., 1955), 366–77.

[46] Special message to Legislature, March 8, 1893, in Hogg, *Addresses and State Papers*, Robert C. Cotner, ed. (Austin, Tex., 1951), 335, 340.

[47] *Ibid.*, 343.

[48] Both Woodward, *Origins of the New South*, and Tindall, *Emergence of the New South*, deal with the issue of discriminatory freight rates. A full monographic account of the political response of the South may be found in Robert A. Lively, *The South in Action: A Sectional Crusade Against Freight Rate Discrimination* (Chapel Hill, N.C., 1949). See also David Potter, "The Historical Development of Eastern-Southern Freight Rate Relationships," *Law and Contemporary Problems*, XII (1947), 416–48.

[49] Clarence Danhof, for example, has concluded that the "conspiracy" thesis that underlay the long campaign against discriminatory freight rates "must be considered an unfortunate episode—a resurgence of crude sectionalism—that diverted the attention of some of the South's ablest [leaders] from constructive approaches to the region's problems." Danhof, "Four Decades of Thought on the South's Economic Problems," in Melvin Greenhut and W. T. Whitman, eds., *Essays in Southern Economic Development* (Chapel Hill, N.C., 1964), 7, 50. His judgment rests in part on the foundation-stone fact that only a very small proportion of southern production was directly affected by the cost-plus basing and similar rate discriminations.

[50] *Papers of Walter Clark*, A. L. Brooks and H. T. Lefler, eds. (2 vols., Chapel Hill, N.C., 1948), I, 479.

[51] *Ibid.*, 480.

[52] Letter of Clark to Marion Butler, Feb. 3, 1898, in *ibid.*, 327.

[53] For example, *Ex parte Thornton*, 4 Hughes 220, 12 Fed. 538 (C.D., E. D. Va., 1882); *Asher v. Texas*, 128 U.S. 129 (1888); *Robbins v. Taxing District of Shelby County*, 120 U.S. 489 (1887). On the history of the anti-drummer laws and their fate in the courts and legislatures, see the excellent study by Stanley C. Hollander, "Nineteenth Century Anti-drummer Legislation in the United States," *Business History Review*, XXXVIII (1964), 456–78. The landmark case was *Ward v. Maryland*, 12 Wall. 418 (U.S. 1871).

[54] A systematic search in the published proceedings of the national Board of Trade, with a view toward identifying evidences of southern regionalism and the southern positions on federalism issues, reveals that southern representatives participated regularly from 1868 to 1877; then, from 1877 to 1890, southern representation was minimal. In the 1890s only a few southern cities sent delegates, and many of them participated little in the debates.

One issue on which the southerners did speak out regularly when it was debated, however, was the question of anti-drummer legislation.

[55] *Proceedings of the Second Annual Meeting of the National Board of Trade, Held in Cincinnati, December 1860* (Boston, 1870), 43.

[56] So argued by Richard Lathers, representing the Charleston Board of Trade, in *Proceedings of the Third Annual Meeting . . . Held at Buffalo, December 1870* (n.p., 1871), 89–90.

[57] Petitions of the 1880s in the *Congressional Record* as cited by Hollander, "Anti-Drummer Legislation," 494, n. 109.

[58] See *McCready* v. *Virginia*, 94 U.S. 391 (1867).

[59] Texas enacted in March 1893 its Perpetuities and Corporation Land Law, requiring all private corporations whose main purpose was land speculation and development to sell off their holdings within fifteen years. Texas, *Laws* (1893), 466–7. This measure was passed in response to a campaign by Gov. Hogg aimed at alien landowners and corporate speculators. Texas was one of several states (mainly western) to enact legislation restricting alien ownership. See Hogg, *Addresses*, 180; Scheiber, "Xenophobia," 656–7; Clements, "British Investment and American Legislative Restrictions in the Trans-Mississippi West," *Mississippi Valley Historical Review*, XLII (1955), 207; Sullivan, "Alien Land Laws: A Reevaluation," *Temple Law Quarterly*, XXXVI (1962), 29.

[60] Robertson, in Texas *House Journal*, 1907, at 92, quoted in James A. Tinsley, "Texas Progressives and Insurance Regulation," *Southwestern Social Science Quarterly*, XXXVI (1955), 239. The Robertson Law of 1907 required all incorporated insurance companies doing business in Texas to invest within the state, in securities and property, at least 75% of the reserves set aside for payment of policies issued in Texas. The law was tested by referendum in 1916 and upheld. It was finally repealed in 1963. See Thomas A. Crosson, *A History of the Robertson Law and its Effect upon Life Insurance in Texas* (M.A. thesis, University of Pennsylvania, 1951).

[61] Crosson, *Robertson Law*, 10. See also H. Roger Grant, *Insurance Reform: Consumer Action in the Progressive Era* (Ames, Iowa, 1975), 65.

[62] See works cited in note 1; and Scheiber, "Federalism and the Economic Order."

[63] Pete Daniel, *The Shadow of Slavery: Peonage in the South 1901–69* (Urbana, Ill., 1972). See also Harold Woodman, "Sequel to Slavery: The New History Views the Postbellum South," *Journal of Southern History*, XLIII (1977), 23–54; and Frenise Logan, "The Movement of Negroes from North Carolina, 1876–1894," *North Carolina Historical Review*, XXXVI (1956), 45–65.

[64] Woodman, "Sequel to Slavery," *passim*; Goldfield, *Cotton Fields and Skyscrapers*, 80–138. Some evidence on how southern courts extended tort and nuisance immunity, in the context of national trends much in the same direction, is conveniently available in the important article by Paul M. Kurtz, "Nineteenth Century Anti-entrepreneurial Nuisance Injunctions—Avoiding the Chancellor," *William and Mary Law Review*, XVII (1976), 621–70.

[65] See Woodward, *Origins of the New South*, *passim*; Douglas F. Dowd, "A Comparative Analysis of Economic Development in the American West and South," *Journal of Economic History*, XVI (1956), 558–74.

[66] Woodward, *Origins of the New South*, 61–62; see also discussion in Nicholls, *Southern Tradition*, 106–9.

[67] Woodward, *Origins of the New South*, 310.

[68] Ronald D. Eller, *Miners, Millhands, and Mountaineers: Industrialization of the Appalachian South, 1880–1930*, at 210–11.

[69] *Ibid.*, 234–5. See also J. Morgan Kousser, *The Shaping of Southern Politics: Suffrage Restriction and the One-Party South, 1880–1910*, (New Haven, Conn., 1974).

[70] In a recent article, J. Mills Thornton III has argued that in the Reconstruction South farmers carried an unprecedentedly high burden of land taxation. His argument fails to

take account of differential spending by function among the southern states, and seems to oversimplify the issue of why Redeemer governments failed (or found it politically impossible to do otherwise) in the provision of a decent level of human services at the state level. Nonetheless, a judgment as to the "real" (as opposed to nominal constitutional) autonomy of the southern states— i.e., the real potential in terms of fiscal resources and not only constitutional authority—and the degree to which they could have pursued different policies must take account of fiscal base, tax effort, types and effectiveness of expenditures. See Thornton, "Fiscal Policy and the Failure of Radical Reconstruction in the Lower South," J. Morgan Kousser and James M. McPherson, eds., *Region, Race, and Reconstruction: Essays in Honor of C. Vann Woodward* (New York and Oxford, 1982), 349–94. Such a full accounting is not attempted here.

[71] This view was contended for at the 1983 conference on the Legal History of the South, in discussion of this paper by Prof. Grady McWhiney of the University of Alabama. How many southerners, taken in by "the gospel prosperity," "took their places at the table . . . [and] became the agents or hired attorneys of the invading capitalists," is discussed in an article that portrays the New South leadership as having sold out southern ideals, such as the author sees them, in the article by Francis B. Simkins, "The South," in Merrill Jensen, ed., *Regionalism in America* (Madison, Wisc., 1965), 147, 167.

[72] See Logan, "The Movement of Negroes from North Carolina."

[73] See discussion of state base in note 70 above.

[74] Dewey W. Grantham, Jr., *Hoke Smith and the Politics of the New South* (Baton Rouge, La., 1958), 156–79.

[75] Hearden, *Independence and Empire*, 45. Hearden contents that sectional animosity and rivalry were the wellsprings of southern pro-industrialization rhetoric. For a different view, see Paul M. Gaston, *The New South Creed: A Study in Southern Mythmaking* (New York, 1970).

[76] See Woodward, *Origins of the New South, passim*. The disillusionment and contention that control of the economic order was being taken away from southern governments began early in response to railroad consolidations and the penetration of northern railroad capital in the 1870s and 1880s. As early as 1882, for example, the Rev. R. L. Dabney attacked the developments in the southern railroad sector in terms that were even more applicable, as Allen Moger has written, to the situation ca. 1900: "Once the Commonwealth owned all the highways by water and by land. . . . Now the highways are the property of great carrying corporations who command more men as their disciplined employees than the government's own standing armies, before whose revenues the whole incomes of commonwealths are paltry trifles, to whose will legislatures hasten to bow. Each of these roads points virtually to New York. To . . . one corner of Wall Street in that city, centre all their debts, their loans, their revenues, their chief management." (Address of 1882, quoted in Allen Moger, "Railroad Practices and Policies in Virginia after the Civil War," *Virginia Magazine of History and Biography*, LIX (1951), 423, 457n.) A valuable economic and business history that considers the history of manufacturing promotion and investment is Jack Blicksilver, *Cotton Manufacturing in the Southeast: An Historical Analysis* [Georgia State College of Business Administration, Bureau of Business and Economic Research, *Bulletin*, No. 5] (Atlanta, 1959).

[77] A variety of interpretations has been placed before the scholarly public in recent years as to continuity or discontinuity of planter control of politics and the course of economic change, as to the relationships between older elite elements and "intruded" new elite elements from the North and from the southern middle class, and as to the importance of ideology, especially the force of what is commonly designated (though seldom satisfactorily explained) as "hegemony." It is worth remembering, too, that often great variations from one locale to another, in the configuration of social and political relationships, may confound generalizations on these points. Nonetheless, from a review of this literature, I contend that autonomy and the substantial capacity to have made very different policy choices—with significantly different policy outcomes—remained with the southern states.

Especially important in the very large recent literature are: Dwight Billings, Jr., *Planters and the Making of the "New South"* (Chapel Hill, N.C., 1979); Jonathan Wiener, *Social Origins of the New South: Alabama, 1860–1885* (Baton Rouge, La., 1978); essays in Robert C. McMath, Jr., and Orville Burton, eds., *Toward a New South? Studies in Post–Civil War Southern Communities* (Westport, Conn., 1892). A number of the most prominent recent studies receive critical treatment in Woodman, "Sequel to Slavery." For an especially useful local study, centering on the stock-fencing laws, changing concepts of property rights, and class conflicts in the context of legal culture, see Steven Hahn, "Common Right and Commonwealth: The Stock-Law Struggle and the Roots of Southern Populism," in Kousser and McPherson, eds., *Region, Race and Reconstruction*, 51–88.

[78] Grantham, "The Contours of Southern Progressivism," *American Historical Review*, LXXXVI (1981), 1035, 1051.

[79] The classic study is Arthur S. Link, "The Progressive Movement in the South, 1870–1914," *North Carolina Historical Review*, XXIII (1946). 172–96. See also Link, "The South and the 'New Freedom': An Interpretation," *American Scholar*, XX (1951), 314–24; and the important corrective to some of Link's views, Richard Abrams, "Woodrow Wilson and the Southern Congressmen, 1913–1916," *Journal of Southern History*, XXII (1956), 417–37.

[80] Herbert J. Doherty, Jr., "Voices of Protest from the New South, 1875–1910," *Mississippi Valley Historical Review*, XLII (1955), 45–66.

[81] See Tindall, *Emergence of the New South*; Grantham, "Contours."

[82] See text at notes 98–104.

[83] The sectional vote on the bill is discussed in text at note 90.

[84] Abrams, "Woodrow Wilson."

[85] 50 *Congressional Record* (63rd Cong., 1st Sess.), 4804.

[86] *Ibid.*, 4806.

[87] *Ibid.*, 5098. On the pressure that led to Wilson's accepting farm credit provisions, see Arthur S. Link, *Woodrow Wilson and the Progressive Era, 1910–17* (New York, 1954), 49–50.

[88] 50 *Congressional Record*, 4865.

[89] *Ibid.*

[90] *Ibid.*

[91] 51 *Congressional Record*, 1230, 5129.

[92] How intra-sectional southern rivalries colored the debate in this second phase may be garnered by reference to the legislative record, especially the following: 63rd Congress, 2nd Session, *Senate Documents*, No. 485 (*Letter from the Reserve Bank Organization Committee. . . .*) (Washington, 1914); and debates in 51 *Congressional Record*, 6344–85 (April 7–8, 1914), 6417–44 (April 8, 1914).

[93] James C. Malin, "The Background of the First Bills to Establish a Bureau of Markets, 1911–1912," *Agricultural History*, VI (1932), 107–29. See also Theodore Saloutos, *Farmer Movements in the South, 1865–1933* (Berkeley and Los Angeles, 1960), 184–235.

[94] Malin, "Background," 120–21.

[95] Saloutos, *Farmer Movements, passim.*

[96] Grantham, "Contours," 1041–45.

[97] See, for example, Doherty, "Voices of Protest"; Sheldon Hackney, *Populism to Progressivism in Alabama* (Princeton, N.J., 1969); Tindall, *Emergence of the New South*.

[98] See the strident condemnation of New South industrialists on this question by one of the region's leading reform voices, in Alexander J. McKelway, "The Child and the Law," *Annals of the American Academy of Political and Social Science*, XXXIII, Suppl. (1909), 65ff. Also, Elizabeth H. Davidson, *Child Labor Legislation in the Southern Textile States* (Chapel Hill, N.C., 1939); Tindall, *Emergence of the New South*, 16–17, 322–23. The statistics compiled by some of the state governments and cited by Davidson (and then by Tindall) were disputed widely in the South by reformers as distorted and designed to cover up the widespread use of child workers. See, for example, Doherty, "Voices of Protest," 61–2 (on how

National Civic Federation findings were attacked by McKelway); and McKelway's and accompanying articles in *Annals*, 33, Suppl. (1909), cited above, this note.

[99] So, too, were the human effects of such minimum standards indisputable. See Arden Lea, "Cotton Textiles and the Child Labor Act of 1916," *Labor History*, XVI (1975), 485–94; and, on the political and constitutional struggles over child labor in that era more generally, the fine study by Stephen B. Wood, *Constitutional Politics in the Progressive Era: Child Labor and the Law* (Chicago, 1968).

[100] See Wood, *Constitutional Politics*, 48–51; also, on the general economic background, Blicksilver, *Cotton Manufacturing*.

[101] Wood, *Constitutional Politics*, 47–51; U.S. Congress, House of Rep., 63rd Congress, 2nd Session, Committee on Labor, *Hearings . . . on H.R. 12292, A Bill to Prevent Interstate Commerce in the Products of Child Labor, and for Other Purposes, May 22, 1914* (Washington, 1914), 85–89 (testimony of Lewis Parker, mill owner, Greenville, S.C.); U.S. Congress, House of Rep., 64th Congress, 1st Session, Committee on Labor, *Hearings . . . on H.R. 8234, A Bill to Prevent Interstate Commerce in the Products of Child Labor, and for Other Purposes, January 10, 11, and 12, 1916* (Washington, 1916), 49 (testimony of Danville, Va., textiles executive: "It [the bill] invades the constitutional right of each State to regulate conditions within its own borders. . . .), 139, 153 *et passim*.

[102] Wood, *Constitutional Politics*, 51.

[103] Minority Report, House Committee on Labor, *supra* note 101, at 11. Italics added.

[104] Testimony of William W. Kitchin, in House Committee on Labor, *supra* note 101, at 153. Of course, there was also the positive defense, to wit, that labor in the mills was much to the benefit of the children themselves, their often-widowed mothers, and the communities in which the mills were situated. See testimony of David Clark, owner of the *Southern Textile Bulletin* of North Carolina, Senate Committee on Labor, *supra* note 101, at 12, 16–17.

[105] Mario Einaudi, *The Roosevelt Revolution* (New York, 1959); Edward S. Corwin, *Constitutional Revolution, Ltd.* (Boston, 1941).

[106] Alfred H. Kelly, Winfred A. Harbison, and Herman Belz, *The American Constitution: Its Origins and Development* (6th edition, New York and London, 1983), 501–22; Harry N. Scheiber, "American Federalism and the Diffusion of Power: Historical and Contemporary Perspectives," *University of Toledo Law Review*, IX (1978), 619–24, 644–48.

[107] Tribe, *American Constitutional Law*, *passim*.

[108] See Theodore Saloutos, *The American Farmer and the New Deal* (Ames, Iowa, 1982), 150–91 *et passim*; Tindall, *Emergence of the New South*, 391–432.

[109] Selznick, *TVA and the Grass Roots* (reprint edition, New York, 1966).

[110] For some of the anomalies, however, especially in the way in which public works expenditures and the newly institutionalized welfare and Social Security benefits may have had a much greater proportional effect than relief *per se*, see the discussion in Tindall, *Emergence of the New South*, 473–97.

[111] Saloutos, *American Farmer and the New Deal*, 212 (regarding the Electric Home and Farm Authority restricted experimentally to Mississippi, Alabama, Georgia and Tennessee), 218 (on the disproportionate advantage to the South of Rural Electrification programs), *et passim*. See also Edward L. Schapsmeier and Frederick H. Schapsmeier, "Farm Policy from FDR to Eisenhower: Southern Democrats and the Politics of Agriculture," *Agricultural History*, LIII (1979), 352–62.

[112] This is a main theme of James T. Patterson, *The New Deal and the States: Federalism in Transition* (Princeton, N.J., 1969).

[113] Tindall, *Emergence of the New South*, 649.

[114] Harvey S. Perloff *et. al.*, *Regions, Resources and Economic Growth* (Baltimore, Md., 1960), 274–78, 282.

[115] Carl Abbott, *The New Urban America: Growth and Politics in Sunbelt Cities* (Chapel Hill, N.C., 1981), 15–27; Walt W. Rostow, "Regional Change in the Fifth Kondratieff Up-

swing," in David C. Perry and Albert Watkins, eds., *The Rise of Sunbelt Cities* (Beverly Hills, Calif., and London, 1977), 83–93 (esp. Table 3 at p. 93). That the new industrial era did not, in fact, by any means end exploitation of labor as a lure or as a reality of life in the South, is stressed by Goldfield, *Cottonfields and Skyscrapers*, 191–94; see also Perry and Watkins, "People, Profit, and the Rise of the Sunbelt Cities," 293–99.

[116] As also offered, of course, by municipal and state governments, or industrial development authorities, in other states. See Public Interest Research Group, *Bidding for Business: Corporate Auctions and the Fifty Disunited States* (mimeo, Washington: PIRG, 1979); and U.S. Advisory Commission on Intergovernmental Relations, *Regional Growth: Interstate Tax Competition* (Washington, 1981). A fascinating account of how state planning agencies, initially established to maximize efficient use of resources, conservation, and orderly development, shifted to "developmental" agencies bent on luring capital investment from outside, is in Albert Lepawsky, "Government Planning in the South," *Journal of Politics*, X (1948), 554–62.

[117] See works cited note 115, *supra*; and data in U.S. Advisory Commission on Intergovernmental Relations, *Regional Growth: Flows of Federal Funds* (Washington, 1980), 55 (Table I).

[118] Peter A. Lupsha and William J. Siembieda, "The Poverty of Public Services in the Land of Plenty: An Analysis and Interpretation," in Perry and Watkins, eds., *Rise of Sunbelt Cities*, 169–90.

[119] Regional governors' conferences (the South's dates from the 1930s campaign against the Interstate Commerce Commission and differential freight rates), bloc organization on regional lines in Congress, and other forms of regionally based political institutionalization of interests—both public-sector and private-sector—implement this regional developmental strategy. See, for example, the report, "Federal Spending: The North's Loss Is the Sunbelt's Gain," *National Journal*, VIII (June 26, 1976), 878; Neil Peirce, "Northeast Governors Map Battle Plan for Fight Over Federal Funds Flow," *National Journal*, VIII (Nov. 27, 1976), 1965; Charlie Jean, "North vs. South: Second War Between the States," *Southern Exchange*, V (1978), 6; Leonard U. Wilson, *State Strategies for Multistate Organizations* (*State Planning Series*, Council of State Planning Agencies, Vol. 8, Washington, 1977). See also Kent A. Price, ed., *Regional Conflict and National Policy* (Baltimore, 1982).

The Virginia State Debt
and the Judicial Power of the United States
1870–1920

JOHN V. ORTH

THE CIVIL WAR determined the nature of the federal Union, but when the arms fell silent, many questions remained unanswered. The reconstruction of southern society proved to be beyond the might or will of the conquering North. As martial ways yielded to occupations of peace, controversies again assumed legal form. In no area was this more apparent than in litigation that surrounded the settlement of public debts of the southern states.

Impoverished by war and defeat, the states of the old Confederacy staggered under the burden of antebellum debts contracted in more prosperous times. Some states, subjected to hated Reconstruction governments, saw their debts dramatically increased by new borrowing. Forcibly reunited in a federal system that protected all forms of property except slavery, the indebted states later sought legal means to repudiate—or in their language, to "readjust"—their obligations. Because of a little known constitutional amendment dating from the early years of the republic, most southern states succeeded in evading a large part of their debts. But the Commonwealth of Virginia did not share the happy fate of its fellow debtors. For decades the Old Dominion was involved in litigation—first in defense of its debt-reducing statutes known as the Coupon Killers, then in opposition to its neighbor and offspring, West Virginia. In the course of these legal battles the United States Supreme Court determined the nature of the judicial power of the United States.

I

When the fighting began at Fort Sumter in 1861, Virginia carried a large public debt, as befitted an old and prosperous state.[1] War brought the usual rapid increase of indebtedness, but defeat relieved Virginia of liability on this portion of the debt. During hostilities, however, the state had suspended payment on the legitimate antebellum debt, which by 1865 had increased substantially as a result of the compounding of unpaid interest. By the end of the war, Virginia's debt, including accrued interest, exceeded $41 million.[2]

More than any other state in or out of the Union, Virginia had been ravaged by war. An unhealthy percentage of the young white male population had been killed or maimed. Livestock and farm implements had been stolen or destroyed. The slaves had, of course, been emancipated without compensation to their owners. The body politic itself had been dismembered: one-third of the Old Dominion was now the separate state of West Virginia. All of these developments reduced the state's economic resources and lessened its ability to raise the taxes required to support the government and to repay the large antebellum debt.

Reconstruction ended early in Virginia. By 1869 self-government was restored. The Redeemers were self-proclaimed Conservatives, dedicated to good government and sound money.[3] Under the leadership of Governor Gilbert C. Walker, a northern businessman trying to attract northern capital, the Conservatives responded to the legacy of debt by enacting the Funding Act of 1871.[4] The Commonwealth denied its liability on one-third of the antebellum debt, attributing that to the new government in Wheeling, but offered bondholders certificates to be paid "in accordance with such settlement as shall hereafter be had between the states of Virginia and West Virginia."[5] As to the balance, the Commonwealth offered the bondholders an attractive deal: they could exchange old bonds for new ones called consolidated bonds, or "consols" for short, maturing in 34 years and paying the then-high rate of six percent interest. Coupons attached to the bonds represented the interest, and as a further inducement to the bond-holders to make the exchange, these coupons were "receivable at and after maturity for all taxes, debts, dues, and demands due the state."[6] The coupons were an earnest of repayment. Because they were receivable for the state's taxes, the coupons were in effect a first lien on the state's revenue. They had to be honored before money could be raised for the current expenses of government. There would always be a market for coupons clipped from the bonds, and prices in that market would always be buoyant. The slightest discount from face value would make it in the economic interest of taxpayers to buy.

The carrying charges on the debt, even excluding the share as-signed to West Virginia, soon proved to be politically unaccept-able.[7] The coupons, denounced as the "cut-worms of the Trea-sury,"[8] sapped the Commonwealth's income and threatened the state's ability to fund its newly mandated statewide system of free elementary schools.[9] For the next two decades the two issues—public schools and repayment of the debt—were inextricably linked. In political terms the issue was often whether to pay the capitalists or the schoolteachers. In the uncompromising words of one governor committed to paying the debt: "Free schools are not a necessity. They are a luxury . . . to be paid for, like any luxury, by the people who wish their benefits."[10] But public education had its own constituency, and political pressure in favor of default built rapidly.

Until the end of the 1870s the debate was contained within the Conservative Party, although the powerful faction in favor of readjustment often had its way. In 1872 the General Assembly overrode a gubernatorial veto and repealed the section of the Funding Act that made coupons receivable in payment of state taxes.[11] The judges of the Virginia Supreme Court of Appeals, however, represented an earlier tendency in Conservatism and held the new statute unconstitutional.[12] Their reasoning was sim-ple: the state's bond was its contract; the Federal Constitution de-nied to the state the power to pass any "Law impairing the Ob-ligation of Contracts";[13] the repealer, impairing the bondholders' contract, was void.

The Commonwealth did, of course, stop the issuance of new consols. Those bondholders who failed to make the switch in time went remediless. The state withdrew its generous offer before acceptance, so there was no contract with them. In place of consols the late-comers were offered bonds known as "peelers" that lacked coupons receivable in payment of state taxes.[14] In the ensuing controversy few bondholders accepted the peelers, and little interest was paid on them.[15] Lacking the leverage of the consols' coupons, the peelers had a claim of low order on the impecunious debtor.

Legal and political attention then focused on whether the state could default on the tax-receivable coupons. In 1873 the General Assembly, with the blessing of the newly elected Conservative governor, Gen. James Lawson Kemper, C.S.A., imposed a tax on the coupons and ordered the tax collectors to deduct it from the coupons as they were tendered.[16] The effect, of course, was to reduce the rate of interest on the bonds. By this time the state judiciary had come to terms with the new political tendency and upheld the tax. But the state courts are not the final arbiters of rights under the Federal Constitution, and in 1881 in *Hartman* v. *Greenhowl* the U.S. Supreme Court reversed the Virginia court and declared the tax to be a violation of the Contracts Clause.[17]

Before the legal proceedings were over, however, an attempt was made to readjust the debt by agreement with the bondholders. In 1879 the General Assembly passed the McCulloch Act,[18] named in honor of Hugh McCulloch, former U.S. Secretary of the Treasury and subsequently agent for the bondholders.[19] The McCulloch Act provided for funding the debt into bonds yielding three percent interest for ten years, four percent for twenty years, and five percent for ten years. In the shorthand of the day the new bonds were known as "ten-forties."[20] Some bondholders made the exchange, but many awaited further legal and political developments.

In 1879, unable to contain any longer the raging debate on fiscal policy, the Conservative Party split into warring factions. Known for their attachment to the Funding Act of 1871, the Funders were filled with zeal for the good name of Virginia and were convinced that it was legally impossible to default on the coupons. Their opponents, dedicated to the cause of repudiation, styled themselves "Readjusters."[21] In 1879 the Readjusters won control of the General Assembly; two years later they captured the governorship. In short order they sent to the U.S. Senate two arch-Readjusters, William Mahone and H. H. Riddleberger. With state government now in their control, the Readjusters set about to kill the coupons.

II

At first glance, the probability for the success of the Readjusters must have appeared high. Legal precedents from the 1870s, especially in cases involving similar attempts in Louisiana, augured well for Virginia. Louisiana had recovered self-government as a result of the Compromise of 1877. In 1879 Louisiana's Redeemers, the legendary Bourbons, sought to scale down the state debt inherited from the hated Carpetbaggers and Scalawags. The first order of business was to summon a constitutional convention to replace the Constitution of 1868. Ignoring an appeal to uphold the "fair fame and name" of Louisiana,[22] convention delegates added to the Constitution of 1879 an extraordinary provision known as the Debt Ordinance.[23] This provision repealed the guarantees of the state debt contained in an amendment to the preceding constitution and reduced the interest the state would pay.

During the decade of the 1880s, holders of Louisiana state bonds challenged the Debt Ordinance in a series of federal cases. At the outset the plaintiffs' prospects looked good. Louisiana had unmistakably entered into valid contracts with its creditors; the Debt Ordinance clearly impaired the obligation of those contracts. The Supreme Court, moreover, had held Louisiana liable in an 1876 case, *Board of Liquidation* v. *McComb*,[24] in which the state challenged the jurisdiction of the federal courts on the basis of the infrequently cited Eleventh Amendment. By its terms that amendment deprives the national judiciary of power over "any suit in law or equity, commenced or prosecuted against one of the United States by Citizens of another State." But the amendment had long been interpreted not to apply to suits against officers or instrumentalities of the state, and in *McComb* the Court wasted few words defending its jurisdiction. While Louisiana's legal argument on behalf of the Debt Ordinance looked insubstantial, its position as a matter of practical politics was more secure. The Bourbons controlled state government, and the federal courts lacked adequate enforcement power. In the Compromise of 1877 the Republicans had conceded, among other things, home rule to the South in return for the peaceful inauguration of Rutherford B. Hayes as the nineteenth President. The necessary corollary of this concession was the removal of the Union army of occupation. The judges could issue what orders they pleased, but enforcement would require executive or congressional support. The Hayes administration was unlikely to oblige.

Under these circumstances, the Supreme Court retrieved the Eleventh Amendment. In 1883 in *Louisiana ex rel. Elliott* v. *Jumel*,[25] a bondholder sought to compel Louisiana to order the state auditor to pay interest on the state debt in disregard of the Debt Ordinance. The Court distinguished its recent precedent in *McComb* and ignored *Hartman*. The Eleventh Amendment as now interpreted barred federal relief in cases in which a state impaired the obligation of its own contracts.

But the best advised bondholders evidently anticipated a rebuff. Shortly after the Louisiana constitutional convention—at the same time, in other words, that the *Jumel* litigation began—a more imaginative strategy was set in train. The bondholders, many of whom lived in the North, persuaded the legislatures of New Hampshire and New York to enact statutes[26] authorizing their attorneys general to sue Louisiana on behalf of their citizens whose bonds were unpaid. By its terms, of course, the Eleventh Amendment applied only to suits against a state brought by "Citizens of another State." *New Hampshire* v. *Louisiana*,[27] as the consolidated cases were called, offered a technical distinction to justices interested in protecting vested rights such as those claimed by the bondholders. But the Court passed up this opportunity, showing that more than literalism was involved in the interpretation of the newly rediscovered Eleventh Amendment.

The stakes were too high, however, to leave any loophole unexplored. The amendment said nothing about suits against a state brought by its own citizens. It was a simple matter for a Louisianian to sue his state in federal court. In 1890 in *Hans* v. *Louisiana*[28] a dissatisfied bondholder made the attempt, only to be repulsed. In the words of the Court, "the obligations of a State rest for their performance upon its honor and good faith, and cannot be made the subjects of judicial cognizance unless the State consents to be sued."[29] While not explicitly recognized in the Eleventh Amendment, the concept of sovereign immunity barred suits against a state by its own citizens. It was ironic indeed that state sovereignty was a winning argument in the U.S. Supreme Court within a generation of the Civil War.[30]

Since Louisiana repudiated a state debt larger than any other state in the Old Confederacy, it is fitting that that state should have figured in all the leading cases. But the Louisiana story was by no means unique. All southern states repudiated some part of their public debts.[31] North Carolina was close behind Louisiana both in the amount repudiated and in the ensuing litigation.[32] It is worth stressing that readjustment did not affect Reconstruction bonds only. Those unpopular obligations created advantageous opportunities for states to reduce debts of unquestioned validity. North Carolina, for example, was able to scale down to a fraction of their face value millions of dollars worth of bonds issued by the indigenous white government before the War.[33] For these creditors, too, the rehabilitation of the Eleventh Amendment amounted to a legal Appomattox.

III

Those who studied the Supreme Court decisions must have believed that the precedents augured well for the Virginia Readjusters' plans to kill the coupons. Those plans were promptly set in motion. Because the direct route of simple repudiation had been closed by earlier state judicial decisions and the somewhat circuitous route relying on the taxing power had been blocked by the U.S. Supreme Court in *Hartman*, the Readjusters' strategy called for legal ingenuity. The two statutes of 1882 known by the epithet "Coupon Killers"[34] were designed to kill their victims by interfering with the manner of their receipt. Under the guise of suppressing forged, stolen, and invalid coupons, the new legislation prohibited tax collectors from accepting any coupons. The taxpayer who tendered coupons had to pay his taxes in lawful money and then sue the state to compel acceptance of his coupons. The plaintiff had to prove the coupons' validity, and should he prevail, the state's attorney could appeal from court to court. Before he could get his money back, the taxpayer would have to bear the law's delay and expense.

The Coupon Killers attempted to induce bondholders to exchange their consols for other bonds, popularly known as "Riddlebergers" in honor of H. H. Riddleberger, the Readjuster Senator.[35] The law's prohibitions and requirements were necessary because the Riddlebergers yielded only three percent interest, half the return on the older obligations, and Riddleberger coupons were not receivable in payment of state taxes.[36] Although the new bonds were not to mature for fifty years, the state was empowered to redeem them at any time after eighteen years. Not surprisingly, owners of consols did not queue up to make the exchange. Instead, they haled the Coupon Killers into court. But they lost. In 1883, the year of Louisiana's sweeping victories, the U.S. Supreme Court upheld the Virginia statutes in *Antoni* v. *Greenhow*.[37] The justices, it appears, had concluded that southern-state debts were, as a practical matter, not collectible and saw no reason to single out the Old Dominion for special treatment.[38] With the disingenuous explanation that the statutes left the owners of coupons with "an adequate and efficacious remedy,"[39] the Court found no violation of the Contracts Clause.

The Readjusters seemed to have discovered a route out of the labyrinth of debt in which the Funders had wandered. Although the Readjusters lost the legislative elections in 1883, the victorious Funders-Conservatives (newly reorganized as Democrats) showed little of their former zeal for paying Virginia's pound of flesh. In fact, the Democratic solons passed a joint resolution advising the creditors that "any expectation that any settlement of the debt, upon any other basis [than the Riddleberger Act], will ever be made or tolerated by the people of Virginia, is absolutely illusory and hopeless."[40] They quickly followed their opponents' legal victory in *Antoni* with more statutes designed to kill the coupons; for example, a license fee of $1,000 was imposed on sellers of coupons,[41] and lawyers who sued the Commonwealth to collect the coupons were required to buy a special license costing $250.[42] The Democrats also stole the Readjusters' thunder on another issue by providing that the school tax could not be paid in coupons, but "only in lawful money of the United States."[43]

Despite their moribund appearance, the coupons were not dead, thanks to the tireless efforts of a Funder lawyer, William L. Royall. As chief counsel to the bondholders, Royall appeared before the Supreme Court almost every term from 1881 to 1890, twice challenging his own imprisonment by Virginia for championing his clients' cause.[44] In 1885 Royall discovered the key to success. Unlike the bondholders of other southern states, the creditors of Virginia did not need a court order requiring politicians to raise taxes and pay interest. They did not even need to compel the Commonwealth to accept the coupons. All that mattered was the discharge of liability for taxes. The legal strategy was simple. A taxpayer would tender coupons, but when they were refused, he would seek no legal remedy; when in due course he was sued for delinquent taxes, he would defend on the ground that he had in law paid his taxes.[45] In eight cases in 1885 known collectively as the *Virginia Coupon Cases*[46] the Supreme Court accepted Royall's argument.

Readjusting Democrats redoubled their efforts to kill the coupons. Although the Commonwealth had challenged the genuineness of the coupons, it excluded expert testimony on that issue.[47] To close the market for coupons, it required any taxpayer who tendered coupons to produce the bonds from which they had been cut.[48] Any person soliciting or inducing suits against the state was subjected to fine and imprisonment,[49] and lawyers guilty of the offense were to be perpetually disbarred.[50]

Made bold by his victory in the *Virginia Coupon Cases*, Royall took the offensive on behalf of the bondholders. In 1887 he successfully petitioned the federal circuit court in Richmond for a temporary injunction prohibiting Rufus A. Ayers, the Virginia attorney general, from suing taxpayers who tendered coupons. When Ayers defied the order, he was imprisoned for contempt. To Royall's chagrin, however, the U.S. Supreme Court ordered Ayers released.[51] Citing the Eleventh Amendment, the Court disclaimed jurisdiction and refused to be drawn into a struggle with the politicians.

Royall had discovered that he could not force the pace. When Virginia finally moved against those who had tendered coupons, however, he was ready with a strong defense. In 1890, when Louisiana won its final victory, Virginia suffered its final defeat. In the unanimous opinion in *McGahey* v. *Virginia*[52] the U.S. Supreme Court reiterated that the bonds issued under the Funding Act of 1871 constituted contracts between the state and the bondholders. It held that statutes that materially impaired the obligation of these contracts were void and that a taxpayer tendering coupons in payment of taxes was "entitled to be free from molestation in persons or goods on account of such taxes."[53] In what appears to be a concession to the school supporters, however, the Court upheld the act prohibiting the receipt of coupons in payment of the school tax.[54] Concluding its opinion, the Court sententiously observed:

> It is certainly to be wished that some arrangement may be adopted which will be satisfactory to all the parties concerned, and relieve the courts as well as the Commonwealth of Virginia, whose name and history recall so many interesting associations, from all further exhibitions of a controversy that has become a vexation and a regret.[55]

At last the parties negotiated a settlement.[56] New bonds, known as century bonds because they matured in 100 years, were exchanged for consols, peelers, ten-forties and Riddlebergers at the rate of about two for three.[57] Interest on the centuries would be paid without protest at the rate of two percent for the first ten years and three percent thereafter. After two decades the battle with the creditors was finally over. Like all such long drawn-out contests, it left its mark. The debt experience led the Commonwealth to adopt a pay-as-you-go policy that endured well into the second half of the twentieth century.[58]

IV

Virginia was different from Louisiana and other southern states; the Funding Act of 1871 had made it so. Whereas lenders elsewhere had put their trust in promises, albeit of the most solemn constitutional kind, Virginia's creditors had relied on the simple receivability provision. Because of the realities of the federal system, it was harder for the Commonwealth to renege. For this reason it is unrealistic to suggest, as James Tice Moore does in his valuable sociological study of the Virginia debt controversy, that the patricians "could easily have maintained their position by stealing the Readjusters' thunder, defying the courts, and forcibly reducing the interest burden."[59] After 1871 nothing could be as easy for Virginia as for the other southern states. Plaintiffs suing on the bonds of other states had to ask the Supreme Court to order state politicians to do the very acts they had been elected not to do. To enforce such orders the political branches of the federal government would have had to violate the cardinal principle of the Compromise of 1877 and coerce the South. As an excuse not to issue these orders the Court dusted off the Eleventh Amendment. But the plaintiffs' case against Virginia did not require such orders. There was no need to compel the Commonwealth's officers to act; all that was required was a judgment declaring that they had no legal right to take action against the taxpayers who had tendered coupons. The economic effect, of course, was the same. The Old Dominion was just as poor if its income fell or its expenses rose. But the difference in terms of judicial power was substantial. Under the federal system the last word on whether taxes had been paid or not belonged to the judges.[60]

V

The Commonwealth's struggle with its burden of debt was, however, only two-thirds over. In 1871 Virginia had disclaimed liability on one-third of the antebellum debt and had issued certifi-.cates attributable to West Virginia. Although the West Virginia Constitution of 1862 had bound the new state to assume an "equitable proportion" of the public debt of the Old Dominion and had directed the legislature in Wheeling to provide for its payment "as soon as may be practicable,"[61] West Virginia never paid a cent.

During the two decades in which Virginia struggled with its own self-assessed share of indebtedness, it paid little attention to the share putatively owed by the state "made from her rib."[62] Once the Commonwealth had settled with the bondholders, however, it was time to take up the matter with its neighbor. In 1894 the Virginia General Assembly created a Debt Commission to treat with West Virginia.[63] After a half dozen years of fruitless negotiations, it empowered the Commission to accept deposit of the certificates that represented the share attributed to West Virginia and to bring suit if necessary on behalf of the bondholders.[64] Holders of the overwhelming majority of certificates promptly deposited with the Debt Commission.[65]

West Virginia was in no hurry to settle. Over the decades it had grown accustomed to thinking that it had come into existence with a clean slate. Perhaps it believed that loyalty in the Civil War earned it credit in its accounting with the secessionists. Whatever the motive, the Mountain State was unyielding in negotiations. It claimed that its fair share equaled the amount of borrowed money that had actually been spent within the western counties plus "a just proportion" of the ordinary expenses of state government minus taxes paid during the same period.[66] Calculations on this basis varied widely, sometimes showing that West Virginia owed Virginia $4 million and sometimes showing that Virginia actually owed West Virginia $3 million.[67]

The negotiators on behalf of the Old Dominion must have believed that their hand was strengthened by the decision in 1904 in another bond case, *South Dakota* v. *North Carolina*.[68] South Dakota had become the owner of ten North Carolina bonds the easy way—by gift. Since the debtor refused to pay, the bondholder took advantage of the constitutional provision permitting states to sue one another in the U.S. Supreme Court.[69] It might seem that New Hampshire and New York's unhappy experience in 1883 would have foreclosed the plaintiff's suit. But the Court in 1904 was willing to distinguish the earlier case: the two states had acted on behalf of their bondholding citizens, while South Dakota was suing on its own behalf. The Court ordered North Carolina to pay the debt, and the state complied with the judgment.[70]

In 1906 Virginia filed papers opening a legal battle with West Virginia that raged for a dozen years.[71] Virginia asked the Justices to determine West Virginia's part of the state debt and to issue an order requiring payment.[72] West Virginia challenged the Court's jurisdiction. Since the Court had, it argued, no power to enforce a judgment against a state, it had no jurisdiction to issue one. Without a remedy, in other words, there was no right. In a second challenge to the jurisdiction of the Court, West Virginia argued that Virginia had an insufficient interest in the controversy because the debt, if any, was owing not to the Commonwealth but to the owners of the certificates. While finding many precedents opposed to West Virginia's first argument, the Justices dismissed the second with an ipsedixitism: "We are satisfied that . . . we have jurisdiction."[73] The matter was then referred to an officer of the Court known as a "master" for the ascertainment of the facts necessary for decision. In 1911 the Court, using the figures produced by the master, decided to apportion the antebellum debt on the basis of property values, exclusive of slaves. On this reckoning West Virginia owed 23.5 percent of the total.[74] Although the certificates represented one-third of the debt, West Virginia was held liable for only one-quarter; the bondholders lost the difference. At this stage no coercion was applied to West Virginia. As Justice Holmes observed for the Court: "Great States have a temper superior to that of private litigants, and it is to be hoped that enough has been decided for patriotism, the fraternity of the Union, and mutual consideration to bring it to an end."[75]

West Virginia took exception to the calculations, however, and convinced the Court in 1915 to reduce its liability by attributing to it a proportional share of those assets pledged for the retirement of the debt that Virginia held in 1861.[76] While that setoff lessened West Virginia's liability, the Court in the same action increased it by holding West Virginia liable for interest compounded since

1861.[77] In vain West Virginia urged that it had a claim against the United States, derived from Virginia, arising out of the cession of the Northwest Territory in 1783 and that its share would discharge the judgment.[78] Fraternal feelings proved insufficient to move West Virginia to appropriate the necessary sum, so the Court was finally forced in 1918 to consider ways and means of enforcing its judgment. Orders of the Supreme Court are federal orders, sustainable, the Court confidently stated, "by every authority of the Federal government, judicial, legislative, or executive."[79] Judicial power included, the Court hinted, the power to issue an order to the West Virginia legislature requiring it to levy a tax and even the power to levy the tax itself. Before exercising this awesome power, the Court announced its intention to give Congress an opportunity to bring legislative power to bear. Although it was proceeding with all deliberate speed, the Court was clear that West Virginia would eventually be compelled to pay. Any other result would "overthrow the doctrines irrevocably settled by the great controversy of the Civil War."[80] At last West Virginia conceded defeat and paid the certificates, outstanding since 1871.

VI

There are tactics and strategies in law as in war, and justices of the Supreme Court are constrained by circumstances no less than generals in the field. After the end of Reconstruction the justices, whatever their personal feelings about private property, countenanced the repudiation of millions of dollars worth of southern state bonds. But during the same years the Virginia Coupon Killers failed in their mission. The provision in the Funding Act of 1871 making the coupons receivable for state taxes put the creditors of Virginia in position to take advantage of federal judicial power. Although the Court in the 1880s had been unwilling to try to make its writ run in the newly restored southern states, it had fewer misgivings when the lone state of West Virginia was in the dock a generation later. While moving cautiously, it nonetheless moved inexorably to judgment. The chances of making this defendant do justice to its creditors were much better. Compared to investors in other southern obligations, the investors in Virginia securities did well, although the recovery was a long time coming. In the course of the litigation the nation learned important lessons about the judicial power of the United States.

NOTES

[1] On Jan. 1, 1861, the public debt of Virginia amounted to $33,897,074. B. U. Ratchford, *American State Debts* (Durham, N.C., 1941), 197.

[2] Ratchford, *American State Debts*, 198.

[3] See Jack P. Maddex, *The Virginia Conservatives, 1867–1879: A Study in Reconstruction Politics* (Chapel Hill, N.C., 1970), 91.

[4] Virginia, *Acts* (1870–71), 378. The fundable debt amounted to $47,090,867. Ratchford, *American State Debts*, 201. By Act of March 2, 1866, Virginia had acknowledged liability for the antebellum debt and had funded the wartime interest in bonds bearing the same rate of interest as the principal. Virginia, *Acts* (1865–1866), 79.

[5] Virginia, *Acts* (1870–1871), 379.

[6] *Ibid.* By December 1871 the state had issued consols worth $21,610,691, which means that $32,416,036 of old obligations must have been surrendered. Ratchford, *American State Debts*, 201.

[7] The economic burden should not be exaggerated. The census of 1880 showed that the ratio of taxation to true valuation in Virginia was .67 as compared with .70 for the United States and .62 for the southern states. Reginald C. McGrane, *Foreign Bondholders and American State Debts* (New York, 1935), 371–72. On the other hand, per capita taxation in 1880 was more than twice what it had been in 1850. Maddex, *Virginia Conservatives*, 170.

[8] James Tice Moore, *Two Paths to the New South: The Virginia Debt Controversy, 1870–1883* (Lexington, Ky., 1974), 16.

[9] The Virginia Constitution of 1870 (Art. VIII, Sec. 3) required that a public school system be enacted no later than 1876. Between Jan. 1, 1873, and Oct. 1, 1878, the state received coupons worth almost $1,000,000 a year in lieu of taxes. Ratchford, *American State Debts*, 170.

[10] Allen W. Moger, *Virginia: Bourbonism to Byrd, 1870–1925* (Charlottesville, Va., 1968), 34 (quoting Gov. F. W. M. Holliday). It was reported that a "prominent debt payer" declared publicly that it would be better to burn the schoolhouses than to default on the debt. Charles C. Pearson, *The Readjuster Movement in Virginia* (New Haven, Conn., 1917), 62.

[11] Virginia, *Acts* (1871–72), 141.

[12] *Antoni* v. *Wright*, 63 Va. (22 Gratt.) 833 (1872).

[13] U.S., Constitution, Art I, Sec. 10.

[14] Morris Gray, "The Coupon-Legislation of Virginia," *American Law Review*, XXIII (1889), 927. Although Gray spells the name of the new bonds "pealers," they are styled "peelers" in other literature.

[15] Maddex, *Virginia Conservatives*, 219.

[16] Virginia, *Acts* (1872–73), 207.

[17] 102 U.S. 672 (1881).

[18] Virginia, *Acts* (1878–79), 264.

[19] Pearson, *Readjuster Movement*, 52, 85 (n.5).

[20] Ratchford, *American State Debts*, 206, 208, 217–18.

[21] Pearson, *Readjuster Movement*, 96.

[22] William Ivy Hair, *Bourbonism and Agrarian Protest: Louisiana Politics, 1877–1900* (Baton Rouge, La., 1969), 100.

[23] *Sources and Documents of United States Constitutions*, William F. Swindler, ed. (10 vols., Dobbs Ferry, N.Y., 1973–79), IV-A, 214.

[24] 92 U.S. 531 (1876).
[25] 107 U.S. 711 (1883).
[26] New Hampshire, *Laws* (1879), 357; New York, *Laws* (1880), 440.
[27] 108 U.S. 76 (1883).
[28] 134 U.S. 1 (1890).
[29] *Ibid.*, 20.
[30] For more details on Louisiana see John V. Orth, "The Fair Fame and Name of Louisiana: The Eleventh Amendment and the End of Reconstruction," *Tulane Lawyer*, II (1980), 2–15.
[31] For tables showing amounts of repudiated debts, see Ratchford, *American State Debts*, 192, and William A. Scott, *The Repudiation of State Debts* (New York, 1893), 276.
[32] See John V. Orth, "The Eleventh Amendment and the North Carolina State Debt," *North Carolina Law Review*, LIX (1981), 747–66.
[33] B. U. Ratchford, "The Adjustment of the North Carolina Public Debt, 1879–1833," *North Carolina Historical Review*, X (1933), 157–67.
[34] Virginia, *Acts* (1881–82), 10, 37. See "The 'Coupon Killers,'" *Virginia Law Journal*, VII (1883), 513–26.
[35] Moger, *Virginia*, 39.
[36] Virginia, *Acts* (1881–82), 88.
[37] 107 U.S. 769 (1883).
[38] Those who like political explanations of judicial decisions will point out that a Supreme Court dominated by Republicans was upholding Readjuster laws at the time Sen. Mahone was allied with the Republican Party. The political convenience of the result may be conceded. See Moger, *Virginia*, 39. But Mahone had been voting with the Republicans in the Senate since his election in 1879, and his party's legal strategy had nonetheless suffered a setback in 1881 in *Hartman*. Nor do the political facts explain the rulings in 1883 in favor of Louisiana Democrats.
[39] 107 U.S. at 774.
[40] Virginia, *Acts* (1883–84), 7.
[41] *Ibid.*, 590.
[42] *Ibid.*, 597. By comparison, the license fee for practice was $15 for attorneys who had been licensed for less than five years and $25 for attorneys who had been licensed for five years or more.
[43] *Ibid.*, 603.
[44] *Ex parte Royall*, 112 U.S. 181 (1884); *Ex parte Royall*, 117 U.S. 241 (1886). The second Royall Case is a landmark in federal jurisdiction. It marks the beginning of restrictive judicial interpretation of the Habeas Corpus Act of 1867, U.S., Statutes at Large, XIV, 385. See William M. Wiecek, "The Reconstruction of Federal Judicial Power, 1863–1876," *American Journal of Legal History*, XIII (1969), 347. Professor Wythe Holt of the University of Alabama School of Law suggested to me that the case reveals a caution in the exercise of judicial power similar to that shown in the bond cases. Had the Court used the full power conferred by the Habeas Corpus Act, it would have prompted the repeal of the Act. On the principle that half a loaf is better than nothing, it exercised discretion, and the act was spared.
[45] William L. Royall, *Some Reminiscences* (New York, 1909), 120.
[46] 114 U.S. 269 (1885).
[47] Virginia, *Acts* (1885–86), 36.
[48] *Ibid.*, 40.
[49] *Ibid.*, 249.
[50] *Ibid.*, 384.
[51] *In re Ayers*, 123 U.S. 443 (1887).
[52] 135 U.S. 662 (1890).
[53] *Ibid.*, 684.
[54] *Ibid.*, 716–20.

[55] Ibid., 721.

[56] Virginia, *Acts* (1891–92), 533.

[57] The exact rate of exchange was 19 to 28. Thereafter, the funded debt was $31,469,054. Ratchford, *American State Debts*, 216–17.

[58] Moger, *Virginia*, 42.

[59] Moore, *Two Paths*, 26. In his occupational profiles of the two groups Moore shows that many more of the Funder leaders had legal experience than had the Readjuster leaders. Of 67 prominent Funders, at least 54 had been lawyers or had studied law. Of 125 prominent Readjusters, 50 had studied or practiced law. Moore, *Two Paths*, 28 (n. 1), 48 (n. 6). Perhaps the patricians understood the legal realities better than their opponents did.

[60] For further reflections on the nature of judicial power, see John V. Orth, "The Interpretation of the Eleventh Amendment, 1798–1908: A Case Study of Judicial Power," *University of Illinois Law Review* (1983), 423–55.

[61] West Virginia, Constitution of 1862, Art. VIII, Sec. 8.

[62] Thomas Reed Powell, "Coercing a State to Pay a Judgment: Virginia v. West Virginia," *Michigan Law Review*, XVII (1918), 2.

[63] Virginia, *Acts* (1893–94), 867.

[64] Virginia, *Acts* (1899–1900), 902.

[65] Of the $15,481,690 of certificates outstanding, $13,173,435 were deposited. Ratchford, *American State Debts*, 219.

[66] The West Virginia position dates from the 1861 ordinance of the Unionist convention providing for the formation of the state. Virginia, *Acts* (1861, extra session), 58.

[67] James G. Randall, "The Virginia Debt Controversy," *Political Science Quarterly*, XXX (1915), 566.

[68] 192 U.S. 286 (1904).

[69] U.S., Constitution, Art. III, Sec. 2.

[70] See Robert F. Durden, *Reconstruction Bonds and Twentieth Century Politics: South Dakota v. North Carolina* (Durham, N.C., 1962).

[71] *Virginia* v. *West Virginia*, 206 U.S. 290 (1907); 209 U.S. 514 (1908); 220 U.S. 1 (1911); 222 U.S. 17 (1911); 231 U.S. 89 (1913): 234 U.S. 117 (1914); 238 U.S. 202 (1915); 241 U.S. 531 (1916); 246 U.S. 565 (1918).

[72] 206 U.S. 290 (1907).

[73] *Ibid.*, 321.

[74] 220 U.S. 1 (1911).

[75] *Ibid.*, 40.

[76] 238 U.S. 202 (1915).

[77] As of July 1, 1915, the West Virginia debt was calculated to be $12,393,929, of which $4,215,622 was principal and $8,178,307 interest. *Ibid.*, 242.

[78] 246 U.S. 567–79 (1918).

[79] *Ibid.*, 601.

[80] *Ibid.*, 603.

Part III
Law and Race in Southern History

Forging the Shackles:
The Development of
Virginia's Criminal Code for Slaves

PHILIP J. SCHWARZ

As VIRGINIA'S LEGISLATORS created and modified a distinctive criminal code and separate criminal courts for Virginia slaves during the seventeenth, eighteenth, and nineteenth centuries, they kept three considerations in mind. The first was their objective of maintaining racial slavery as a labor and social system.[1] Another was the degree to which they could apply the principles of the English common law as well as the changing varieties of Anglo-American and American law[2] to the distinct institutions or "positive" laws of slavery.[3] The third consideration—to which historians have given the least attention[4]—involved those illegal actions of slaves to which so many lawmakers believed criminal prosecutions were the necessary response.

The writing of the criminal code, the creation of the slave courts, and the trials of numerous slaves produced a large body of court cases, numerous appeals, and many expressions of opinion about them.[5] Several historians have analyzed the manner in which the laws, courts, and cases reflect white leaders' diverse ideas, values, or fears concerning those actions of slaves that authorities deemed dangerous.[6] Others have explained the relationship between Anglo-American law and the slave law and courts. Few historians, however, have attempted to explain how the statutes, judicial bodies, and criminal convictions also reflect the actions, ideas, values, and fears of slaves.[7] Those Virginia slaves convicted of crimes by white judges, like slaves convicted of crime everywhere, affected the manner in which legislators and jurists stated, modified, and applied the legal assumptions of and institutional prerequisites for slavery.[8] The white supremacist, pro-slavery ideology of the masters was not sufficient to cause the perpetuation of the slave code and courts over nearly two centuries. The actions of a significant number of slaves—especially as perceived by many white legislators and judges—also influenced the creation and modification of the slave court system.

Denied citizenship and legally defined as passive extensions of the wills of their owners, slaves nevertheless stood trial for crimes. Because of this aspect of "slave crime,"[9] some scholars appear to regard slave codes and courts as nothing more than instruments of planter hegemony. This has encouraged a preoccupation with the law and courts rather than with the actions of slaves. For example, various proponents of labelling theory would probably argue that white authorities' definition of slave crime was completely political. Authorities "created" crimes, especially in a system such as the slave courts with its jurisdiction over regular offenses and with "status" offenses, for which only slaves could be tried, and they also sentenced slaves to discriminatory punishments.[10] Indeed, according to labelling theory, authorities created crime in response to the behavior of those members of society who most threatened leaders' rule. Such labelled deviants often forced leaders of society to articulate their norms, partial and self-interested though they might be. In prosecuting slaves, therefore, white authorities were conscious only of the threat that some slaves presented to slavery.

A complete historical explanation of Virginia's criminal code and courts for slaves must acknowledge that lawmakers and judges were also reacting to the threat certain slaves presented to life, limb, or property. The penal system for slaves served the dual functions of preserving slavery and protecting people or property. The administration of the criminal justice system for slaves in Virginia was not completely political. Yet the political aspects of that system were the most significant.

Because of the political nature of whites' use of slave codes and courts as a means of slave control, some historians treat the actions of slaves convicted of crimes as solely political. For them, all

such behavior was conscious resistance to slavery.[11] This argument is largely true, even though it ignores that behavior of slaves
which resulted from self-interested motives, irrationality, or impulse. Most of the behavior for which slaves suffered court-or-
dered punishments was a response to various forms of oppressive
slave control. As such, it was either politically motivated or had
a political impact. Moreover, many white authorities ironically
attached political importance to all "slave crimes." These authorities politicized such crimes by treating them as special cases because of the threat such behavior directly or indirectly presented
to slavery.[12] Whether slaves convicted of crimes had consciously
acted against slavery or for themselves alone, their behavior had
a political effect. The very manner in which many pro-slavery authorities treated all the illegal behavior of slaves helped to assure
that all "slave crimes" would have a political dimension, no matter
what the motives were of the slaves involved.

As long as slavery existed in Virginia, white authorities wrote
criminal statutes and prosecuted certain slaves in response to the
actions of those slaves. Political and social change[13] also influenced this legislative and judicial process. Another reason for
changes in the interaction between convicted slaves and white authorities is that the amount of slaves' illegal behavior differed over
time. Regardless of the exact number of slave felons or misde-
meanants, there were clearly enough at any time for legislators to
justify writing the slave laws as they did. Conversely, there were
also times in which threatening or dangerous slave behavior decreased to the extent that white judges believed it safe to lighten
sentences and legislators to introduce ameliorative features into the
slave code and court system.[14] There were, for example, enough
slaves who killed whites to lead lawmakers to go to great lengths
to proscribe their behavior. It was the relative number of "slave
crimes," not the absolute number, that made all the difference.
We cannot know the absolute number, but the trial records do allow us to chart the relative number over time.[15]

Most of the evidence concerning the kind of slave behavior that
led white officials to create some special definitions of felonies or
misdemeanors is in records of the criminal trials of slaves. With a

few exceptions, these trials took place in Virginia's segregated county courts of oyer and terminer.[16] The more than 4,000 trials on which this study is based include 1,988 cases from every available county record covering 1706 to 1785, 787 trials from 1786 to 1800 in Brunswick, Dinwiddie, and Henrico counties and the city of Richmond as well as from the records of the representative counties of Essex, Henry, Southampton, and Spotsylvania for 1786 through 1865,[17] and 1,423 convictions from the files of the state auditor and governor, 1785 to 1865.[18] These trial and conviction records contain somewhat biased evaluations but relatively accurate descriptions of the behavior of nearly 4,000 Afro-Virginian slaves.[19] The records contain the best available evidence over time of slaves' challenges to or conflicts with the slave code and courts. (Other evidence concerning such slave behavior is in a variety of manuscript sources.)

One of the most important factors for slaves to consider before engaging in illegal behavior was the degree of risk involved. Convicted slaves faced a variety of risks between the 1600s and 1800s because of several fundamental modifications in the penal system. These included legalization of benefit of clergy for slaves in 1732, institution of the "reduced" sentence of transportation in 1801, and abolition of benefit of clergy for slaves in 1848.[20] The first and second changes legitimized an amelioration in sentences that had begun earlier through other means.[21] Over time, those two changes made possible a rather steady decline in the number of executions of slaves for capital offenses. Before the 1730s, about two-thirds of slaves convicted of felonies received the death sentence. From the 1730s to the 1780s, the percentage dropped to 42.3. Of 131 slaves condemned to death and granted neither benefit of clergy nor pardons between 1785 and 1799, only one escaped the gallows. By the 1850s, however, only 14.6 percent of condemned slaves actually hanged.

Abolition of benefit of clergy in 1848 created a new kind of danger, which some convicted felons had not faced previously. The number of transportees in the 1850s was nearly double that for the 1840s, while the number of executions decreased by twelve. Many lesser factors also influenced convictions of slaves for major crimes. These included the degree of control slaveowners exer-

cised over the courts and changes in the public accountability of
the governor when he chose to pardon condemned slaves, to re-
prieve others for sale and transportation or for labor on the public
works, or else to carry out their execution.[22]

Why did some slaves still take these risks? Those slaves who attacked white people or property usually acted with a purpose and
not just on impulse. There is a pattern of resistance in the behavior of most of them, which justifies the ascription of political motivation to many of their actions. While some irrational activity
took place,[23] many killings, poisonings, thefts, uses of arson, and
attempts to rebel were efforts to oppose the means of maintaining
slavery or attempts to attack slavery itself. For example, slaves
convicted of large thefts most frequently singled out the necessities of food and clothing.[24] They often secured for themselves what
some owners either failed or refused to provide for them. Similarly, killings or attempted killings of whites by slaves typically,
although not always, resulted from a slave's refusal to endure further whippings or intolerable abuse of other kinds.[25] Many poisonings,[26] uses of arson,[27] and other forms of attack were products
of the same resolution, while slaves' threats and attempts to rebel
usually proceeded from a generalized sense of grievance combined with a strong belief in the necessity of resorting to collective
violence as the only possible means of ending their slavery.[28]

The conflict between often purposeful, aggressive slaves and
generally powerful white authorities began in the seventeenth
century as the number of slaves in Virginia increased steadily and
then dramatically, making them more than half of the labor force
before 1700. During the seventeenth century, there were a few
slaves whose behavior prompted local officials to try to suppress
them.[29] There were also several who provoked a governmental response that prefigured the judicial control of slaves. Outlying
slaves—that is, those who ran away from their owners yet lived
secretly and "off the land" for long periods—who were plunder-
ing livestock and storehouses and occasionally threatening whites
sometimes led the keepers of the colony's centralized institutions
to react with *ad hoc* executive directives, laws, and finally some
separate courts.[30]

The caretakers of public safety eventually rejected *ad hoc* actions of the royal government as inadequate. White authorities' evaluations of certain slave behavior led to *ad hominem* legislation. In 1669, the House of Burgesses, with the approval of Governor Berkeley and King Charles II's Privy Council, declared that the "obstinacy" of many blacks precluded their being "supprest" by "other than violent means." White owners of black slaves would therefore become the law for their human property. Before 1788, if they should kill slaves in the process of "correcting" them, they could not even be held accountable for manslaughter. Thus did owners acquire the nearly unimpeachable authority to punish all lesser, as opposed to major, crimes or offenses that they believed had been committed by slaves.[31] The Burgesses went further in 1680 and 1681, prohibiting "dangerous" assemblies of slaves and setting the penalty of thirty lashes for slaves who were found guilty of "lifting a hand" against a Christian. In order to deal with the problem of outlying slaves, the same act allowed persons with "lawfull authority" to kill such slaves should they resist capture. The legislators then decided in 1691 to empower any two justices of the peace in the county quorum to issue a warrant to the county sheriff to use any force necessary, including killing, to suppress such offenders, with the colony paying the owners compensation for any "property" so destroyed.[32]

The majority of the legislators moved the logic of the developing criminal code for slaves another step toward complete control one year later. The 1692 "Act for the More Speedy Prosecution of Slaves Committing Capital Crimes" announced in its title and preamble that both jury trials in the counties and general court proceedings in Jamestown were ineffective responses to slaves accused of committing common law capital offenses. The only means of providing "condign punishment" that would deter other slaves, making them return to work and "be affrighted" to violate the criminal code, was a separate court of oyer and terminer, which, like the similar form of courts that was about to be used against witches in Massachusetts, could fully hear and determine such cases and also exercise the power to execute the condemned.[33]

With the creation of the oyer and terminer courts in 1692, the House of Burgesses institutionalized the provincial county governments' response to slave behavior they deemed most dangerous. Installation of the system was a response to the behavior of some slaves over the years before 1692; each subsequent trial[34] would be a reaction to an accusation against a specific slave, and each conviction would reflect several judges' opinion that a fellow slaveholder's "possession" had indeed committed a dangerous capital offense. In 1705 the government promised financial compensation to the owners of executed slaves as an inducement to report offenders, or at least not to cover for them out of fear of losing a capital investment. Thereafter, there was a good chance that a court of oyer and terminer would be the normal means of responding to slaves accused of particularly threatening or destructive behavior.[35] Moreover, the need to apply to the legislature for compensation for condemned slaves as well as the opportunity, after 1748, for owners to appeal sentences of death to the governor and council kept colonial and later state officials involved in the criminal justice system for slaves.[36]

The cycle of lawmaking, trials, convictions, sentences, and punishments concerning major stealing by slaves, the most commonly prosecuted capital offense, is typical of the cycle of all "criminal" slave behavior. The common law defined breaking and entering (burglary) and theft, of course, but the positive law of slavery attached special penalties to the various categories of stealing by slaves.[37] Between 1706 and 1739, about two-thirds (98) of the 148 slaves known to have stood before judges of oyer and terminer did so because the King's attorney was prosecuting them for stealing. Nearly two-thirds (64/98) of the defendants were found guilty, with 40 receiving the sentence of death.[38] Two hundred nineteen, or just over one-third, of the 616 found guilty of a felonious theft, usually combined with burglary, between 1740 and 1784 also were condemned.[39] This was a major offense for free people as well as for slaves in the eighteenth century. The risks were high for anyone convicted of burglary. Even authorities in the "Golden Age" of Virginia could hang slaves convicted of burglary who had taken, in one case, assorted goods worth only 21s. 6d. current money, or, in another instance, a coat, a pair of breeches, a hat, a handkerchief, silver worth three shillings, and one chamber pot.[40]

Just as the courts of oyer and terminer and the special penalties for slaves convicted of major stealing were responses to slave violations of statutes against theft, so the manner in which the many slave courts dealt with such actions over time was a reaction to the perceived level of threat and damage. In the first place, only five percent of the slaves convicted of stealing before 1785 had "taken and carried away" something from their owners. The courts clearly regarded stealing outside the home plantation as the only kind that merited their regular attention. Plantation authorities could normally deal with slaves' thefts from their owners. Moreover, there were so few prosecutions for breaking and entering with intent to steal, as opposed to burglary combined with stealing, that lawmakers decided in 1772 that those convicted of the lesser offense could plead for benefit of clergy.[41]

Indeed, the royal government's conferral of the privilege of benefit of clergy on slaves in 1732 affected the nature of justices' responses to stealing by slaves. Almost by itself, the willingness of many judges to grant benefit to slaves convicted of burglary and stealing accounts for the lower proportion of convicts sentenced to hanging between 1740 and 1784 as compared to 1706 to 1739. Judges made it possible to grant benefit in many cases simply by reducing the valuation of goods that the defendant was charged with stealing. About one-third of those convicted of theft received the death sentence before the 1770s; thereafter the portion lowered slightly to approximately one-quarter, staying at that level for several decades.

While separate penalties for slaves and free white people meant that slaves accused of stealing faced the risk of harsher punishments, the risk decreased over time. White authorities could see that the harshest punishments would not lower the amount of major stealing by slaves.[42] Also, beyond that increase which resulted from population growth, they could perceive no rise in major property crimes after the eighteenth-century amelioration in punishments.

The institution of transportation in 1801 allowed the most dramatic lightening of sentences to occur. Sixteen convicted burglars went to the gallows between 1795 and 1799; only one did from 1800 to 1804. Thereafter, only 28 slaves convicted of property crimes were executed through 1865. Most of them had been convicted of highway robbery rather than the kinds of stealing that endangered property alone. When the state legislature abolished benefit of clergy for slaves in 1848, the number convicted of stealing and sentenced at least to transportation might have risen sharply. But it did not. Instead, it dropped: 33 were exiled and none were executed during the 1850s, as opposed to 55 transported and two hanged in the 1840s. White authorities grew more relaxed but were by no means indifferent about slaves found guilty of major crimes against property; certain slaves continued to engage in that kind of behavior, especially in rapidly growing cities such as Richmond.[43]

Whenever a slave killed a white person, especially one in authority, fear was a natural reaction. Was it realistic? The trial records indicate that such killings occurred regularly. No fewer than 266 slaves were convicted of killing at least 183 whites from 1706 to 1864.[44] The objective of most of the slaves found guilty of murdering whites was normally fairly clear. Killing appeared to them to be the only means of preventing the white victim from continuing to victimize the slave. Quite commonly the convicts had told either fellow slaves or some other third party of their refusal to be whipped or otherwise abused again by an owner or overseer. Impulse played a part in some attacks, but there were a large number of trials in which witnesses claimed the defendants had explicitly stated before the homicide that they intended to take desperate measures, including killing, in order to control a specific white enemy.[45] The semi-political nature of some of these mortal attacks is significant. Conspiracies of slaves to kill other slaves or free blacks were extremely rare; conspiracies—that is, collective decisions—to kill whites were quite regular.

Such killings happened frequently enough and without warning to spread fear out of all proportion to the number of victims they claimed. Consequently, the official responses were sometimes rather harsh. In general, however, court action distinguished among some of the kinds of killing. Eighteenth-century judges almost always sentenced principals in the killing of whites to be hanged, only once convicting a slave of homicide by mis-

adventure and almost never lowering the offense to manslaughter.[46] Before 1765 justices found ways to convict slaves of manslaughter when they had killed other slaves. The House of
Burgesses recognized the pro-slavery, white-supremacist logic of
this practice in a 1765 law that allowed benefit of clergy for slaves
convicted of manslaughter against a slave. Manslaughter was now
a legal category for killing of slaves by slaves, but it would be a
long time before legislators or judges would allow convictions for
second-degree murder when the victim was white.[47] After the
sanction of transportation became available in 1801, judges used
it to exile accessories instead of granting them benefit of clergy;
judges even convicted a few slaves of second-degree murder or
manslaughter of whites in the 1850s, allowing them to be transported.[48]

During the same years, however, lawmakers reacted strongly
to their perception of the threat of murderous behavior by slaves.
A year after the 1822 Vesey conspiracy in South Carolina, legislators in the Old Dominion made it a capital offense for a slave to
assault a white with intent to kill, yet the law still allowed conferral of benefit on convicts. The number of slaves transported or
executed after being found guilty of this crime tripled during the
next quinquennium (1825 to 1829). After the Nat Turner Revolt
of 1831, however, a revision in the slave code assured that the same
convicts would be unable to plead their clergy.[49] Thereafter they
were generally transported, and a few were executed. While the
abolition of benefit of clergy for slaves in 1848 allowed, sometimes forced, oyer and terminer judges to give more severe sentences than before to slaves convicted of infanticide[50] or of killing
other slaves, the main concern of authorities continued to be the
ability of some slaves to destroy their white rulers.[51]

There is a connection between slave insurrections and slaves'
often mortal attacks on whites, which historians of slavery, who
have focused mainly on the most famous and large slave insurrections, have largely ignored.[52] To those whites who feared slave resistance, any killing or attempted killing of a white authority by
a slave looked a little like an insurrection in miniature. Indeed, before the law and the courts, any slave conspiracy to kill a white

owner, overseer, or official had some of the characteristics of an insurrection. In one sense, both slaves and white authorities recognized this. Between 1706 and 1865, at least twice as many Virginia slaves were convicted of being involved in successful conspiracies to kill one or more white people than were found guilty of being directly and actively involved in insurrectionary plotting that led to killings.[53] At least 98 slaves were convicted of being involved in conspiracies that resulted in the killing of white people between 1786 and 1865 alone. Most were politically significant killings. More than two-thirds of the convicted slaves had killed their owners or members of their owners' families. Seventeen of the remaining 32 slaves were convicted of killing their overseers or some other person in authority, such as a hirer; several of the other fifteen slaves might have been so convicted. Moreover, lawmakers constantly made clear that a conspiracy of slaves to kill a white person resembled a conspiracy to rebel. From 1723 to 1865, the Old Dominion outlawed both kinds of conspiracies in the same laws and required the same penalties for each.[54]

But the behavior of both rebellious slaves and repressive judges also reflected the challenge to white supremacy inherent in most killings of whites by slaves. Two of the peaks in convictions of slaves for murdering whites occurred in the 1790s, after the Santo Domingo rebellion of 1791 and just prior to Gabriel's massive plot of 1800, and in the 1820s, contemporary to the Vesey conspiracy of 1822 and preceding the Turner insurrection of 1831. Other high points were during periods of intense slave organizing or rumors of organizing.[55] The lawmakers who tightened the slave code's strictures against attempted murder of whites responded to general trends in slaves' attacks on whites and not just to the Vesey plot and the Turner insurrection. Attacks of this nature apparently decreased after the early 1830s; so did hangings of slaves for killing or trying to kill whites.

Fear influenced greatly the cycle of slave convictions. As a significant number of whites in early Virginia grew to dread being killed by slaves, governmental leaders took extraordinary precautions to suppress the reality behind that fear as well as to calm the fear itself. In doing so, they tried to spread fear among slaves.

Public executions were supposed to terrify slaves into subordination. Throughout the eighteenth century, authorities in Virginia fell back on the oldest European sanctions in order to increase the horror of execution. At least two slaves were burned to death,[56] while sheriffs hung the corpses of twenty other slaves in chains, burned their corpses to ashes, displayed their quartered bodies in several locations, or stuck their heads on poles which they erected at crossroads.[57] After 1800 such forms of execution nearly disappeared, except when performed by vigilantes after insurrection trials.[58] Instead execution itself became the most terrible punishment available.

Rebellious Afro-Virginians had only so much opportunity to terrify whites in return. They never did outnumber Euro-Virginians. Yet there were more slaves than white residents in many counties and male slaves above the age of sixteen frequently lived in greater force alongside white males. Had slaves been able to stockpile arms, undergo military training,[59] and maintain security against slave informers, they certainly could have mounted a successful revolt. Since this was rather obvious to slaveholders, however, they made certain to suppress any signs of a conspiracy to rebel, including "loose talk." Among the variety of preventative measures and sanctions at their disposal were the slave code and courts. The laws of 1680 and 1681 against assemblies and slaves' attacks on white people were the first line of defense. By 1723 they were clearly inadequate. During the fourteen years between 1709 and 1723, sixteen slaves stood trial in special courts and the General Court for offenses related to rebellion. Only two of them were hanged, although the fate of three is unknown. Another eight were transported out of the colony, a sentence not allowed previously, but which *ad hoc* legislation quickly made possible. The special action taken against these rebels was a hint that the central government had not decided what should be the normal procedure concerning suspected slave insurrectionaries.

The convicted conspirators of late 1722 moved the burgesses to make up their minds and create new shackles that judges could fasten onto dangerous slaves for years to come. As if giving emphasis to the cyclical nature of slaves' conflicts with the criminal code and courts in Virginia, Governor Drysdale explained the need for this new statute. The laws of the colony, he told legislators in early 1723,

> seem very deficient in the due punishing any Intended Insurrection of your Slaves: You have had a late Experience of the Lameness of them, I am persuaded you are too well acquainted with the Cruel dispositions of those Creatures when they have it in their power to destroy or distresss, to let slip this fair Oppertunity of makeing more proper Laws against them. . . .

The representatives quickly obliged Drysdale by creating a new capital crime. Should six or more slaves "consult, advise, or conspire, to rebel or make insurrection, or plot or conspire, the murder of any person or persons whatever," they would receive the death penalty without benefit of clergy.[60] Five capital sentences which followed in 1730 and 1732 reiterated the point that authorities would use any law and all force in response to the only effective force that slaves might hope to employ against slavery itself.[61] From 1740 to 1784, at least 21 slaves stood trial for insurrection and conspiracy. As in other kinds of trials, the judges found ways to vary their responses according to circumstances. While they condemned eight slaves to hang for rebellion and could no longer use the penalty of transportation, they reduced the verdict of fourteen others to a misdemeanor, allowing no more than a whipping.[62]

Slave insurrections presented American revolutionaries with a problem. At the same time that the new republicans attempted to introduce ameliorative, humanitarian features to the slave code, their wish to protect their new country made them claim they had to suppress revolutionaries whom they deemed illegitimate.[63] It was slave rebels rather than such leaders as New England's Daniel Shays who worried Virginia's leaders. A significant number of slaves had developed their own motives for trying to achieve independence. The cycle of conspiracy, fear, legislation, court action, and even military maneuvers that followed was the most intense in the history of the slave society of Virginia. Between 1785 and 1831, prosecutors charged at least 237 Afro-Virginians with conspiracy to make insurrection. One hundred twenty-seven slaves received various punishments, with hanging suffered by 74. Due in part to the concern of ex-revolutionary and slaveholder Thomas Jefferson, the very penalty of transportation used for rebels in the early 1720s became available once again in 1801, allowing judges and the government to send 45 convicted insurrectionaries into exile.[64] Virginia's legislators also recognized the possibility of white or free black complicity. Their 1798 law required the death penalty for any free person who joined in a slave conspiracy.[65]

After 1831, however, there was an abrupt reversal of the earlier trend toward rebellion. Only twelve convictions came to the attention of state authorities from 1832 to 1865. Eleven slaves were transported and one executed.[66] Ironically this change occurred in the context of the South's anti-abolitionist campaign and many insurrection scares. It is possible only to speculate that either the harsh reaction, both judicial and private, to the Turner episode intimidated slaves, or that greater emphasis among slaves on running away to the free states or Canada deflected their energy from futile, insurrectionary resistance. Almost all of the convictions of slaves for insurrection after 1831 were actually for seditious speech or plotting. No court concluded that any slaves had taken action.

The ability of white leaders to create and enforce the slave code makes it obvious that slaves did not control the criminal justice system any more than they dominated slaveholders. Neither were they merely passive sufferers. The victimized and oppressed are not necessarily weak and helpless. Their problem is always that they have less power than their oppressors. Slaves accused of major crimes had several sources of strength in their struggle with dominant whites. Some bondsmen remembered or inherited conceptions of African tribal law and courts against which they could measure the injustice of slave codes and courts.[67] Others—conjurers, exhorters, and preachers—possessed special knowledge of poisons or held power among slaves that allowed them to mobilize large or small groups against whites.[68] A good many slaves lived within supportive communities whose members would cover up running away and other behavior proscribed by whites. Some even had access to their own informal judicial systems, where they could enforce their customary laws on slaves who threatened or injured other slaves.[69] Finally, they all could use their bodies in attempts to undermine white power in several ways. They lacked some essential kinds of power, however. Most had neither guns nor military training. Perhaps as significant was their total lack of government-supported laws and official courts where they could forcefully sustain their own definitions of crime.

Historians of slavery have quite appropriately pointed out how white supremacist ideology and the pervasive demand for protection of the peculiar institution as well as of people and property fostered the creation and development of oppressive slave codes and courts. Scholars need to complete their analysis of this process of legal development, however, with a comparative explanation of how the purposeful behavior of a significant number of rebellious slaves led white authorities in Virginia and elsewhere to create and develop special statutes and institutions for slaves. Had slaves not engaged in such behavior, white officials would not have gone to such pains to defend bondage. But those slaves who were convicted of major crimes because of their effort to preserve their own lives, safety, welfare, or interests forced white lawmakers and judges to put on paper and declare in open court their increasingly circular justification for the legalized ownership and total, forceful subordination of human beings. The special laws and courts existed to maintain slavery as a social and labor system, but slavery itself continued to exist only because slaveowners created and perpetuated special laws. When slaves consciously opposed this system, they attacked the legal foundation of slavery itself. Ironically, even those slaves who acted irrationally or without any intention of challenging slavery or the authorities of the slave society of Virginia ended up threatening slavery as well as property or people.

NOTES

[1] Previous treatments of the law of slavery have appeared in, among others: David B. Davis, *The Problem of Slavery in Western Culture* (Ithaca, N.Y., 1964); A. Leon Higginbotham, *In the Matter of Color: Race and the American Legal Process: the Colonial Period* (New York, 1978); Winthrop D. Jordan, *White Over Black: American Attitudes Toward the Negro, 1440–1812*

Table 1

Slaves Convicted of Violent Murder and Hanged or Transported, Virginia, 1785–1864

	Number of slaves convicted				Number of victims			
	Owners or owners' family	Other authorities	Other whites*	Total convicted	Owners or owners' family	Other authorities	Other whites*	Total victims
1785–1789	2	0	1	3	1	0	1	2
1790–1794	0	6	4	10	0	2	3	5
1795–1799	12	0	7	19	11	0	6	17
1800–1804	7	4	5	16	6	2	4	12
1805–1809	3	7	6	16	2	3	3	8
1810–1814	5	0	3	8	4	0	2	6
1815–1819	8	3	2	13	2	3	2	7
1820–1824	8	4	11	23	7	3	9	19
1825–1829	20	2	8	30	8	2	8	18
1830–1834	8	1	6	15	2	1	4	7
1835–1839	9	2	10	21	5	2	9	16
1840–1844	5	0	1	6	4	0	1	5
1845–1849	4	2	4	10	2	2	2	6
1850–1854	4	0	9	13	4	0	8	12
1855–1859	2	2	4	8	2	1	5	8
1860–1864	3	0	1	4	2	0	1	3
1785–1864	100	33	82	215	62	21	68	151

SOURCES: Condemned Slaves, boxes 1–10, VSL, supplemented by county court order and minute books and materials in VEPLR, VSL.

*Some of the victims among "Other whites" were probably authorities such as overseers, hirers, constables, etc., but full identification was

(Chapel Hill, N.C., 1968), 48–52, 83; Thad W. Tate, *The Negro in Eighteenth-Century Williamsburg* (Williamsburg, Va.,1965), 91–113; Mark Tushnet, *The American Law of Slavery, 1810–1860: Considerations of Humanity and Interest* (Princeton, N.J., 1981); William M. Wiecek, "The Statutory Law of Slavery and Race in the Thirteen Mainland Colonies of British America," *William and Mary Quarterly*, 3d Ser., XXXIV (April 1977), 258–80.

² Tushnet, *The American Law of Slavery*, contains a provocative discussion of the connections between slave codes and other laws. An exhaustive review of the literature appears in A. E. Keir Nash, "Reason of Slavery: Understanding the Judicial Role in the Peculiar Institution," *Vanderbilt Law Review*, XXXII (Jan. 1979), 7–218. See also Elizabeth Fox-Genovese and Eugene D. Genovese, *Fruits of Merchant Capital: Slavery and Bourgeois Property in the Rise and Expansion of Capitalism* (New York, 1983), 337–87.

³ Positive law refers to statutory law, as opposed to common law.

⁴ Exceptions include Michael S. Hindus, *Prison and Plantation: Crime, Justice and Authority in Massachusetts and South Carolina, 1767–1878* (Chapel Hill, N.C., 1980), and Douglas Greenberg, *Crime and Law Enforcement in the Colony of New York, 1691–1776* (Ithaca, N.Y., 1976), 72–76, 138–39, 142, 149–52.

⁵ Appeals of convictions of slaves could not be made until the 1850s. *Peter v. the Commonwealth*, 2 Va. Cases (4 Va.) 330 (1823).

⁶ I am not assuming the existence of a unified set of values and fears. Among the best discussions of this subject are Eugene D. Genovese, *Roll, Jordan, Roll: The World the Slaves Made* (New York, 1974), 25–49, and Bertram Wyatt-Brown, *Southern Honor: Ethics and Behavior in the Old South* (New York, 1982), 362–434.

⁷ Genovese, *Roll, Jordan, Roll*, at 30, 587–657, is an exception.

⁸ Throughout the process by which legislators created Virginia's slave code, they insisted that they were responding to extreme behavior rather than against a group, class, or caste. See, for example, William Waller Hening, ed., *The Statutes at Large: Being a Collection of All the Laws of Virginia from the First Session of Legislature in the Year 1619* (13 vols., Richmond, 1810–1823), II, 481–82; *Acts Passed at a General Assembly, 1831* (Richmond, Va., 1832), 20–22.

⁹ Standard definitions of crime do not necessarily apply to actions of slaves that were responses to oppression but that still resulted in criminal convictions. The quotation marks do not solve the problem of defining and evaluating such behavior; they merely reflect its existence.

¹⁰ See Richard Quinney, *Critique of Legal Order: Crime Control in Capitalist Society* (Boston, 1974); Stanton Wheeler, "Trends and Patterns in the Sociological Study of Crime," *Social Problems*, XXIII (1976), 525–34.

¹¹ See, e.g., Sterling Stuckey, "Through the Prism of Folklore: The Black Ethos in Slavery," *Massachusetts Review*, IX (1968), 432; Earl E. Thorpe, *The Mind of the Negro* (Baton Rouge, La., 1961), 79; Merle Gerald Brouwer, "The Negro as a Slave and as a Free Black in Colonial Pennsylvania," (Ph.D. dissertation, Wayne State University, 1973), 180, 192, 310–33.

¹² Even a slave's killing of another slave threatened the social and economic order owners wished to maintain and also destroyed the owner's capital investment.

¹³ For recent treatments of such change, see Alan Kulikoff, "The Colonial Chesapeake: Seedbed of Antebellum Southern Culture?" *Journal of Southern History*, XLV (Nov. 1979), 513–40; Ira Berlin, "Time, Space, and the Evolution of Afro-American Society on British Mainland North America," *American Historical Review*, LXXXV (Feb. 1980), 44–78; David R. Goldfield, *Urban Development in the Age of Sectionalism, 1847–1861* (Baton Rouge, La., 1971), 1–8.

¹⁴ At some times, the number of convictions indicated there was so much more of this kind of killing that assembly delegates tightened up even the laws concerning attempted murder of whites. Laws of 1823 and 1832: *Supplement to the Revised Code of the Laws* (Richmond, Va., 1833), 234, 247. At other times, however, the incidence of convictions for this

sort of homicide was sufficiently low that lawmakers allowed courts to convict slaves of second-degree murder even when the victim was white. See, for example, trial of Bob, alias Robert, for a Saturday night stabbing, Dec. 15, 1856, Lancaster County Order Book, 1854–1866, 117, 119; also Condemned Slaves, box 9, VSL, and Virginia Executive Papers, Letters Received (hereafter referred to as VEPLR), which is arranged by date. Similarly, several enslaved killers of whites were transported during the ante-bellum years. See, for example, trial of Jere, Dec. 5, 1835, Pittsylvania County, Condemned Slaves, box 6. Unless otherwise indicated, all county court minute and order books are on microfilm at VSL.

[15] The problem of the "dark figure" of unrecorded crimes is formidable. See J. M. Beattie, "Towards a Study of Crime in 18th Century England: A Note on Indictments," in Paul Fritz and David Williams, eds., *The Triumph of Culture, 18th Century Perspectives* (Toronto, 1972), 299–314, and V. A. C. Gatrell and T. B. Hadden, "Criminal Statistics and Their Interpretation," in *Nineteenth Century Society*, E. A. Wrigley, ed. (Cambridge, Eng., 1972), 336–96.

[16] Tate, *The Negro in Eighteenth-Century Williamsburg*, 93–96, remains the best description of the Virginia courts of oyer and terminer for slaves. From 1692 to 1786, designated white Virginians, usually justices of the peace, heard capital trials of slaves under commissions of oyer and terminer, which the governor issued on a case-by-case basis before 1765 and as open-ended empowerments after that. The same system, controlled exclusively by county justices, covered all felony trials of slaves from 1786 to 1865.

[17] David H. Flaherty, "A Select Guide to the Manuscript Court Records of Virginia," *American Journal of Legal History*, XIX (April 1975), 112–37, provides a description and listing.

[18] The records of the auditor are Condemned Slaves, boxes 1–10, VSL. The governor's records are in VEPLR, VSL, which contains letters received by all governors, filed by date, as well as many trial records, filed either by date or in separate files for "Pardons," usually found after the December files for each year. Legislative Petitions, VSL, which are filed by county, then by date, contain some appeals.

[19] Weighed against Kennth M. Stampp's reasonable tests for the historical accuracy of the kind of "white source" these trials represent, the trials stand up fairly well. They reflect the pressure for accurate *description* more than for distortion, they often contain first-hand testimony, and they were recorded soon after the event. Stampp, "Slavery—the Historian's Burden," in Harry P. Owens, ed., *Perspectives and Irony in American Slavery*, (Jackson, Miss., 1976), 169. In three random samples of fifteen cases from three periods (1760–1763, 1768–1771, and 1783–1785), the average number of days between event and trial was, respectively, 26, 24, and 19.

[20] Hening, *Statutes at Large*, IV, 325–27; *The Code of Virginia* (Richmond, 1849), 753; Landon C. Bell, "Benefit of Clergy," typescript, VSL, Library Division; Tate, *The Negro in Eighteenth-Century Williamsburg*, 94–96; William K. Boyd, "Documents and Comments on Benefit of Clergy as Applied to Slaves," *Journal of Negro History*, VIII (Oct. 1923), 443–47. At least 314 slaves received benefit of clergy from 1733 through 1785. Also see Samuel Shepherd, *The Statutes at Large of Virginia, from October Session 1792, to December Session 1806, Inclusive* (3 vols., Richmond, Va., 1835), II, 279–80.

[21] For example, Tom stood trial in 1714 for burglary of a house in the daytime and stealing goods worth more than twenty shillings, but the oyer and terminer justices convicted him only of petty larceny and sentenced him to 39 lashes. Lancaster County Court Order Book, 1713–1721, 40–42. Before legalization of transportation, pardons saved many slaves. Between 1782 and 1786, for example, the governor and council pardoned 41 slave convicts. *Journals of the Council of State of Virginia*, H. R. McIlwaine and Wilmer L. Hall, eds. (vol. 1– , Richmond, Va., 1931–), III, *passim*.

[22] A. G. Roeber, *Faithful Magistrates and Republican Lawyers: Creators of Virginia's Legal Cul-*

ture, 1680–1810 (Chapel Hill, N.C., 1981); Tadahisa Kuroda, "The County Court System of Virginia from the Revolution to the Civil War" (Ph.D. dissertation, Columbia University, 1969), 274–86, 313–25; Francis N. Thorpe, ed., *The Federal and State Constitutions, Colonial Charters, and Other Organic Laws . . .* (7 vols., Washington, 1909), VII, 3843–44, 3849; Harrison M. Ethridge, "The Jordan Hatcher Affair of 1852," *Virginia Magazine of History and Biography*, LXXXIV (Oct. 1976), 446–63; trial of Elvira, April 22, 1864, Petersburg Hustings Court Order Book, 1861–1867, 372–78, also Condemned Slaves, box 9; *In re Elvira*, 16 Gratt. (57 Va.) 561 (1865), reprinted in Helen T. Catterall, ed., *Judicial Cases Concerning Negro Slavery* (5 vols., Washington, 1924–1926), I, 254. See also Revisors of the Code of Virginia (John M. Patton and Conway Robinson), *Report of the Revisors of the Code of Virginia Made to the General Assembly in July, 1849, Being Their Final Report, and Relating to the Criminal Code* (Richmond, Va., 1849), 990.

[23] Gerald W. Mullin, *Flight and Rebellion; Slave Resistance in Eighteenth-Century Virginia* (New York, 1972), 58–60. For example, Jemmy was convicted of murdering his master, mistress, and their three children by beating them to death. Trial of Jemmy, Jan. 19, 1754, Surry Criminal Proceedings, 39–41, Surry County Courthouse, Surry, Va.

[24] Between 1740 and 1784, nearly 80 percent of items that court clerks identified as stolen were food, clothing, or livestock. For slaves executed or transported between 1785 and 1831, the comparable figure was 68.5 percent; from 1830 to 1864, it was 60 percent. Countless slaves made an ethical distinction between permissible "taking" from owners and reprehensible "stealing" from other slaves. See, for example, *Minutes of the Baptist Association, in the District of Goshen: Held at Bethel Meeting-House, Caroline County, Virginia . . . 1816* (Fredericksburg, Va., 1816), 7–8.

[25] See trial of Sam, Sept. 22, 1809, Montgomery, Condemned Slaves, box 3, also VEPLR; trial of Jim, January 14, 1808, Campbell, Condemned Slaves, box 2, also VEPLR; trial of Giles, Nov. 1, 1847, Henrico, Condemned Slaves, box 8, also VEPLR, and *Richmond Enquirer*, Nov. 5, 1847, 2, and Dec. 14, 1847, 4.

[26] For example, trial of Tom, Dec. 7, 1807, Albemarle, Condemned Slaves, box 6, also VEPLR.

[27] See trial of William, Aug. 3, 1796, Frederick, Condemned Slaves, box 1, also VEPLR, and John Marshall, *The Papers of John Marshall*, Herbert A. Johnson et al., eds. (vol. 1– , Chapel Hill, N.C., 1974–), III, 36–38.

[28] Herbert Aptheker, *American Negro Slave Revolts* (New York, 1974); Eugene D. Genovese, *From Rebellion to Revolution: Afro-American Slave Revolts in the Making of the Modern World* (Baton Rouge, La., 1979); Johnston, *Race Relations in Virginia*, 30–41; Jordan, *White Over Black*, 111–12, 122, 392–401; Mullin, *Flight and Rebellion*, 140–63; Stephen B. Oates, *The Fires of Jubilee: Nat Turner's Fierce Rebellion* (New York, 1975); Tate, *The Negro in Eighteenth-Century Williamsburg*, 109–113.

[29] See, for example, Charles City County Court *Order Book, 1664–1665*, 604–05, 617–18.

[30] *Minutes of the Council and General Court of Colonial Virginia*, H. R. McIlwaine, ed. (2nd ed., Richmond, Va., 1979), 502, 520; Aptheker, *American Negro Slave Revolts*, 164–66; Middlesex County Court *Order Book, 1680–1694*, 486–87, 535, 537, 546–47, 572–73; (Old) Rappahannock County Court *Order Book, 1689–1692*, 335, transcript, VSL; *Executive Journals of the Council*, I, 86–87; Catterall, *Judicial Cases*, I, 79.

[31] Hening, *Statutes at Large*, II, 270; IV, 132–33; XII, 681. Trials and convictions of whites for murdering slaves were regular but not frequent.

[32] Hening, *Statutes at Large*, II, 481–82, 492–93; III, 86–88.

[33] Hening, *Statutes at Large*, III, 102–103. Warren M. Billings, "Pleading, Procedure, and Practice: The Meaning of Due Process of Law in Seventeenth-Century Virginia," *Journal of Southern History*, XLVII (Nov. 1981), 577, places this creation in the context of previous use by Virginia governors of the oyer and terminer commission.

[34] From 1692 to 1765, judges had to apply to the provincial government for each com-

mission. After that, the governor issued blanket commissions. Hening, *Statutes at Large*, VIII, 187.

[35] Hening, *Statutes at Large*, III, 269. Examples: *Legislative Journals of the Council of Colonial Virginia*, H. R. McIlwaine, ed. (3 vols., Richmond, Va., 1918–1919), III, 1596–1600.

[36] Hening, *Statutes at Large*, VI, 106, XII, 345; *The Code of Virginia*, 1860, 841; Shepherd, *Statutes at Large*, II, 280.

[37] For summaries of burglary statutes, see George Webb, *The Office and Authority of a Justice of the Peace* (Williamsburg, Va., 1736), 63, 208–10, and Richard Starke, *The Office and Authority of a Justice of the Peace* (Williamsburg, Va., 1774), 61–67, 327–30.

[38] Early white Virginians regarded burglary in combination with theft as quite serious no matter who was accused, partly because of the English precedents. See Sir Leon Radzinowicz, *A History of the English Criminal Law and Its Administration from 1750* (3 vols., London, 1948–1956), I, 139–42, 147–48, 150–51, 155, 157.

[39] It is only irregularly possible to verify that such sentences were carried out. Thus it is impossible to tabulate the actual number of hangings before the 1780s, when the auditor's records become comprehensive. When it was possible to verify executions, I have so indicated.

[40] Trial of Tom, Feb. 19, 1777, Sussex County Court Papers, 1774–1777, Bundle 1, VSL microfilm; Sussex County Sheriff's Accounts, 1777, *ibid.*; trial of Ben, Sept. 16, 1779, Powhatan County Court *Order Book, 1777–1784*, 120–21, 145.

[41] Hening, *Statutes at Large*, VIII, 522.

[42] For example, statutes concerning hog stealing rattled the sabre over the years—one in 1748 threatened capital punishment for a third offense—but hog stealing by slaves persisted. Hening, *Statutes at Large*, II, 129, 440–41, III, 179, 276–79, VI, 121–24; Philip J. Schwarz, "Gabriel's Challenge; Slaves and Crime in Late Eighteenth-Century Virginia," *Virginia Magazine of History and Biography*, XC (July 1982), 296–97.

[43] Of all slaves executed or transported for stealing between 1785 and 1831, 16 percent were clearly from cities; between 1830 and 1864, at least 33.9 percent were from cities. From 1785 to 1864, Fredericksburg, Richmond, and Petersburg had the highest rates of major convictions per population.

[44] Should the slave of one owner kill the slave of another, the victim's owner could not sue the killer's owner. This increased the chance that slaveowners would prefer criminal trials of slaves suspected of killing other slaves rather than settling for private punishments. See *American Digest*, XLIV, cols., 1054–1058, 1325.

[45] See note 25.

[46] Accomack County Court *Order Book, 1731–1736*, 99; trial of Bob, March 30, 1768, Mecklenburg County Court *Order Book, 1765–1768*, 480.

[47] See Lancaster County Court *Order Book, 1721–1729*, 192–93. The 1765 change: Hening, *Statutes at Large*, VIII, 139.

[48] See note 14.

[49] *Ibid.*

[50] The only extant record of an infanticide conviction before 1785: Brunswick County Court *Order Book, 1772–1774*, 184–85; *Legislative Journals of the Council*, III, 1598. Between 1785 and 1848, ten slave women were executed or transported for infanticide; ten more were executed or transported between 1850 and 1859.

[51] Killings of whites by slaves were common knowledge in some counties. See, e.g., Captain Richard Irby, "Extracts from Old Places and Old People," 1899, typescript, in looseleaf notebook, Nottoway County, Virginia, Library. (I am indebted to Professor Marijean Hawthorne for this reference.)

[52] Aptheker, *American Negro Slave Revolts*, and Johnston, *Race Relations in Virginia*, are exceptions.

[53] Some 23 slaves were executed and another 20 transported upon being convicted of com-

plicity with the Turner revolt. At least 138 slaves were convicted of being involved in conspiracies to murder that resulted in the death of whites between 1706 and 1865.

[54] Hening, *Statutes at Large*, IV, 126; Shepherd, *Statutes at Large*, I, 122–25, II, 77–78; *Acts of the General Assembly of Virginia*, 1847–1848 (Richmond, Va., 1848), 125; *Code of Virginia*, (2nd ed., Richmond, Va., 1860), 753.

[55] The number of whites killed by convicted slaves, by decade, was as follows: 1790s, 22; 1800–1809, 20; 1810s, 13; 1820s, 37; 1830s, 23; 1840s, 11; 1850s, 20. See Table One.

[56] Trial of Eve, Jan. 23, 1746, Orange County Court *Order Book, 1743–1746*, 454–55, 1746–1747, 99, 103; unidentified female slave, *Virginia Gazette*, Feb. 4 and 27, 1737. Such executions occurred in eighteenth-century England as well. Radzinowicz, *History of the English Criminal Law*, I, 210–13.

[57] Courts whose records have survived ordered quartering in only two cases. Trial of Tom, Feb. 25, 1755, Amelia County Court *Order Book, 1751–1755*, 210–11; trial of Mercer, July 28, 1768, Frederick County Court *Order Book, 1767–1770*, 90. See also trials of Stepney and George, Jan. 15, 1760, Accomack County Court *Order Book, 1753–1763*, 317–18 (hanging in chains), and trial of Tom, Nov. 9, 1763, Augusta County Court *Order Book, 1763–1764*, 324–26. Tom's sentence was carried out. *Ibid.*

[58] One instance in which condemned slaves' heads were displayed on poles: trials of Frank and James, June 15, 1809, Mathews, Condemned Slaves, box 2, also VEPLR.

[59] In 1777, four Essex County slaves were condemned and five otherwise punished for engaging in military drills. Essex County Court *Order Book, 1773–1782*, 316. (I am indebted to Professor Harry M. Ward for originally informing me of this reference.)

[60] *Journals of the House of Burgesses*, 1723–1726, 360; Governor Drysdale to the Board of Trade, Dec. 10, 1722 and June 29, 1723, Great Britain, Public Record Office, Colonial Office, 5, 1319: fols. 83–84, 114; Mr. West's report to the Privy Council, July 31, 1723, *ibid.*, fols. 97–100; Hening, *Statutes at Large*, IV, 126.

[61] 1730 and 1732 execution sentences: Governor Gooch to Board of Trade, Sept. 14, 1730 and proclamation of Oct. 28, 1730, Colonial Office, 5, 1322: fols. 158, 161–63, 212–13; James Blair to the Bishop of London, May 14, 1731, and Governor Gooch to same, May 31, 1731, Correspondence of the Bishop of London, 110–11, Fulham Palace Papers, 15; Spotsylvania County Court *Order Book, 1730–1738*, 106, 118.

[62] For example, trial of Will, Aug. 4, 1752, Surry County Criminal Proceedings, 29–32; trial of Tom, April 4, 1753, York County Court *Order Book, 1752–1754*, 204–05; trial of Will, Aug. 19, 1785, Mecklenburg County Court *Order Book, 1784–1787*, 392. See also note 59.

[63] Peter Joseph Albert, "The Protean Institution: The Geography, Economy, and Ideology of Slavery in Post-Revolutionary Virginia" (Ph.D. dissertation, University of Maryland, 1976); David Brion Davis, *The Problem of Slavery in the Age of Revolution* (New York, 1975); Genovese, *From Rebellion to Revolution*, 82–137; Duncan J. McLeod, *Slavery, Race, and the American Revolution* (London, 1974); Jordan, *White Over Black*, 375–426.

[64] See note 20.

[65] Shepherd, *Statutes at Large*, II, 77. An 1848 revision stated that death would be the penalty whether a rebellion occurred or not. *Acts of the General Assembly of Virginia, 1847–1848* (Richmond, Va., 1848), 124. See also James Hugo Johnston, "The Participation of White Men in Virginia Negro Insurrections," *Journal of Negro History*, XVI (April 1931), 158–67.

[66] See, for example, Southampton County Court *Order Book, 1839–1843*, 210, 217, 220–23, also Condemned Slaves, box 7; "A List of Slaves and Free persons of color . . .," and "Slaves Transported and Executed—pd for—1 Oct. 40 to 30 Sept. 41," *ibid.*, box 10; Virginia Council Journals, 1840–1841, 85, VSL; trial of Beverley, Feb. 1, 1857, New Kent, Condemned Slaves, box 9, and *Governor's Biennial Messages to the General Assembly of . . . Virginia, December 7, 1857* (Richmond, Va., 1857), 174.

[67] Philip J. Schwarz, "The Adaptation of Afro-American Slaves to the Anglo-American Judiciary," paper delivered at the Forty-first Conference of the Institute of Early American History and Culture at Millersville (Pa.) State College, April 1981.

[68] See trials of Matthew, Old Matt, and Daniel, Dec. 23, 1816, Cumberland, Condemned Slaves, box 3, also VEPLR.

[69] Space prohibits support for this. The possibility is apparent in Joseph P. Reidy, "'Negro Election Day' & Black Community Life in New England," *Marxist Perspectives* (Fall 1978), 102–17.

"Society is not marked by punctuality in the payment of debts":[1] The Chattel Mortgages of Slaves

THOMAS D. MORRIS

Introduction

Gogol's hero in *Dead Souls*, Chichikov, clambered about the Russian countryside in the early nineteenth century buying titles to dead serfs who had not been removed from the census roles. He planned to mortgage them to raise capital. C. Duncan Rice has argued that the use of persons as collateral has been a characteristic of most unfree societies.[2] Studies of the law of slavery, however, have not probed very far into the commercialization of slavery.[3] This is certainly true about the history of slaves as collateral or security for debts in the American South, even though there is an enormous body of case law on the subject. This essay is a modest effort to open inquiry into this problem by an examination of that law;[4] and this, in turn, hopefully will throw some light on the larger problem of understanding a society resting upon property rights in man.

The Law of Chattel Mortgages

The mortgaging of slaves in nineteenth-century America must be seen within the context of an emerging general contract law, which broke away from property law and appeared in the 1800s as a separate legal category.[5] A law of obligation, tort and contract, arose altogether separate from the law of real property, which had been the cornerstone of the early common law.[6] Obligations, in contract law, were created out of expectations the law would protect,

147

"expectations of good faith which arise out of particular transactions between individual persons."[7] This legal development came with the rise of a market economy.

The theoretical foundation of this new legal category was the will theory of contract. Free individuals entered into contracts to advance their future expectations, and the state must not interfere with such transactions, except under extraordinary circumstances.[8] A strong statement of the theory appeared in John Joseph Powell's 1790 work, *Essay Upon the Law of Contracts and Agreements*. In his view, "it is the consent of parties alone, that fixes the just price of any thing, without reference to the nature of things themselves, or to their intrinsic value. . . . Therefore a man is obliged in conscience to perform a contract which he has entered into, although it is a hard one."[9]

Juristically, the notion of property in Anglo-American thought has been that it is a "bundle of rights" that could be divided among different persons. These rights could be of two general kinds: legal or equitable. These were the result of the quirks of English legal history and meant simply that the rights would be upheld in a common law court, or in a court of chancery. The emerging contract law was largely a product of law, not equity, and was moving toward what C. B. Macpherson has called the mature possessive market society.[10] The difficulty was that equitable rules, at the same time, remained those that had been fashioned in a pre-market, paternalistic society.[11] Even though equity was under considerable attack in the early 1800s, it still retained force so that what existed was an uneasy co-existence of disparate styles of legal thought.

Perhaps a good illustration of the tension would be to juxtapose a remark of Chief Justice John Marshall for the U.S. Supreme Court with one from Judge Francis Taliaferro Brooke of Virginia. The case before Marshall was a transaction for the transfer of land. (Although the case did not involve slaves, it was often cited in southern cases that did.) The problem was to distinguish a conditional sale from a genuine mortgage. According to Marshall, "To deny the power of two individuals, capable of acting for themselves, to make a contract for the purchase and sale of lands defeasible by the payment of money at a future day, or, in other words, to make a sale with a reservation to the vendor of a right to repurchase the same land at a fixed price and at a specified time, would be to transfer to the Court of Chancery, in a considerable degree, the guardianship of adults as well as of infants." In an 1839 Virginia case, on the other side, Judge Brooke argued that the transaction before him was a mortgage of slaves and not a conditional sale because the "borrower," to use his phrase, "might in some sense be said to be the slave of the lender." [12]

Although mortgages were originally the creation of law, equity asserted a role, and by the 1800s the supervision of mortgage transactions was one of its major functions. Still, much remains unclear because the history of mortgages in English law remains unwritten. Legal scholars, nevertheless, have sketched a cameo. By the 1600s there were two forms that used land as a security for a loan: the *vadium vivum* and *vadium mortuum* (or "mort" gage). Under the first, the creditor took possession of the property and used its profits to pay off the debt. When the debt was repaid, the land was restored to the debtor. The other form, which existed early, was a dead or "mort" gage because if the debtor did not repay the debt at the proper time, the land became the property of the creditor: it was dead to the debtor. Under this form the creditor took the rents and profits from the land as well as the debt, which then amounted to a disguised interest seen by some as "usurious and sinful." Commercial pressure, however, led to its legal acceptance. By the 1600s the mortgage had become the more common form (although the *vadium vivum* survived). The general rule was that the creditor got the legal title to the property, the debtor usually retained possession, and the creditors' right would be reconveyed to the debtor if he paid on time. If he did not, he lost the property forever. [13]

It was the creation of an "equity of redemption" that gave a debtor the right to redeem his land whenever he could, even after failure to pay on time. By the end of the 1700s, if not sooner, equity set a twenty-year limit in order to discourage stale claims. While debtors were given this vital equitable right, creditors received a remedy as well—the right of foreclosure. They could go into equity to force the debtor to pay or forever lose the equity of redemption.[14] Those involved in commercial investment, however, did not consider this a happy solution. Businessmen, as Stewart Macauley has argued, will avoid court actions if at all possible.[15] The horrors described in Dickens' mordant story of the equity case of *Jarndyce* v. *Jarndyce* in *Bleak House* are ample testimony of the reason they would avoid equity in particular. By the end of the eighteenth century, conveyancers often inserted a clause in mortgage contracts giving the creditor the right to seize and sell the property upon failure to pay on time. Such a clause bypassed the cumbersome foreclosure process.[16]

By the late 1700s all of this applied only to transactions involving land: there was no body of *chattel* mortgage law. As late as 1766 Adam Smith wrote in his *Lectures on Jurisprudence* that "pledges property regard moveable subjects and mortgages immoveable." Chancellor Kent in his *Commentaries on American Law*, written in the 1820s, cited only one English chancery case in which personal property was a proper subject for mortgage, and that case was decided after 1800. Justice Henderson in *Falls* v. *Torrence*, (N.C., 1826) said nothing could be learned from English decisions, "personal property not being the subject of mortgage." Six years later Justice Whyte in *Overton* v. *Bigelow* (Tennessee, 1832), relying solely on Kent, said that "Negroes may be the subject of mortgage, as well as real estate." On the other hand, John Powell, a critical figure in the rise of the will theory of contract, had written in his *Treatise on the Law of Mortgages* (1799) that "every thing which may be considered as property . . . may be the subject of a mortgage."[17]

Chattel mortgage law, then, was in gestation. In the early common law, personal property was customarily pledged, not mortgaged. Under a pledge the creditor took possession of the property but acquired no title. If he derived any profit from its use, the profit had to be used to liquidate the debt. Since the debtor remained the owner, he had a lifetime to redeem the property, unless special terms were inserted in the agreement.[18] The pledge was to personal property what the *vadium vivum* contract was to land, and it also fell into relative disuse with the spread of a market society.

Before a body of chattel mortgage law would emerge, however, thought about chattels in general had to undergo transformation. The English legal historian J. H. Baker has observed that "the common law took the strict view that no estates could be created in chattels, because it was contrary to the nature of ownership that the owner for the time being should not be able to do what he liked with the chattel, including its destruction."[19] How could a mortgagee acquire a legal estate in slaves if no estate could exist in chattels?

By the 1800s English law had been transformed. The reasons for this shift are unclear, but a reasonable guess would be that chattels (personal property) had risen in importance in the late 1700s with the spread of an industrial market society. Personal property no longer meant simply things like linen, jewels, or cows. It now included such things as stocks.

This change in the way people thought about chattels played a role in the rise of capitalism. The precise relationship between the ownership of slaves and this process is not clear, but a reasonable conjecture would be that it was close. Slaves, after all, always had been viewed as of much more value (and social importance) than things like bedsheets or stock animals. If this interpretation is accurate, slavery played a critical part in the emergence of market capitalism (in a slightly different although parallel manner to that discussed by Eric Williams). It played a major role in the change in legal thought about property, and it preceded the spread of national commodities markets.

One fact that confuses this neat conjecture is that during the establishment of slavery in the 1600s slaves were often defined as real property, not as chattels personal. This was true in Barbados, South Carolina, and in Virginia (which did not change the definition of slaves to chattels personal until the early 1790s).[20] This experience might have persisted even after the legal definition was changed. The whole process requires more study, but what is clear is that the strict, early common-law view had eroded by the 1800s; the way was open for a body of mortgage law in which estates could be created in chattels by virtue of the mortgage contract.

Southern courts, in any case, adopted one of two theories when they had to say precisely what it was that was created when a slave was mortgaged: the legal estate or the lien. Under the first theory, the creditor held a legal estate while the estate of the debtor was entirely equitable. A mortgage was seen as a conveyance of legal title to property as it was in the case of land. The alternative theory was that a mortgage was not really a conveyance and did not confer an estate upon the creditor but merely created a lien on the property of the debtor.

Maryland, one of the most commercial of the southern states, was the strongest legal theory state. South Carolina's equity court, on the other side, held in an 1847 case that, although a creditor might in some sense be the "legal owner," he was not considered in equity "as in any manner . . . the owner of the slaves." Georgia also held that title was in the mortgagor (the debtor). Other states and jurists wobbled. In one Alabama case, for instance, two jurists wrote opinions. (The third disqualified himself so that there was no judgment of the court.) One held that the debtor was the legal owner against all persons except the mortgagee and that the mortgage created a mere chattel interest. The other held that the creditor became the absolute legal owner upon failure to pay.[21]

Conditional sales, whose history also remains unwritten and clouded in obscurity, were woven into the story of chattel mortgages. Conditional sales, which in the form of the installment contract or purchase on time have become one of the foundations of our modern credit economy, were defined during the 1700s as sales with the seller holding the right to repurchase the property at a particular time.[22] If he did not, he lost all claim. The purchaser took possession from the outset. Equity courts did not look with favor upon such sales because the seller might in fact be a person in severe economic difficulty who was forced to sell his property for a price well below its real value. The problem was that the debtor, economically weak, would be unlikely to be able to repurchase at all and would then lose his property for a price well below the market value. To protect people against such oppressive contracts, equity courts acted on the assumption that if a transaction was unclear (whether it was a mortgage or a conditional sale) they would rule it a mortgage.[23] This rule, and the fear of the conditional sale, arose before the rise of national commodities markets, which transformed the functions and theory of these contracts.

One more legal instrument needs to be mentioned to understand the law of chattel mortgages. This is the trust deed, which is a transfer of property to trustees, who hold the entire estate (legal and equitable), to carry out the purposes of the trust: this could include the power to sell the property for the benefit of creditors or to receive rents and profits to be applied to the liquidation of debts. While there is an enormous body of chattel mortgage case law, slave owners often used the trust deed as the "fundamental equivalent" of the mortgage. They were quite frequent in Mississippi and Alabama, for example. In Alabama the courts referred to the trust deed as a "virtual mortgage" so that these two categories collapsed into one another.[24]

Since pledges of slaves rarely occurred and because the line between mortgages and trust deeds was often wiped out, the greatest difficulty faced by southern courts was whether a contract was a conditional sale or a chattel mortgage. It is in these cases that we can see the conflict between the old equitable paternalism and the emerging will theory of contract, which became one of the legal foundations of the market capitalism of the 1800s.

The analytical problem was that the language in a contract was not always helpful. All courts, therefore, tried to cut through the inartfully drawn contract (a frequent problem in the nineteenth-century South) to the intention of the parties. In a major exception to accepted common law procedure, equity had long held that it was proper to admit oral testimony in order to explain a contract. Although some jurists were not happy with this equitable rule, most accepted it. The most hostile was the commercially oriented state of Maryland. In *Watkins* v. *Stockett's Admin.* (1820), for instance, the court held that "parol evidence is inadmissible to vary or contradict the clear, certain, and unequivocal import of a written instrument."[25] Other courts held that even an absolute sale could be a mortgage in fact and oral testimony would be admitted to show the parties understood the transaction that way. (The point was to protect the vulnerable seller or mortgagee from oppression and fraud by money lenders.)[26] One of the strongest statements, however, came from another strong, commercially oriented state, Louisiana. In the 1848 case of *Boner* v. *Mahle*, Justice Slidell fell back upon the civil code and rejected references to English equity. Louisiana policy, he noted, "prefers that cases of individual hardship should sometimes occur, rather than the daily transactions of the people and their titles to immovable property, should be exposed to the uncertainty which would result from permitting written contracts to be questioned upon oral testimony."[27]

What a court might do with oral testimony, whether it would lean toward equitable paternalism or market individualism, was largely a result of the ideology of particular jurists. Whichever way they leaned, nevertheless, analysis would be built upon what one justice called the "indicia of a mortgage."[28] These did not, however, eliminate the discretionary component of judging.

One apparently clear measure was that there had to be a debt for the contract to be a mortgage. A mortgage, by definition, was a security for a debt due. But at a time when the conditional sale was gaining legitimacy, even this got muddled. The reason was that the debt could be the price or the balance of the price paid for a slave.[29] Despite such a collapse of legal notions into one another, courts heroically went ahead with the attempt to distinguish the two transactions.

One of the norms most often used was whether or not a difference of some magnitude existed between the price paid for the slave and the actual market value. If the money the seller received was far below the market value of the slave, a strong presumption would arise that the court was dealing with a mortgage, and not a conditional sale. Even this, however, was not as objective, or as firm, as it might appear at first glance. The price criterion was a remnant of the older "just price" concept, but this notion was losing its force. "Just price," Powell had observed in his 1790 work on the law of contracts, was to be found in the consent of the parties; and, even if the contract appeared to some to be a hard one, a person was bound to perform it. Equity, nevertheless, continued to use the price standard. In their supervisory role, judges could transform what in fact had been oppressive sales into mortgages. Their "guardianship of adults" would continue, and they would preserve the notion of a just price by requiring an adequate price as a measure of a sale. At the time when the notion of objective value outside the consent of parties was collapsing, however, even this was less than solid.

The North Carolina court observed in 1840, for instance, that what was needed was a "gross disproportion." The next year this was given more form: a price of one-half or less of the market value would be "gross." The inadequacy of price standard had emerged at least as early as 1798 in Virginia, but the North Carolina cases of the early 1840s appear to be the first that tried to define what was "inadequate." What this would be for most jurists would depend upon facts and their sense of the fairness of a given transaction. In the North Carolina case, for example, the slave was valued at the current market rate of $400, but sold for $311. The court saw this simply as a good deal for the purchaser and ruled that it was a conditional sale. In 1857 Justice Nash of North Carolina suggested that the experience of business people would be a proper aid: the circumstances of the "sale" had to be such as "to the apprehension of men versed in business, and judicial minds, are incompatible with the idea of an absolute purchase, and leave no fair doubt that a security only was intended."[30]

The collapse of the idea of just price and the flabbiness of its equitable reflection, the inadequacy standard, left the way open for the development of a general law of contract based upon the will theory. Still, in the case of slave mortgaging this was not at all complete: many southern jurists were not so eager to embrace the market as was Justice Nash. Despite its fuzzy contours, the inadequacy norm still found a place in slave mortgage cases down to the Civil War. The tension between equitable paternalism and market individualism was also reflected in cases concerned with the recording of slave sales and mortgages, problems of possession, and the equity of redemption, among others.[31]

Recording of slave sales and mortgages was required throughout the South by statute, but this did not stop inquiry. What was the effect of a registry? Ruffin, for the North Carolina court, ruled that it was an essential element in a valid mortgage. Other courts ruled that if a third party knew of a mortgage, even if it were not recorded, that was enough.[32] One of the most revealing discussions came in an 1857 Louisiana case, *Johnson* v. *Bloodworth*. Justice Spofford for the majority argued that "registry laws are artificial rules, the creatures only of positive legislation. As they tend to multiply forms in the transmission of property, and to restrict the natural right of man to do what he will with his own, they have seldom, if ever, been extended by judicial construction to cases not within their plain and obvious intendment." A third person, the court held, who accepted a mortgage from a "naked possessor without a recorded title" only to find himself ousted by a superior title "has only himself to blame." Chief Justice Merrick dissented. "The policy of our law," he wrote, "has always been to place property directly in commerce, and protect the possessor in good faith in his title and property . . . The sanctioning of the principles contended for would render insecure the most important interests, and would . . . fill with alarm the holders of mortgage securities and the owners of real estate, slaves and moveables."[33]

As this case suggests, possession was often a problem in mortgage disputes. Possession was *always* transferred in a conditional sale, but in a mortgage it might or might not be. The form the problem took most often in southern courts involved the question of fraud against third persons (those individuals other than the mortgagee who had dealings with the debtor). Was it a fraud if the mortgagor retained possession of a slave before a debt became due? Was it a fraud if he retained it after the due date? Registry laws did not resolve the problem.

The most striking discussion of the matter of possession came in South Carolina. In 1835 the court held that "it is the common understanding and practice of the country that possession shall not be taken till condition broken."[34] Aside from the fact that this was not the common practice everywhere (Texas is a notable exception),[35] the court said nothing about the more crucial issue of possession after default. In 1839 the court conceded that possession was normally an appropriate measure of title. The case of slaves, however, was different because in South Carolina slaves "partake more of the nature of realty" so that mortgages of slaves came more under the rules of real property than did other chattels; and possession was not a measure of title to real estate.[36] Analytically this left the way clear to a rule that possession after default did not amount to fraud. The decision came in 1844. Judge Frost noted that

> the presumption of fraud from possession by a mortgagor after condition broken, would be arbitrary, because contrary to almost universal experience. The habits of society are not distinguished by such punctuality in the payment of debts, or such rigor in enforcing the rights of creditors, as to justify any such presumption from the default of the debtor, or forbearance of the creditor. Mortgages commonly remain unsatisfied for a longer or shorter time after the debts secured by them have become payable; and investments are sometimes permanently so continued.

This was a different world from that inhabited by the pettifoggers and money pinchers portrayed by Dickens. It was all too much for Justice Wardlaw who, dissenting alone, argued that possession after breach without notice of the mortgage was a fraud on subsequent creditors.[37]

Possession in the creditor created its own analytic problems. As early as 1791 the Virginia court affirmed that a mortgagee in possession after failure to pay was valid. (That this even had to be said shows the *paternalism* of equity.) Nevertheless, the court believed that creditors often would not take possession because the debtor had his equity of redemption. Up to twenty years after failure to repay the loan, a creditor who took possession would have the expense of raising and "improving" the property for someone else. (Female slaves, after all, would bear children.) This happened so often that the mortgagee's claim of presumption of title after a long possession did not impress the court.[38]

The North Carolina court in 1830 also believed that creditors would not want possession since they would be subjected to an accounting. Ruffin added that debtors would not want to part with their property. He concluded that "no mortgagee or mortgagor ever yet made a contract, upon which the possession was to change immediately, unless it were the veriest grinding bargain that could be driven with a distressed man, who had no way to turn."[39] Perhaps. But there are many cases in southern courts in which possession was transferred even before default. Were these actually conditional sales transformed by courts into mortgages? There can be no answer to this, but it should be clear that possession (before or after default) was not an inflexible measure of a fraud, or of the existence of a mortgage or conditional sale. The remarks about possession, nonetheless, suggest that equitable paternalism persisted, however weakly, alongside a spreading market individualism.

Class Relations Among Whites and the Mortgaging of Slaves

These rules of law in the area of mortgages, of course, were adaptations of English legal and equitable traditions. There was possibly no more important feature of that law than the equity of redemption. No one openly argued that this equitable right ought to be abolished, but there was severe pressure on the length of time allowed debtors to redeem their slaves. Down to the 1820s the old twenty-year rule appears to have held firm. Fissures then began to appear. During that decade, for example, the Virginia court began to show uneasiness. Although it gave no reason, the court held that a suit brought thirteen years after failure to repay was really too late.[40]

Creditors increasingly began to plead statute of limitations bars to the assertion of the right to redeem. Tennessee refused to accept the argument that the legal three-year limit in personal property actions could be pleaded in an equity court. Missouri went the other way and held that the statutory bar did apply. This was necessary to "preserve property, and promote the peace and welfare of the people." More curiously, the court held that it was unclear whether redemption would even be allowed, whether it could be foreclosed in equity, or whether "when the time is passed, the estate in a chattel is indefeasible." Missouri simply had no chattel mortgage law as late as this 1834 case. Unrestrained by any equitable tradition the court accepted the statutory bar and added that, in its judgment, poverty was not a sufficient excuse for a suit's delay. Missouri's hostility was extreme, but the equity of redemption rarely escaped even in more sensitive courts. Kentucky and Arkansas, for instance, judicially set up a five-year limit if the possession of the creditor was "adverse," that is, if he refused to admit the existence of a mortgage.[41]

Several states modified the time to redeem by statute. In Georgia it was four years, and in Alabama (by analogy to the limit in the legal action of debt) it was set at six. The most rigorous arrangement was in North Carolina. In an 1826 case Judge Henderson upheld the twenty-year period, but the legislature immediately set a ten-year limit. In 1829 there was a severe drop in the price of slaves, and the following year the legislature imposed a two-year statutory limit on the equity of redemption.[42]

During the 1850s several cases reached the state's highest court that involved the 1830 scheme. In 1851 Ruffin noted that "the period of two years seems to be short, and, it may be feared, will not unfrequently operate severely on the necessitous people, who are compelled to mortgage slaves." Nevertheless, that was the law, and the plaintiff's case came within it so that the court could provide no relief. Justice Pearson, in a later case, suggested that the rule could be hard but "we cannot help it—*six lex ita scripta est.*" Ruffin and Pearson, generally sensitive to the "necessitous," were not happy with the rule. The same was not true of Nash. He wrote that the delay in the case before him (eight years) was "unreasonable" because the mortgagor "might lie by any length of time at his pleasure, according to the maxim in equity, once a mortgage always a mortgage, a maxim which in its operation as applied to female slaves, has often been attended with disastrous consequences to mortgagees." The distance between the Virginia court of 1791 and Justice Nash could not have been greater.[43]

Social relationships among whites, then, could be seen by a jurist like Nash in terms of market relationships, but others continued to see them in terms of a more complete human relationship based upon relative social position. Justice Ruffin, for example, ruled in 1859 that the transaction before him was a mortgage. To arrive at this conclusion he took into account the relative positions of the parties to the contract. The debtor in the case was needy, illiterate, and "in the power of the other party."[44] Probably the most outrageous case in the appellate records is *Esham* v. *Lamar*, an 1849 Kentucky case.[45] A Maryland couple migrated to Kentucky with a slave girl they owned. When they arrived, they found themselves without money for even the basic necessities. A former Maryland neighbor persuaded them to "sell" the girl to him for $25. The court declared the transaction to be a mortgage, and gave the couple the right to redeem their slave. Time and again southern jurists found a debtor to be a needy person, or what seems to have been one of their favorite words, "necessitous." Reduced to this level, the debtor, to use Justice Brooke's phrase, "might in some sense be said to be the slave of the lender."[46]

The recognition of a social hierarchy, not just market calculations, did play a role in the way jurists dealt with contracts to mortgage or sell slaves. A paternalistic social system grounded upon the ownership of human beings did find expression in the courts that would protect whites, in some cases at least, from being dealt with as though they were as powerless as slaves. Such a world view, however, lived in uneasy alliance with a market individualism that was seeping into the cases involving contracts for the transfer of slaves.

Slaves and the Emergence of a Law of Chattel Mortgages

T. R. R. Cobb, the pro-slavery legalist from Georgia, ended his study of the law of slavery in 1859 as follows: "[having] concluded our view of the negro slave as a person, we shall hereafter consider of those rules of law to which as property he is subject. In that investigation we shall find that his nature as a man, and his consequent power of volition and locomotion, introduce important variations in those rules which regulate property in general." The promised study never appeared. Cobb was killed in late 1862 at the battle of Fredericksburg in a war that pitted a moral system he tried to defend against one that rejected the idea of property rights in man.[47] We will never know if he meant to include mortgage cases in his defense. Still, there are some cases that support his conclusion.

A severe strain upon the slave system of the South, as well as upon the Union as a whole, was presented by the fugitive slave. Courts on occasion had to deal with this even in mortgage cases. In *Webb and Foster* v. *Patterson* (Tennessee, 1846), for instance, Justice Green noted that equity would not usually rescind a contract because of the suppression of truth "in relation to the moral character of a slave." A mortgage was different because the parties "are to account with each other." When a slave owner knew his slave to be a runner and he concealed the fact, the court ruled, the person who took the slave as security would not bear the expenses of recovery. *Keas* v. *Yewell* (Kentucky, 1834) is even more revealing. A creditor tried to foreclose the equity of redemption but failed because the slave had run away. "The casualty," Justice Nicholas wrote, "by which the slave was lost, is a peril incident to the very nature of such property; and therefore in contracts or covenants concerning such property, the peril should never be presumed to have been intended to be guarded against, unless so expressly stipulated." The creditor bore the loss.[48]

In Kentucky, Maryland, and Louisiana the question arose whether or not a mortgagee had the right to hold the issue of mortgaged slaves as security. In every case the court rested its decision upon the principle of *partus sequitur ventrem*, the status of the child is derived from the mother. Louisiana's court reinforced this principle with a reference to the Code which prohibited the sale of children under ten away from their mothers. (The children in the case were all under ten.) Maryland's court grounded its ruling on the legal theory of mortgages. Since the mortgagee was the legal owner, he was entitled to the offspring. The court concluded the case *Evans* v. *Merriken* with this observation: "We will only remark in conclusion, that we are happy to find that in this instance, the law of the land, and the law of nature, so far from being at variance, are in perfect harmony; and that whilst on the one hand, full and ample justice will be administered to the honest creditor, the claims and feelings of nature will not be violated on the other."[49] This decision represents neither a rejection of commercialism nor of slavery, and it is not one to support the Cobb thesis—no rule of law was adjusted to the humanity of the slave. But it does show the ambivalence that could exist because of a social system built upon property rights in man. Unease, however, played no role in the legal reasoning of the court.

Nevertheless, the humanity of the slave sometimes did skew a decision, and here is where Cobb might have found some support. Justice Reese of Tennessee, for instance, ruled the contract before him to be a mortgage, not a conditional sale, because "the slave was one of peculiar value, worth not less than $1,000; he had been brought up from infancy with the complainant, who was a young man, and they were reciprocally attached to each other." This could backfire, however, as it did in *Harrison* v. *Lee* (Kentucky, 1822). The court there found a conditional sale because the evidence showed that the debtors' supposed unwillingness to part with the slave "is rebutted, by proving that Sam, by an act of rebellion, had given him great offence, which induced him to declare he would sell him, and that he should remain no longer on his premises."[50]

Another dimension of this situation was explored by Chancellor Harper in *Bryan* v. *Robert* (S.C., 1847). A bill for the specific performance of a contract could not be upheld in the case of a mortgagee of slaves. "He is not supposed to know anything of the peculiar qualities of the slaves," Harper wrote, "except that he might form an estimate of the market values of such slaves, and certainly not to have the same attachment, or knowledge of their character and qualifications, as the owner, who has been in possession of them, and has been deprived of it."[51]

Courts then did recognize the communalism within the world built by masters and slaves, but at least in cases of chattel mortgage it was usually limited to the special circumstances of favored slaves. A notable case that perhaps points to a wider understanding was *Flowers* v. *Sproul* (Kentucky, 1819). The court ruled that the intention of the parties should be decided "as well from the subject matter of the contract" as from other circumstances. Here the court abandoned the rule that equity would find a mortgage in a doubtful case. The problem was the equity of redemption. It was unfair and injurious to the fortune and prospects of the mortgagee and his family. But, a ruling that the contract was a mortgage (with the right to redeem) would also be devastating to the subjects of the contract:

> as slaves, though property, are intelligent and sympathetic beings; they interchange sentiments, mingle sympathies, and reciprocate, with their possessor and the members of his family, all the social regards and kind attentions which endear the members of the human family to each other, and bind them in the social state. The agonies of feeling, as well on the part of the slaves as of their possessors, inseparable from a sudden disruption of those social relations, ought not to be lightly regarded by the judge who, after the lapse of many years from its date, is called upon to decide whether a contract for slaves be a contract of mortgage or conditional sale.[52]

The irony is that the equitable paternalism of the Kentucky court in *Flowers* pointed to the same legal result as the market individualism of other jurists, such as Nash in North Carolina: the validation of the conditional sale.

Despite such gestures toward the humanity of slaves, it should never be forgotten that, where the subject matter of mortgages was property rights in man, we are dealing with a legal history filled with human misery. Buried within all the legal discussions about possession, adequacy of price, and equity of redemption could be broken slave families. It must be put in the conditional, of course, because slaves could live and die without ever knowing that they had been mortgaged. Nonetheless, it takes only a casual reading of a random selection of cases to see the blunted morality created by a social system resting upon slavery. Case after case refers to a thirteen-year-old girl, a ten-year-old boy, or other minors. One case will have to stand as a symbol. Thirty years after *Flowers*, the Kentucky court decided the case of *Lee* v. *Fellowes & Co.* The court ruled that sales of mortgaged property under execution could not be sold in gross as they had been in this case. A sale in gross (i.e., of all the slaves together) could, of course, preserve the family and personal relations of those involved. In the view of the court, however, "a sale in gross would be often detrimental to the best interests of debtor and creditor. . . ." It, therefore, upheld a lower court decree disregarding the earlier sale in gross and ordered a new sale of the slaves individually.[53]

Conclusion

After referring to the collapse of equitable doctrines in the early 1800s, Morton Horwitz concluded that "in one of the greatest triumphs of form over substance common law judges during the nineteenth century . . .`began to treat these transactions as conditional sales, thus entirely freeing this economic relationship from regulatory and paternalistic equitable mortgage doctrines."[54] The story of the mortgaging of slaves, however, is not a clear example of the rise of formalism. Equitable maxims, such as "if there is doubt the court will find a mortgage," did persist, although the use of them begin to sound rather hollow by the 1850s. It is true, nevertheless, that market notions controlled the way some southern jurists dealt with "these transactions." It is also true that chattel mortgage law was so confused that the boundaries between pledges, mortgages, trust deeds, and conditional sales were often fuzzy. Because the weight of traditional legal thought was none too heavy, the way was open for the commercialization of slavery, at least in the area of mortgage relationships.[55]

Nonetheless, commercialization was not a completed process on the eve of the Civil War. Tushnet, building his study of the law of slavery upon the Marxian analysis of slave society communalism worked out by Genovese, has suggested a different trend. "The motivating principle of bourgeois law is an undifferentiated individualism," he argued, "while the motivating principle of slave law is a differentiated communalism." Ultimately the tension between these would be resolved, but this did not mean that "any particular resolution was likely." Earlier on, Tushnet was more conclusive: "In light of the suppleness of the law over extended periods, there is little doubt that such a law [an autonomous law of slavery] would have been created." But the time needed was not there. Had a "rationalized law of slavery" been erected it would have meant a basic transformation in the notion of property. "It would no longer be defined as the expression of individual will, subject to regulation only for the most pressing social goals. Instead, property, at first only in slaves but eventually in everything, would be defined as the delegation by society as a whole of certain limited authority to 'owners,' who would be charged with exercising that authority only in socially prescribed ways."[56]

To argue for some model of "pure" slave law, however, is to approach the problem ahistorically. Paternalistic communalism may characterize a slave society during one phase of its history, and this may be reflected in the legal system. But it has had to contest against other value systems, such as market individualism. There is, of course, no necessary antipathy between slavery and commercialism, nor is there a necessary correspondence; the relationship can be close and congenial, or it can be distant and tense. In all events, it is a relationship that must be worked out.

Sidney Mintz has argued that the assimilation of the slave to property in law is related to "the level of technical development and the accompanying institutional apparatus, including the economic system," and the property component in slave law is related to the "labor needs of an emerging capitalism."[57] To the extent that cases involving the mortgaging of slaves in nineteenth-century America throw any light on this, they suggest that a "rationalized law of slavery" had little chance to emerge. The concept of property as the expression of individual will was never stronger than in the mid to late 1800s. It was deeply rooted in English law[58] and in law of northern states, and it was expressed in these cases when southern courts began to validate the conditional sale, which they did more and more.

Deeply rooted in the spread of market individualism in southern legal experience was a growing tension in moral notions. What a complete triumph for market ideas in the southern courts (and a complete victory did not occur) might have meant for the social and moral order of the South we can never know. Instead of a prolonged intellectual transformation, that order collapsed in violence. In any event, the morality of keeping promises (an idea central to market individualism) was especially strong in mid-nineteenth-century American legal thought, even if the contract was quite lopsided. Such a notion, however, stood against moral values peculiar to a communal society resting upon property rights in man. At its best, this latter moral order could come out in the communalism in the *Flowers* case or in the concern of jurists to protect the "necessitous" from being reduced to the powerlessness of the slave.

Less often as the war approached, however, did the courts choose to sit as guardians of adults. Indeed, even though southern proslavery writers and jurists showed increasing concern about the separation of slave children from their mothers (a point hammered on by the abolitionists),[59] southern courts faced with "mortgages" of slaves on a day-to-day basis showed concern less and less. Opinion after opinion in the last years before the war totally ignored broken slave families: the property rights, legal or equitable, of the owners were the sole concern—something Chichikov would have understood only too well.

NOTES

[1] *Fishburne* v. *Kunhardt* 2 Speers (S.C.) 556 (1844).

[2] C. Duncan Rice, *The Rise and Fall of Black Slavery* (Baton Rouge, La., 1975), 381. This, however, is arguable; see, for example, Pierre Dockes, *Medieval Slavery and Liberation* (Chicago, 1982), 4ff.

[3] Studies of the law of slavery, of course, all recognize the importance of the property element. Moses I. Finley, for instance, has written that the core of slavery "is the totality of powerlessness in principle, and for that the idea of property is juristically the key— hence the term 'chattel slave.' " *International Encyclopedia of the Social Sciences* (14 vols., New York, 1968), XIV, 307. George M. Stroud anticipated this definition when he noted that ". . . the cardinal principle of slavery—that the slave is to be regarded as a thing—is an article of property—a chattel person—obtains as undoubted law in all of these states." *A Sketch of the Laws Relating to Slavery* (New York, 1968: originally published, 1856), 11. This effort to define slavery in juristic terms, however, has been criticized as too Western in orientation. It also fails to pay enough attention to the particular functions of the institution over time. There is an extensive literature. Among those that should be consulted would be Dockes, *Medieval Slavery*, 4ff; Suzanne Miers and Igor Kopytoff, eds., *Slavery in Africa: Historical and Anthropological Perspectives* (Madison, Wisc., 1977), 11–22; Moses I. Findley, *Ancient Slavery and Modern Ideology* (New York, 1980), 72ff; Arnold A. Sio, "Interpretations of Slavery: The Slave Status in the Americas," *Comparative Studies in Society and History*, VII (1965), 289–308; Mark Tushnet, *The American Law of Slavery, 1810–1860: Considerations of Humanity and Interest* (Princeton, 1981); Kenneth M.Stampp, *The Peculiar Institution: Slavery in the Ante-Bellum South* (New York, 1956), Chapter 5; Eugene D. Genovese, *Roll, Jordan, Roll: The World the Slaves Made* (New York, 1974), 25–49; A. E. Keir Nash, "Reason of Slavery: Understanding the Judicial Role in the Peculiar Institution," *Vanderbilt Law Review*, XXXII (Jan. 1979), 1–218; Stanley M. Elkins, *Slavery: A Problem in American Institutional and Intellectual Life* (2nd ed., Chicago and London, 1968). Where these studies have gone into some detail they tend to focus upon the use of law to control slaves and upon emancipation. Tushnet's recent study is a notable exception, but he did not examine the use of slaves as security for debts or as collateral.

[4] This is especially true because the focus is upon the case law. A critical problem that

remains, for example, concerns the actual function of slave mortgages in the South. Robert H. Skilton, "Developments in Mortgage Law and Practice," *Temple University Law Quarterly*, XVII (1943), 342, noted that mortgages could be used as a means to economic advance or as a cushion against economic decline. Case law does not show adequately whether this was also true of slave mortgages. What is needed is a close study of the recorded mortgages in southern states over a period of time. As a *very* modest start I have looked at all the mortgages registered in Fairfield District, South Carolina, in the mid-1850s. These records suggest that Skilton's remark does apply. Fairfield, Co., Office: Clerk of Court (as Register of Mesne Conveyance); Deeds, 1854–1856, Microfilm Reel C 311, South Carolina Department of Archives and History.

⁵ For example, see J. H. Baker, *An Introduction to English Legal History* (2nd ed., London, 1979), 263–300; S. F. C. Milsom, *Historical Foundations of the Common Law* (London, 1969), 271–316; and Morton J. Horwitz, *The Transformation of American Law, 1780–1860* (Cambridge, Mass., 1977), 160–211.

⁶ For a study of slave torts see Thomas D. Morris, " 'As If the Injury was Effected by the Natural Elements of Air, or Fire': or Slave Wrongs and the Liability of Masters," *Law Society Review*, XVI (1981–1982), 569–99.

⁷ Baker, *Introduction to English Legal History*, 263.

⁸ A powerful statement of the philosophical underpinning is David Hume, *A Treatise on Human Nature*, ed., L. A. Selby-Bigge (Oxford, 1958: originally published in 1739), 526. Patrick Atiyah, *The Rise and Fall of Freedom of Contract* (Oxford, 1979), is a brilliant study that shows how the theory became widespread about the turn of the century.

⁹ Cited in Horwitz, *Transformation of American Law*, 160–61.

¹⁰ One of the critical "postulates" in the model of a mature possessive market society is that "each individual's capacity to labour is his own property and is alienable." This differs from a customary or status society in which "the whole labour force is tied to the land, or to the performance of allotted functions, or (in the case of slaves) to masters. The members of the labour force are thus not free to offer their labour in the market: there is no market in labour. (There may be a market in slaves, but a market in slaves comprises only an exchange relation between masters, not between slave and master, and is therefore not a market relation between all the persons concerned.)" C. B. Macpherson, *The Political Theory of Possessive Individualism: Hobbes to Locke* (Oxford, 1962), 49, 54.

¹¹ Horwitz, *Transformation of American Law*, 265.

¹² *Conway's Executors and Devisees* v. *Alexander* 7 Cranch 237 (1812); *Moss* v. *Green* 10 Leigh (Va.) 251 (1839). Keir Nash has described Brooke as occupying the extreme conservative position among Virginia judges of the late 1820s. "Reason of Slavery," 145.

¹³ Alan Harding, *A Social History of English Law* (Gloucester, Mass., 1973), 106–07; James Kent, *Commentaries on American Law* (4 vols., Boston, 1830), IV, 136–37.

¹⁴ Sir William Holdsworth, *A History of English Law* (16 vols., London, 1966 reprint), V, 330–32; VI, 663–64.

¹⁵ Stewart Macaulay, "Non-contractual Relations in Business: A Preliminary Study," *American Sociological Review*, XXVIII (1963), 55–67.

¹⁶ John Joseph Powell, *A Treatise on the Law of Mortgages* (2 vols., London, 1799) I, 13; Kent, *Commentaries*, IV, 139. Lawrence M. Friedman, relying upon Skilton's pathbreaking study of mortgage law, suggested that these clauses were often voided in southern courts so that the trust deed became the "functional equivalent" of the mortgage with a power of sale clause. *A History of American Law* (New York, 1973), 217. I have not found this to be the case in slave mortgage cases before the Civil War, however. Power of sale clauses were upheld, to give only a couple of examples, in *Planters & Merchants Bank* v. *Willis* 5 Ala. 770 (1843); *Wootton* v. *Wheeler* 22 Tex. 338 (1858).

¹⁷ Adam Smith, *Lectures on Jurisprudence*, eds., R. L. Meek, D. D. Raphael, and P. G. Stein (Oxford, 1978: originally published in 1766), 471; Kent, *Commentaries*, IV, 144, fn. a; *Falls* v. *Torrance* 11 N.C. 196 (1826); *Overton* v. *Bigelow* 3 Yerger (Tenn.) 513 (1832); Powell, *Law of Mortgages*, 25.

168   *The Chattel Mortgages of Slaves*

[18] Kent, *Commentaries*, II, 578.

[19] J. H. Baker, "Property in Chattels," *Selden Society*, XCIV (1978), 217. See also his discussion of chattel property in the *Introduction to English Legal History*, 315–36.

[20] See, for example, M. Eugene Sirmans, "The Legal Status of the Slave in South Carolina, 1670–1740," *Journal of Southern History*, XXVIII (1962), 462–73; Elsa Goveia, *The West-Indian Slave Laws of the 18th Century* (Barbados, 1973), 21. Goveia refers to slaves as real property for some purposes and mentions laws regulating the mortgaging of slaves in the West Indies, especially 4 Hening, *Statutes at Large of Virginia*, 222–28; 5 Hening, *Statutes at Large*, 432–43. This latter law was an attempt to define slaves as personal "estate" but was disallowed by the crown. The changed definition in Virginia is easily available in the *Revised Code of the Laws of Virginia* (2 vols., Richmond, 1819), I, 432ff.

[21] *Jamieson* v. *Bruce* 6 G. & J. (Md.) 320 (1834); *Bryan* v. *Robert* 1 Strob. Eq.(S.C.) 334 (1847); *Davis et al.* v. *Anderson* 1 Ga. 176 (1846); *Bates* v. *Murphy* reported with *M'Gowen* v. *Young* 2 Stew (Ala.) 162 (1832); see also *Hannah, Admin.* v. *Carrington et al.* 18 Ark. 185 (1856).

[22] As late as the 1830s Chancellor Kent (using the early definition) referred to the chattel mortgage as a more "benign" contract than the conditional sale. Kent, *Commentaries*, IV, 144, fn. e. By mid-century such sales were taking on new contours. A standard legal dictionary gave as a common example of such sales the so-called sale and return, "that is, the vendee is to return all that he does not sell. So goods may be sold on trial; the vendee is then to try them, and return them, if unsuitable, without a reasonable time," John Bouvier, *Institutes of American Law* (2 vols., Philadelphia, 1882; first published in 1851), I, 239. By the 1930s the Corpus Juris dealt with "so-called contracts for sale and return, or sales with agreements to repurchase" (the earlier forms of the conditional sale) as something other than a conditional sale. The latter was defined (following the Uniform Conditional Sales Act) as "a contract for the sale of personal property under which possession is delivered to the buyer, but title is retained in the seller until the performance of some condition, usually the payment of the purchase price," 55 C. J. 1193. Finally, by the mid-twentieth century a standard treatise on sales noted that "the term 'conditional sale' has many different meanings. As used in current installment sales of chattels, it usually takes this form: a contract to sell when the buyer completes payment of all installments of the purchase price," Lawrence Vold, *Handbook of the Law of Sales* (2d ed., St. Paul, Minn., 1959), 281. Throughout the years before the Civil War, southern courts continued to use the earlier definition of a sale with the right of repurchase.

[23] Kent, *Commentaries*, IV, 144; Sample cases include *Turnipseed* v. *Cunningham* 16 Ala. 501 (1849); *Poindexter* v. *McCannon* 1 Dev. Eq. (N.C.) 373 (1830); *Secrest* v. *Turner* 2 J. J. Marsh (Ky.) 471 (1829); *Barnes* v. *Holcomb* 12 Smedes & M. (Miss.) 306 (1849).

[24] Friedman, *History of American Law*, 217; *A. Pope & Son, et al.* v. *Wilson, et al.* 7 Ala. 690 (1845).

[25] *Watkins* v. *Stockett's Admin.* 6 H. & J. (Md.) 435 (1820).

[26] Among cases illustrating the admissibility of parole evidence are *Prince* v. *Bearden* 1 A.K. Marsh. (Ky.) 169 (1818); *Secrest* v. *Turner* 2 J. J. Marsh. (Ky) 471 (1829); *Ross* v. *Norvell* 1 Wash. (Va.) 14 (1791); *Overton* v. *Bigelow* 3 Yerger (Tenn.) 513 (1832); *Kent* v. *Allbritain* 4 How. (Miss.) 317 (1840); *Thompson* v. *Chumney* 8 Tex. 389 (1852); *Hudson* v. *Isbell* 5 Stew. & P. (Ala.) 67 (1833). Cases showing hostility to the rule are fewer, but the following should be examined: *Thompson* v. *Patton* 5 Littell (Ky.) 74 (1824); *Ransone* v. *Fraysers Exec.* 10 Leigh (Va.) 592 (1840); and *Montany* v. *Rock* 10 (Mo.) 506 (1847).

[27] *Boner* v. *Mahle* 3 La. Ann. 600 (1848). Louisiana, of course, was a civil-law not a common-law state, and that meant that the system of mortgaging was subject to different rules. The term "mortgage" in that state covered a wide variety of liens, including those created by courts. It was not limited simply to an agreement between two private individuals. A good introduction to the overall Louisiana civil-law system is George Dargo, *Jefferson's Louisiana: Politics and the Clash of Legal Traditions* (Cambridge, Mass., 1975).

[28] *Turnipseed* v. *Cunningham* 16 Ala. 501 (1849).

[29] Of the 24 cases of slave mortgages recorded in Fairfield District, South Carolina, be-

tween 1854 and 1856, six appear quite clearly to be actual sales. In January 1855 six men mortgaged slaves to Mary A. Ellison. The terms of these "mortgages" make it clear that they were in fact purchases of slaves. The purchasers then gave Ellison a "mortgage" on the slaves she just sold to secure the balance of the price. Fairfield Co., Office: Clerk of Court; Deeds, 1854–1856, Reel C 311, S.C. Dept. of Archives and History.

[30] *Lewis* v. *Owen* 36 N.C. 241–42 (1840); *McLaurin* v. *Wright* 37 N.C. 69 (1841); *Colvard* v. *Waugh* 3 Jones Eq. (N.C.) 335 (1857); *Chapman* v. *Turner* 1 Call (Va.) 280 (1798). See also *English* v. *Lane* 1 Port. (Ala.) 328 (1835), where the court held that "a greatly inadequate price" does not by itself void a sale but that a "gross inadequacy" might imply fraud. Two years before, the court, in *Hudson* v. *Isbell* 5 Stew. & P. (Ala.) 67 (1833), held that a "very great inadequacy of the price" strongly suggested that the contract was a mortgage and not a conditional sale.

[31] The areas discussed are illustrative of attitudes; this does not, of course, mean that others would not be. One problem, for example, was whether or not a mortgagor's "rights" were subject to execution by creditors other than the mortgagee. In *McGregory & Darling* v. *Hall* 3 Stew. & P. (Ala.) 397 (1833), the court ruled that they could be, even though the "ancient doctrine" was that a court of law could not touch an equitable estate. The reason was that this rule had been "giving way" in the case of real estate mortgages, and, in the view of the court, no distinction between real property and personal property need be made. Tushnet, therefore, appears to be in error when he observes that "southern courts accepted or rejected analogies to real property depending solely on whether the substantive rules could be supported independently by appeals to humanity." *The American Law of Slavery*, 174. Cases upholding the liability to execution are *Wootton* v. *Wheeler* 22 Tex. 338 (1858); *McIssacs* v. *Hobbs* 8 Dana (Ky.) 268 (1839). Examples of courts ruling the other way would be *King* v. *Bailey* 8 Mo. 332 (1843); *Thornhill* v. *Gilmer* 4 Smedes & M. (Miss.) 153 (1845). In *Prewett* v. *Dobbs* Smedes & M. (Miss.) 432 (1850) the court held that a right of redemption in a slave was not subject to a general execution in satisfaction of debts, but was liable to be distrained and sold in satisfaction of rent due.

[32] *Fleming* v. *Burgin* 37 N.C. 430 (1843). On the other side see *Youngblood* v. *Keadle* Strob. (S.C.) 121 (1846); *Guerrant* v. *Anderson* 4 Rand. (Va.) 208 (1826); *Dearing* v. *Watkins* 16 Ala. 20 (1849); *Hughes* v. *Graves* 1 Littell (Ky.) 317 (1822).

[33] *Johnson* v. *Bloodworth* 12 La. Ann. 699 (1857).

[34] *Gist* v. *Pressley* 2 Hill's Eq. (S.C.) 319 (1835).

[35] In *Thompson* v. *Chumney* 8 Tex. 389 (1852), the court noted that the contract "was in fact a loan of money, with the understanding that the services of the negro should be received in satisfaction of interest on the money loaned—a character of mortgage very common in this country. . . ."

[36] *Maples* v. *Maples* Rice Eq. (S.C.) 300 (1839). A solitary case in contrast is *Robertson* v. *Campbell* 8 Mo. 365 (1844) in which the court refused to apply the rules of real-property mortgages to slaves. It declined to separate slaves from other chattels. In its view the difference in rules between land and chattel mortgages arose "partly from the inferior value and importance of personal property, and partly from a reluctance to impose any unnecessary restrictions upon its transfer."

[37] *Fishburne* v. *Kunhardt* 2 Speers (S.C.) 556 (1844). On Frost see Benjamin F. Perry's sketch in U. R. Brooks, *South Carolina Bench and Bar* (2 vols., Columbia, S.C., 1908), I, 129. Frost had someone else collect his legal fees for him while he was in practice. His sensibilities, however, did not prevent him from becoming the president of the Blue Ridge Railroad Company.

[38] *Ross* v. *Norvell* 1 Wash. (Va.) 14 (1791).

[39] *Poindexter* v. *McCannon* 1 Dev. Eq. (N.C.) 373 (1830). Examples of cases involving possession by mortgagee before debts were paid are the following: *Byrd* v. *McDaniel* 33 Ala. 18 (1858); *Kent* v. *Allbritain* 4 How. (Ala.) 317 (1840); *Kea* v. *Council* 55 N.C. 286 (1856); and *Bailey* v. *Carter* 42 N.C. 200 (1851).

[40] *Roberts Admin.* v. *Cocke, Exec. of Thompson* 1 Rand. (Va.) 121 (1822).

[41] *Perry* v. *Craig* 3 Mo. 516 (1834); *Overton* v. *Bigelow* 3 Yerger (Tenn.) 513 (1832); *Kenwick* v. *Macey's Exec.* 1 Dana (Ky.) 276 (1833); *Ewell* v. *Tidwell* 20 Ark. 136 (1859). In *Sullivan* v. *Hadley* 16 Ark. 129 (1855) the court gave a mortgagee three years to bring a bill to foreclose. This was the time to commence an action at law for the possession of slaves.

[42] *Humphries* v. *Terrell* 1 Ala. 650 (1840). The Georgia scheme is mentioned in the Alabama case. Also see *Falls* v. *Torrance* 11 N.C. 196 (1826).

[43] *Bailey* v. *Carter* 42 N.C. 200 (1851); *Robinson* v. *Lewis* 45 N.C. 63 (1852); *Colvard* v. *Waugh* 3 Jones Eq. (N.C.) 335 (1857).

[44] *Wilson* v. *Weston* 4 Jones Eq. (N.C.) 350 (1859).

[45] *Esham* v. *Lamar* 10 B. Mon. (Ky.) 43 (1849).

[46] *Moss* v. *Green* 10 Leigh (Va.) 251 (1839).

[47] Thomas R. R. Cobb, *An Inquiry into the Law of Negro Slavery* (New York, 1968: originally published in 1858), 317. On Cobb see the entry in Allen Johnson, ed., *Dictionary of American Biography* (22 vols., New York, 1928–1958), III, 247.

[48] *Webb and Foster* v. *Patterson* 7 Humphreys (Tenn.) 431 (1846); *Keas* v. *Yewell* 2 Dana (Ky.) 248 (1834).

[49] *Boner* v. *Mable* 3 La. Ann. 600 (1848); *Hughes* v. *Graves* 1 Littell (Ky.) 317 (1822); *Evans* v. *Merriken* 8 G. & J. (Md.) 39 (1836).

[50] *Ballard* v. *Jones and Ingram* 7 Humphreys (Tenn.) 439 (1846); *Harrison* v. *Lee* 1 Littell (Ky.) 190 (1822). See also *Overton* v. *Bigelow's Admin.* 10 Yerger (Tenn.) 48 (1836); *May & May* v. *Eastin* 2 Pot. (Ala.) 414 (1835).

[51] *Bryan* v. *Robert* 1 Strob. Eq. (S.C.) 334 (1847). The modern common law does not compel specific performance of contracts in the future: it awards damages for the breach of contract. Baker, *Introduction to English Legal History*, 263. Horwitz added that "the moment at which courts focus on expectation damages rather than restitution or specific performance to give a remedy for nondelivery is precisely the time at which contract law begins to separate itself from property," *Transformation of American Law*, 174.

[52] *Flowers* v. *Sproul et al.* 2 A. K. Marsh. (Ky.) 54 (1819).

[53] *Lee* v. *Fellowes & Co.* 10 B. Mon. (Ky.) 117 (1849).

[54] Horwitz, *Transformation of American Law*, 266.

[55] Friedman noted that "security devices became almost indistinguishable. It was another example of the principle that nothing—neither small specks of technicality nor large stains of legal logic and jargon—was allowed to interfere in the 19th century with what judges or the dominant public saw as the highroad to progress and wealth." *History of American Law*, 474.

[56] Tushnet, *American Law of Slavery*, 35, 230–31. See also, Eugene D. Genovese, *The World the Slaveholders Made: Two Essays in Interpretation* (New York, 1969), especially Part 2: "The Logical Outcome of the Slaveholders' Philosophy."

[57] Sidney Mintz, Review of *Slavery* by Stanley Elkins, *American Anthropologist*, LXIII (1961), 580. See also, Sio, "Interpretations of Slavery," 304.

[58] An excellent discussion is Atiyah, *Rise and Fall of Freedom of Contract*.

[59] A fine analysis of the effort to reform the law of slavery (indeed, it is one of the only ones) is Genovese, *Roll, Jordan, Roll*, 49–70. John Belton O'Neall, *The Negro Law of South Carolina* (Columbia, 1848), 18; Cobb, *Law of Negro Slavery*, 246. Georgia in 1854, and Alabama in 1852, adopted statutes to prohibit the separation of slave children from their mothers; in the case of Georgia it was applied to children five or under, and in Alabama to children ten and under. Howell Cobb, *A Compilation of the General and Public Statutes of the State of Georgia* (New York, 1859), 636–37; John J. Ormond, Arthur P. Bagby, George Goldthwaite, *The Code of Alabama* (Montgomery, Ala., 1852), 392. The Louisiana Code has already been mentioned. The only case I have found in which this rule had any application to a mortgage case was *Boner* v. *Mable* 3 La. Ann. 600 (1848).

Organizing Civil Rights Litigation:
The NAACP's Experience

MARK V. TUSHNET

IF THE PROBLEM of the twentieth century is the color line,[1] the southern confrontation with racism in the law represents only an early stage in the penetration of that problem throughout American society. Indeed, an examination of the sustained challenge brought against the southern system of racial segregation by the National Association for the Advancement of Colored People (NAACP) illuminates more general problems of law, race, and society. This essay, based upon a study of the NAACP's challenge to segregated schools, frames the inquiry by examining a small incident in that challenge. By doing so, it opens up interesting questions about the ethics of public interest law, the sociology of litigation, and, in the end, about the constraints legal premises place on the use of law to effect social change.

Almost everyone knows that the Supreme Court held segregation unconstitutional in *Brown* v. *Board of Education of Topeka.*[2] Fewer people know that the case was initially planned to challenge segregation in Wichita. The reasons for the change illuminate important issues. In July 1950 the NAACP and its lawyers decided to pursue what they called the direct attack on segregation, a challenge to the legality of separate facilities for blacks or whites without regard to the supposed equality of such facilities.[3] For fifteen years they had been attacking segregated graduate and professional schools and had just won major victories in the Supreme Court.[4] In addition they had successfully sued in urban areas throughout the South to equalize the salaries paid to black

and white teachers. It would have been difficult to continue along
the same lines. Every observer seems to have thought that the 1950
decisions provided the opportunity for a new direction in the
NAACP's litigation, and the organization's limited resources made
it unlikely that extending the salary campaign to rural areas would
be worthwhile. Although the NAACP could have decided to challenge segregation in elementary and secondary schools by seeking
to equalize their physical facilities, it chose instead, in a relatively
uncontroversial decision, to attack legal segregation directly.

Lawsuits are not dreamed up by lawyers acting on their own,
though. The NAACP needed a real plaintiff and an actual location
for the direct attack. At first it seemed that Wichita, Kansas, was
the place. Since 1948 an active member of the Wichita branch had
been urging the NAACP's national office to begin a lawsuit there.
The state Conference of Branches of the NAACP met and endorsed a Wichita lawsuit by a vote of 7–2, the minority believing
that Topeka would be a better site.[5] After that vote, however, a
previously submerged conflict within the black community surfaced. Black teachers had supported the salary equalization campaign because their ideological and economic interests coincided
in that issue. The direct attack on segregation ruptured that unity,
for the black teachers knew that white parents would strenuously
resist having their children taught by black teachers.[6] The Wichita teachers mobilized for the regular election of board members
for the NAACP branch and took over the board. Without solid local support, the NAACP's national office was unwilling to proceed, and attention rapidly shifted to Topeka, where the black
community had already begun to organize in opposition to a high-
handed school administration.

This incident sets the framework for developing some of the
major themes in the NAACP's litigation campaign. The concerns
of the Wichita teachers recapitulated concerns that had arisen at
the outset of that campaign in the 1920s and early 1930s. The
campaign began after the NAACP negotiated to receive a grant from
the American Fund for Public Service, often called the Garland
Fund after the young radical who had created it with legacies of
$1.3 million from his father and grandfather.[7] The Garland Fund

was devoted to supporting "producers' movements" and to "the protection of minorities." Particular decisions were strongly influenced by Roger Baldwin, the Fund's chief administrator and a close adviser to Garland. During this period Baldwin had a quite radical position on politics,[8] which combined two elements relevant to the NAACP's legal activities. First, Baldwin's experience with conscientious objectors and anti-war activists during World War I led him to believe that it was extremely important to provide legal defense for leftists under attack. Second, he insisted on the importance of self-mobilization and especially of workers' self-mobilization, in bringing about major social change. Thus, to Baldwin, law was primarily to be used in defense of individual rights; it could not effectively transform society.

These views made him skeptical about the NAACP's proposals in the late 1920s to bring a series of coordinated lawsuits to challenge segregation. As the proposal went back and forth between the NAACP and the Garland Fund, Baldwin insisted that it contain some emphasis on workers' mobilization. He surely knew, though, that the language that the NAACP included to satisfy him was largely cosmetic. He continued to prefer attacking the problems of race "from the economic standpoint . . . of the union of white and black workers against their common exploiters." In this decision he may have been influenced by his sense that the struggle for black advance could be best conducted by organizations that divided the labor, that the NAACP should specialize in achieving civil and political rights, and that the more important tasks on the economic front should be left to other groups.[9] Baldwin's position meant that, in the end, the NAACP received only about a quarter of the original grant.

The reduced amount supported an initial planning phase, after which the NAACP decided to support the litigation campaign with its own funds. Nathan Margold, a protégé of Felix Frankfurter, was hired by the NAACP with money from the Garland Fund to develop a legal strategy to attack segregation. He recommended attacks on segregated schools as irremediably unequal because legal remedies were not available to force states to equalize their expenditures on white and black schools. Under the accepted doctrine established first in *Plessy* v. *Ferguson* (1896), separate schools had to be equal. But if inequalities were irremediable, separate schools could not be maintained.[10] Margold's report was persuasive, and the NAACP sought a talented lawyer to join it as its first staff attorney to conduct litigation. Baldwin, still overseeing what remained of the grant, objected to the names proposed by the NAACP at least in part because he was unpersuaded that the NAACP's black candidates were as qualified as the white ones he proposed. But eventually Baldwin agreed with the selection of Charles Hamilton Houston, the academic dean at Howard Law School. Houston, a native of Washington, D.C., had graduated from Amherst College and Harvard Law School, where he, like Margold, attracted Frankfurter's attention. Houston practiced law in Washington with his father and then became chief academic officer at Howard Law School, where he aggressively promoted a program to upgrade its academic quality and made it an institution dedicated to providing leaders for the black community.[11]

Houston abandoned Margold's proposal for direct attacks on segregated elementary and secondary schools. He may have thought that the legal theories in graduate school cases and salary cases were more easily established. There were no graduate schools for blacks in most southern states, so that even the "separate" part of "separate but equal" was not satisfied, and the inequality of salary scales was evident. In the 1920s surveys showed that white teachers in Georgia received an average of $97.88 per month while black teachers received $49.41. In North Carolina the figures were $98.20 and $66.53. Two examples of blatant discrimination in salaries came from Louisville and Little Rock. The Louisville Board of Education adopted a salary scale for white teachers and salaries varying according to education and years of experience. The column for black teachers set their salaries at 85 percent of the salaries for whites with equivalent education and experience. In Little Rock the school board paid bonuses in 1941 and 1942 based on a point system taking training and service into account. White teachers received $3 for each bonus point, black teachers $1.50.[12]

Houston also wanted to use litigation to strengthen the NAACP's membership base in the South, both as part of a general community mobilization and as a counter to the influence the Communist Party had on some branches in the North. Salary equalization suits, he thought, would demonstrate to teachers the tangible benefits of NAACP activities and membership.

Until the NAACP had to make choices, it was easy for its leaders to spin out theories about what kinds of suits to bring. With Houston on the staff, however, real choices had to be made, and different legal strategies had different implications for the development of the black community. In 1934 W.E.B. Du Bois, then editor of the NAACP magazine, provoked a major controversy within the organization that indirectly involved litigation strategy.[13] Du Bois argued that, given the existing strength of racist forces, direct attacks on segregation were unlikely to succeed. He argued instead for strategies that would strengthen the black community internally. The institutions of the black community, such as its churches and schools, could provide forums within which leadership talents could be developed. That talent could then be turned to political confrontation with racist forces in the white community. Similarly, the development of the economy of the black community, through such organizations as workers' cooperatives, would enable blacks to secure more equitable treatment in their dealings with the economy of the white community. In contrast, Du Bois thought that the legal strategies proposed by Margold and Houston placed blacks essentially in the position of supplicants requesting paternalistic assistance from nonracist whites. In suggesting that segregation might benefit the black community in the short run, he came close to advocating autarky, or independent development of that community's resources.

The rest of the NAACP leadership rejected Du Bois' initiative, though not without misgivings. Du Bois' argument need not have required him to reject all legal strategies. He did acknowledge the importance of legal defense of individual rights against obvious invasions, such as lynchings. Although Du Bois himself did not pursue the argument to identify legal strategies that promoted the internal development of the black community, it would have been consistent with his position to seek upgrading of black schools by a strategy seeking to equalize expenditures. The NAACP leadership might have been taken to seek a direct attack on segregated schools. Houston's strategy, combining graduate school cases and salary equalization suits, finessed these difficulties.

It was not, as it may seem in retrospect, that salary and graduate school cases rested on legal theories that were easier to develop than the direct attack, which might have proceeded on the basis that per capita expenditures in black and white schools were grossly unequal and had to be eliminated. School boards might have defended differential salary scales by arguing that, because blacks had a lower cost of living than whites, real incomes were in fact equal.[14] In addition, school boards might have tried to defend differential average salaries on merit grounds. After the salary equalization campaign began, many school boards switched to merit rating systems that courts upheld even though they reproduced the discriminatory results. For example, in 1945, South Carolina adopted a four-tier system of teacher certificates, based on the teacher's performance on the National Teacher Examination. In its first year the system gave 90 percent of the white teachers and 27 percent of the black ones salaries at the upper level of the scale. A Florida merit system in 1943 placed 84 percent of the white teachers and 6 percent of the black ones in the highest paid group, and 80 percent of the blacks and 1 percent of the whites in the lowest.[15] On the graduate and professional level, the difficulty was that some states provided scholarships to blacks who wanted to attend out-of-state schools. If the parties agreed that the out-of-state school, for example the law school at the University of Iowa, taught the same nationally oriented curriculum as did the in-state school, such as the University of Missouri's law school, the simple geographical line between the states might not seem important for "separate but equal" purposes.[16]

Thus, the strength of Houston's strategy lay less in the distinctive power of the legal arguments on which it rested than in its place in on-going political controversies within the black community. Equalizing salaries, for example, was a way of improving the economic resources available to the black community. Yet the costs of operating two equal systems, especially at the graduate level where the economies of scale were evident, were widely considered to be so great as to induce southerners to abandon segregation if equality of facilities had to be taken seriously.

Over the next decade, the litigation campaign proceeded, not without complications, but at least to the point where it was fair to say, as internal documents do, that the salary equalization fight had been won. Then in 1950 the NAACP won its major graduate and professional cases in the Supreme Court. The ensuing decision to attack segregation directly seemed easy. By the late 1940s the NAACP had become a mass membership organization. Although the legal staff had formally become an independent organization, the NAACP Legal Defense and Educational Fund, in 1939, the lawyers still shared office space with the executive staff and remained concerned with general membership issues.[17] The growth in the NAACP meant that its legal activity had to move beyond the teachers and applicants to graduate and professional schools. While efforts to equalize facilities might have had broad impact, after the 1950 decisions everyone—the lawyers, the NAACP members, legal and newspaper commentators, and even the Justices of the Supreme Court—thought that the direct attack was the inevitable next step.[18] Finally, it was easy to begin lawsuits without deciding that only a successful direct attack would be a victory. Complaints could be drafted that alleged inequality in facilities and left the remedy—equalization or integration—up to the courts.[19]

It was clear, though, that the day of reckoning would come; the Wichita teachers knew what desegregation would mean to them, as did others.[20] Even leaving the issue of remedy open posed a threat to some in the black community and so raised again the issues that Du Bois had posed: whether black advance could best be achieved by internal development of the black community and whether racist forces were so strong that apparent victories would be dissipated by white resistance.

Those issues can be addressed in a variety of ways. For example, legal action threatened to disadvantage some blacks by making it likely that judgments for the black plaintiffs would cause other blacks to lose their jobs. Deciding on the course to be followed raised ethical issues regarding the role of lawyers. Today public-interest lawyers are often seen as operating independently of any clientele, choosing a course of legal action that the lawyers regard as proper, constrained only by their personal political views.[21] Whether that is true of contemporary public-interest lawyers or not, it was not true of the NAACP lawyers, especially Charles Hamilton Houston and Thurgood Marshall. They were active participants in the rich political life of the black community. Houston and Marshall had professional skills that gave them opportunities to exercise power over some in the community, but they did not do so. They used their skills instead to educate their constituency by vigorous efforts to inform them about the legal theories that the lawyers were advancing, about the advantages and disadvantages of alternative legal approaches, about the specific problems faced by black plaintiffs in other communities, and about the difficulties such as delay and harassment of litigants that were inherent in the kind of litigation campaign to which the NAACP was committed.[22]

In addition, the Wichita incident shows that potential litigants had resources that lawyers needed. Aggrieved blacks could generate individual plaintiffs, conduct investigations of local conditions more easily than could lawyers from New York, and monitor compliance with the day-to-day implementation of settlements and favorable judicial decrees. Finally, the NAACP and its lawyers were part of a dense network of organizations and personal relations within the black community. The network, which included churches, newspapers, and social fraternities, imposed significant limits on the extent to which the NAACP lawyers could depart from what the black community wanted. As the Du Bois example indicates, it is misleading to speak of a unitary black community, but by 1950 the NAACP lawyers plainly did represent a substantial segment, maybe an overwhelming majority, of the black community in the nation and the South.

Another perspective on the issues Du Bois raised is normative. Was pursuit of desegregation litigation the best tactic for advancing the interests of the black community, or would equalization litigation or some other strategy have been more effective? De-

segregation litigation certainly contributed to the self-mobilization of the black community, symbolized by the Montgomery bus
boycott, despite the concern of Baldwin and Du Bois that such
litigation would divert the community from that goal. But there
are other aspects of the outcome worth noting. Desegregation litigation did not strengthen some important elements in the black
community, and equalization litigation might have.[23] Most nota-
bly, the associations of black teachers had provided important resources in the salary equalization cases. They had produced individual plaintiffs, raised money to pay part of the cost of litigation,
and perhaps most important, had developed defense funds that
supported plaintiffs who lost their jobs when school boards retal-
iated against them.[24] Desegregation not only led to the loss of jobs,
as the black teachers had feared, but it also destroyed the natural
ideological and organizational base for such associations. Black
schools persisted in the South, but they no longer had any legitimacy, and, because the stated law was that they were to be eliminated, it was hard to build a stable constituency predicated on
their continued existence. It may be significant in this regard that,
with one minor exception, the NAACP did not challenge the operation of segregated undergraduate institutions, which were important to the cultural life of the black community.[25]

In addition, the NAACP lawyers seriously overestimated the
likelihood that a victory in the Supreme Court could be translated
into actual desegregation in the South. The NAACP lawyers had
faced white evasion of legal mandates before. In addition to discriminatory "merit" systems of teacher pay, states had simply refused to act on the logical implications of court judgments. Perhaps the most dramatic example comes from Maryland, where in
1936 Thurgood Marshall successfully sued the state university to
assure that Donald Murray be admitted to its law school. The state
courts found the out-of-state scholarship system insufficient.
Fourteen years later, Marshall, now with Donald Murray as co-
counsel, sued the university to assure admission of blacks to its
nursing school. The state again raised, and the state courts again
rejected, the out-of-state scholarship defense.[26]

Despite these and similar experiences, the NAACP lawyers remained optimistic. In part, their optimism derived from their immersion in traditional ways of thinking about the law. Race relations law had been predicated on the view, endorsed by the Supreme Court,[27] that rights to equal treatment were personal. That is, each black who was discriminated against was entitled to a remedy that immediately eliminated that discrimination—or at least so it seemed to the NAACP lawyers. The Supreme Court, concerned that immediate desegregation would cause massive social dislocations in the South,[28] abandoned the "personal right" theory in its decision on the appropriate remedy in *Brown*, when it allowed discrimination to persist if the states proceeded "with all deliberate speed" to eliminate it.[29] Perhaps the NAACP lawyers should have anticipated this innovation, predicated as it was on the sensitivity of white liberals to white interests against black ones.[30] But perhaps too that is the perspective that Du Bois would have brought to the issue, a perspective that had been rejected twenty years earlier.

Finally, and perhaps most important in light of the resistance to desegregation that could have been predicted and that later emerged, it may be worth noting a particular cast that the NAACP arguments took. The NAACP's ultimate goal was improving the condition of the black community as a whole. Yet, its proximate goal was improving the condition of particular blacks, such as teachers and those who wanted advanced degrees. That proximate goal made it attractive to seek relief by making arguments predicated on the unfairness of segregation as it affected the potential individual beneficiaries.

Individualistic arguments are natural in our system, and the lawyers had a hard enough time in settling on a legal strategy that promised even modest short-run success. Yet, one can wonder whether in the long run it would have been more effective to cast the legal arguments solely in terms of the ultimate goal, the strengthening of the position of the black community as a whole. Du Bois sought political action to that end. He was concerned that unless blacks gained political power, they would be unable to secure significant improvements in civil rights, or to protect whatever small gains they made in the courts.

White resistance indeed proved as strong as Du Bois feared, as "massive resistance" to desegregation of schools obstructed significant desegregation in the Deep South until the 1970s. By that time the national political climate had changed, to the detriment of blacks, and had done so in part precisely because the black community had found the promise of *Brown* unfilled and adopted new strategies for securing change—demonstrations as well as legal arguments for affirmative action—that the white community found more threatening. Thus *Brown* did not end but only opened a new phase in the black struggle for legal rights.

A different approach to the problem in *Brown* might have given that struggle a different form and may have shortened its course. But though what could be called communitarian political arguments are not hard to imagine, communitarian legal arguments are even today ill-developed. They are being secreted in the interstices of affirmative action cases, where the absence of a direct link between those harmed by overt acts of discrimination and those benefited by the affirmative action programs almost inevitably forces us to look at the interests of the community as a whole.[31] Perhaps the most notable communitarian legal argument in recent years is made in a dissent in *City of Mobile* v. *Bolden*,[32] which comes close to arguing for proportional racial representation. It is not surprising that the dissent was written by Justice Thurgood Marshall.

It is of course unfair to criticize the NAACP and its lawyers for not developing communitarian legal arguments earlier. Such arguments would have led to disputes about the morality of proportional racial representation[33] and reparations.[34] The forms of legal action are highly contentious today precisely because they conflict with the dominant individualist assumptions of liberal society. The NAACP leadership may sensibly have thought that their ultimate goal could be reached without borrowing that kind of trouble. But now, almost fifty years later, it may be worth considering whether they were wrong, whether the black community and the nation would have been better off had the legal attack on segregation proceeded from communitarian premises, whether, that is, Du Bois was right.

NOTES

This article is based on research reported in detail in a forthcoming book, *Segregated Schools and Legal Strategy: The NAACP's Campaign Against School Segregation, 1925–1950*. Funds for the research were provided by the Rockefeller Foundation's program of Fellowships in the Humanities, the American Bar Foundation's Program in Legal History, the Research Committee of the Graduate School of the University of Wisconsin–Madison, and the Georgetown University Law Center. This article directs the reader to materials that are relatively accessible, even in situations in which additional detail is available in the forthcoming book.

[1] W.E.B. Du Bois, *The Souls of Black Folk* (Chicago, 1905), at p. 1.

[2] 347 U.S. 483 (1954).

[3] For details and references regarding this decision, see Mark Tushnet, "Thurgood Marshall as Lawyer: The Campaign Against School Segregation: 1945–1950," *Maryland Law Review*, XL (1981), 411–34.

[4] *Sweatt v. Painter*, 339 U.S. 629 (1950); *McLaurin v. Oklahoma State Regents*, 339 U.S. 637 (1950).

[5] Z. Wetmore to Thurgood Marshall, Sept. 7, 1948, Box II-D-153, NAACP Papers, Library of Congress [hereinafter cited as NAACP Papers]; Minutes of Kansas State Conference of Branches, Sept. 3, 1948, *ibid.*; Franklin Williams to Marshall, Oct. 6, 1948, *ibid.*; Wetmore to Williams, Dec. 24, 1948, *ibid.*

[6] The experience at the Louisville Municipal College in 1950–1951 shows that the teachers' fears were well grounded. The college was founded as a segregated branch of the University of Louisville in 1931. It suffered enrollment declines during World War II, and its trustees, responding in part to threats of litigation as well as to the economic difficulties, decided to close the college in June 1951. Initially the trustees planned to terminate the contracts of all faculty members, including those of four with tenure. After extensive negotiations, a compromise was reached under which some faculty members received positions elsewhere, one at the University of Louisville, and all received favorable financial settlements. See James B. Hudson, III, "The History of Louisville Municipal College" (Ed.D. dissertation, University of Kentucky, 1981).

[7] Information on the Garland Fund can be found in Box I-C-196, NAACP Papers. See also Merle Curti, "Subsidizing Radicalism: The American Fund for Public Service, 1921–41," *Social Service Review*, XXXIII (Sept. 1959), 274–95.

[8] For Baldwin's early career and views, see Peggy Lamson, *Roger Baldwin: Founder of the American Civil Liberties Union* (Boston, 1976), 27–83, 110, 124, 191–92.

[9] Roger Baldwin to L. Hollingsworth Wood, Oct. 21, 1929, quoted in Clement Vose, *Caucasians Only* (Berkeley, Cal., 1959), 42; Nancy J. Weiss, *The National Urban League, 1910–1940* (New York, 1974), 64–70.

[10] The idea of irremediable inequalities reemerged after 1945, when it came to mean, not that legal remedies for unequal expenditures were unavailable, but that the types of injury worked by segregation could not be eliminated by equalizing expenditures. The NAACP first developed this version of the argument in an amicus brief in *Westminster School District v. Mendez*, 161 F.2d 774 (9th Cir. 1947), a case involving segregation of Mexicans in a California school system. See Charles Wollenberg, *All Deliberate Speed: Segregation and Exclusion in California Schools, 1855–1975* (Berkeley, Cal.,1976), 108–35.

[11] See August Meier and Elliot Rudwick, "Attorneys Black and White: A Case Study of Race Relations within the NAACP," *Journal of American History*, LXII (March 1976), 943–44.

[12] "The Negro Common School in Georgia," *The Crisis*, XXXII (Sept. 1926), 248; "The Negro Common School in North Carolina," *ibid.*, XXXIV (May-June 1927), 79, 117; Victor Perry to Thurgood Marshall, Jan. 21, 1938, Box II-L-37, NAACP Papers; *Morris v. Williams*, 149 F.2d 703 (8th Cir. 1945).

[13] On the Du Bois controversy, see B. Joyce Ross, *J. E. Spingarn and the Rise of the* NAACP, 1911–1939 (New York, 1972), 186–98; Raymond Wolters, *Negroes and the Great Depression* (Westport, Conn., 1970), 217–352.

[14] The NAACP had successfully combatted efforts to place cost of living differentials in the codes adopted under the National Industrial Recovery Act; see Wolters, *Negroes and the Great Depression*, 98–106. Occasionally its lawyers mentioned this concern in salary cases; see Leon Ransom to Edward Lovett, May 1, 1937, Box II-D-88, NAACP Papers.

[15] *United States* v. *South Carolina*, 445 F. Supp. 1094, 1102 (D.S.C. 1971); *Turner* v. *Keefe*, 50 F. Supp. 657 (S.D. Fla. 1943).

[16] The Supreme Court found the use of out-of-state scholarships inadequate, though with little supporting reasoning, in *Missouri* v. *Gaines ex rel. Canada*, 305 U.S. 337 (1938).

[17] Between 1940 and 1946 the number of NAACP branches tripled and membership grew from 50,000 to 450,000. Richard Dalfiume, "The 'Forgotten Years' of the Negro Revolution," *Journal of American History*, XLIV (June 1968), 90–106. On the creation of the Inc. Fund, see NAACP Legal Defense Fund, *Thirty Years of Building American Justice* (New York, 1970).

[18] Representative comments can be found in "'Separate But Equal,'" New York *Times*, June 6, 1950; Arthur Krock, "A Historic Day in the Supreme Court," New York *Times*, June 6, 1950; "Jim Crow in Handcuffs," *New Republic*, 122, 25 (June 19, 1950); Bernard Schwartz, "The Negro and the Law in the United States," *Modern Law Review*, XIV (Oct. 1951), 446–61. On the view from within the Court, see Dennis Hutchinson, "Unanimity and Desegregation: Decision-making in the Supreme Court, 1948–1955," *Georgetown Law Journal*, LXVIII (Oct. 1979), 19–24.

[19] As James Nabrit, one of the NAACP's staff lawyers, wrote, "[S]ome of these cases look suspiciously akin to the old equality approach with the direct challenge thrown in." James Nabrit, "Resort to the Court as a Means of Eliminating 'Legalized' Segregation," *Journal of Negro Education*, XX (Summer 1951), 469.

[20] See note 6.

[21] A recent survey of these issues is Bryant Garth, "Introduction: Toward a Sociology of the Class Action," *Indiana Law Journal*, LVII (1982), 379–82.

[22] For example, in the mid-1930s Houston wrote several articles in *The Crisis* whose titles indicate his desire to educate his readers on these matters: "Educational Inequalities Must Go!" *The Crisis*, XLII (Oct. 1935), 300; "How to Fight for Better Schools," *ibid.*, XLIII (Feb. 1936), 52; "Don't Shout Too Soon," *ibid.*, XLIII (March 1936), 79.

[23] Of course, equalization litigation, successes in which might not have been so dramatic to nonparticipants, might not have generated as much fervor in the black community.

[24] See Marshall to Joint Committee of NAACP and Garland Fund, June 17, 1939, Box II-D-91, NAACP Papers.

[25] The exception is *Parker* v. *University of Delaware*, 75 A.2d 225 (Del. Ch. 1950), which was begun after the state college for blacks lost its accreditation.

[26] *University of Maryland* v. *Murray*, 169 Md. 478 (1936); *McCready* v. *Byrd*, 73 A.2d 8 (Md. 1950).

[27] *McCabe* v. *Atchison, Topeka & Santa Fe R. Co.*, 235 U.S. 151 (1914).

[28] Hutchinson, "Unanimity and Desegregation," 50–60.

[29] *Brown* v. *Board of Education*, 349 U.S. 294 (1955).

[30] See Derrick Bell, "*Brown* v. *Board of Education* and the Interest–Convergence Dilemma," *Harvard Law Review*, XCIII (Jan. 1980), 518–33.

[31] See Owen Fiss, "Groups and the Equal Protection Clause," *Philosophy and Public Affairs*, V (Winter 1976), 147–70.

[32] 446 U.S. 55 (1980).

[33] The debates on the extension of the Voting Rights Act in 1982 involved such disputes. The extension as amended provides that voting rights are denied if a class has "less opportunity than other members of the electorate to participate in the political process and

to elect representatives of their choice," allows "the extent to which members of [the] class have been elected" to be taken into account in determining the "less opportunity" question, but denies that there is "a right to have members of [the] class elected in numbers equal to their proportion of the population." P.L. 97–205, sec. 3 (June 29, 1982).

[34] See Boris Bittker, *The Case for Black Reparations* (New York, 1973).

Part IV
Southern Courts, Bench, and Bar

Disorder and Deference:
The Paradoxes of Criminal Justice
in the Colonial Tidewater

PETER C. HOFFER

THE TRADITIONAL SCHOLARLY depiction of court day in the colonial South is a neutral one: fair men doing justice.[1] The emphasis was either upon the exact details of procedure and law, or the recounting of interesting cases and judgments—in effect a "genetic" approach to legal history.[2] Modern scholars have departed from this view to capture the human experience of local law enforcement. Two recently published descriptions of "court day" in colonial Virginia reveal to the reader a "solemn configuration of a symbolic order"[3]: a meeting of justices, jurors, litigants, and suspects combining drama and spectacle with raw power.[4] The rituals of going to law concealed a bargain: paternal protection in exchange for esteem and support. Disorder and crime threatened this exchange of deference for patronage, and the criminal justice system reasserted it. Tushnet, Genovese, and others go a step further in this line of argument, positing a "hegemony" of a planter class over its inferiors, which criminal law and criminal courts maintained. In the latter, sentiment mitigated the full force of discriminatory justice, while still expressing the justness of the class system.[5] If either version of this deference theory is correct, the records of the criminal courts of the colonial South should provide evidence of it.

A unique source upon which to test these propositions survives in the quiet Rappahannock-side county of Richmond, Virginia. It is a record of all criminal proceedings entailing fines or more serious punishments, from 1711 to 1754.[6] The document includes the clerk's own excerpts from the regular sessions of the county court, comprising almost all petty offenses and grand jury presentments, as well as a complete file of examining courts for free persons suspected of felony, and the records of oyer and terminer courts for slaves charged with felony. In the distribution of offenses and the outcomes of cases there certainly is evidence of deference and, behind it, the power of magistrates. But if deference was the rule—if it was willingly offered by inferiors, servants, and slaves—how is one to explain the extent of criminal disorder in Richmond? Surely it is paradoxical that in this community of consensual distinction in dress, housing, wealth, and race, there was more crime than in other colonies, even those with turbulent early modern cities and even more crime than in modern America (with all of its disorderly canons of equality in decoration, locomotion, and address).

Deference, it seemed, was intimately associated with disorder. They were symbiotic, if not casually connected. This hypothesis reveals a second paradox: why did almost no accused free offender, save those tried for felony, demand a jury trial, even when it was their clear right? Why did so many disorderly people confess and seek forgiveness or put themselves upon the court, rather than demand justice from their peers? The answers to the two paradoxes are linked, and they begin with the data itself.

Without reports of crimes by police, the closest the scholar can come to measuring the "rate" of criminal activity is to count presentments, indictments, and orders in the courts. The more serious the crime, of course, the more likely someone would report it to the authorities, but "dark figures of crime" are unavailable in any study.[7] The rate of recorded offenses for any period of time is the number of suspects named in the court over that period of time divided by the population "at risk" to commit those crimes over the same period of time. This population includes adult men and women. The number of people in Richmond County fitting this description can be approximated. Lists of tithables for Virginia counties included all free males over sixteen years and all servants and slaves over sixteen. The number of tithables ranged from 1,555 in 1720 to 1,979 in 1749. Free adult females were not counted among the tithables. To include these women in the rates of recorded crimes one may assume that free adult women were roughly equal in number to free white adult men. This was true in eighteenth-century Maryland and Massachusetts. "Infants" under the law could not be found guilty of committing a felony or homicide and are not included in the "at risk" population calculations.[8]

[handwritten margin note: Are women equally at risk ?]

In Richmond County between 1711 and 1754, the rate of violent offenses, excluding homicides, averaged about 20 per 10,000 adults per year (or would have, if the actual population of adults were 10,000).[9] The rate of noncapital crimes against property averaged almost 12 per 10,000 adults per year. Felony rates (for robbery, burglary, grand larceny, and arson) approached 15 cases per 10,000 adults per year. One must remember that felonies were much more likely to be prosecuted, and hence recorded, than minor property offenses. The homicide (murder and manslaughter) rate averaged 2 per year per 10,000 adults, with, again, few suspicious deaths escaping official scrutiny.

Close examination of periodic fluctuations of property crimes shows a bulge in the years 1729–1739, following hard upon the period of the largest percentage increase in importation of convicts and slaves—the defendants who swelled the dockets in those years. Whether they simply committed more crimes than free laborers or were more carefully monitored and arrested more often for crimes in which the perpetrators were unknown, the justices in the county certainly found more and more servants standing before them in the dock as the century passed. Other variations in the rates within the period 1711–1754 can be explained by careful examination of the record itself and by comparisons of types of crimes with changing economic and demographic conditions.[10]

While the fluctuations in this record of crime present no curiosities, the extent of crime does. For if one were to use Douglas Greenberg's data from the general sessions courts of colonial New York City to calculate theft and violent crime rates, one would obtain figures of between 8 and 9 cases of the former and of the latter per year for every 10,000 adults for the years 1698–1776—and

Greenberg's data is limited to nonfatal assaults and batteries and noncapital property crimes. Richmond's noncapital crime rate was much higher, despite the fact that New York City was noted then, as now, for its disorder, crime, and disdain for deference.[11] There was a similar excess of felony and homicide prosecutions, adjusting for population, in the Tidewater over other regions.

Greenberg does not have complete records for New York's courts of oyer and terminer, but N.E.H. Hull has taken out every case of felony and homicide from the Massachusetts Superior Court of Judicature records, which are complete. From 1711 to 1750, the average felony rate for the entire colony was .70 cases per 10,000 adults per year. The corresponding figure for homicides was .27 per 10,000 adults per year.[12] One must remember that the Massachusetts record included only those cases brought to the grand juries at the highest court by prosecutors or magistrates. The Richmond County figures include all cases "examined" in the county before free defendants were sent to the General Court in Williamsburg as well as all slaves' oyer and terminer trials. One expects the Richmond rate to be larger, for it encompasses those defendants dismissed or summarily punished for a lesser offense in the county. Richmond justices sent only 40 percent of these free defendants on to trial at the capital, and ignoring for a moment the oyer and terminer trials of slaves for felony, one can therefore reduce the Richmond felony rate at most to 6.6 cases per year. (Actually, 9 would be a better correction since oyer and terminer trials of slaves were one-third of the total of felony hearings, and these were functionally, if not procedurally, equivalent to prosecution at the Massachusetts Superior Court of Judicature.) The same calculus would reduce the homicide rate to little more than 1 case per year per 10,000 adults. Even so, the disproportion between the two regions' rates for serious crimes is significant.

Evidence from the records of criminal courts in London and Middlesex County can also be compared with the Richmond Record. The *Old Bailey Sessions Papers* from 1726 to 1756 accurately reported all serious crimes that came before the general gaol delivery and oyer and terminer courts of the city of London and Middlesex County. The rates of indictments for all types of serious crimes varied during these years between 13.1 and 8.9 per 10,000 adults. The figures obtained from Middlesex, including the metropolis, are lower than the rates for Richmond County. Any extreme conclusions must be tempered by realization that densely populated, unpoliced eighteenth-century London probably had a much higher rate of unreported crimes than did Richmond or any other Tidewater county.[13] In mitigation of the growing evidence of Tidewater lawlessness, one must bear in mind again that Virginia examining courts recorded cases that individual New England and English justices of the peace heard and dismissed for lack of evidence without keeping any record.

While it should come as no surprise to students of crime and justice that Virginia Tidewater magistrates heard more reports of crime than do modern police forces, the difference in crime rates between the Tidewater and the northern colonies is noteworthy. How could a society so dedicated and hard-working in its commitment to deference survive such a burden of disorder? Frontiers may be violent places, but by the mid-eighteenth century, Richmond was a veritable backwater.[14] Yet it had far more recorded violence and theft—battery and burglary—than did the newer, western counties of the Old Dominion. Visible differences in class may spur crimes of opportunity and frustration, but Richmond County exceeded the New York City crime rates by a substantial margin.[15] One is driven to wonder if the inhabitants of Richmond really committed so many crimes after all.

There are clues in the data that lead to this very conclusion. The types and proportions of crimes reported and indicted in Richmond were similar to those of rural communities throughout the colonies. There is no abberration—no homicidal maniac or underworld "dangerous class"—in the Richmond record, nor was there a crime wave growing out of an insurrection of any sort. While widening class distinctions were driving some poorer freeholders out of the county, this was not atypical of the older settlements of the American colonies as a whole.[16]

Apparent crime rates may be affected by two factors independent of but not totally unrelated to actual amounts of crimes. The first is community attitudes to crime and criminals. The second is official attitudes toward prosecution. Communities actively concerned about crime, or communities whose opinion leaders express this concern, will report more suspects and give evidence against them more readily than will members of communities who have no interest in catching suspects of crimes. Communities that are antagonistic to criminal officials will hinder efforts to investigate crime and shield suspects. In New York City, for instance, householders rushed to report the comings and goings of free blacks during the slave "rebellion" of 1741, but there were parts of the city where the watch never walked, even during the crisis.[17] Denizens of these neighborhoods did not rush to report crime to the authorities.

The magistrates' willingness to believe reports of particular crimes, order the appearance of witnesses, take testimony, bind over suspects for indictment, and prosecute defendants at trial also varied with type of crime, status of offender, time, place, and circumstance. For example, increased official interest in infanticide led to the veritable explosion of prosecutions for the crime in England after the accession of Elizabeth I. New statutes creating crimes, like 21 James I, c. 27 (1624), which made concealment of a dead bastard by its mother presumptive evidence of murder (without testimony that the child was stillborn or accidentally dead), stimulated prosecutions to a still higher level.[18] The same official animosity against "lewd women" and sexual misconduct that led to the new law also guaranteed that it would result in more prosecutions. With these external influences upon crime reporting in mind, one can search for clues that members of the Richmond County community, and in particular her magistrates, had pressing reasons for increasing their vigilance (and thereby, the number of offenders they forced to come to court) that were not shared by citizens and magistrates in New York, in Massachusetts, or in greater London.

One answer intrudes itself into every discussion of the colonial South: slavery. Michael Hindus has written that slavery made masters and would-be masters "pugnacious."[19] Slavery offered whites an invitation to a legitimate exercise of violence. "Due correction" was excluded by black codes, whose other allowances on the severity of punishment for a special class of slave crimes were unlike anything else in the common law or colonial statute. These laws, as historians Kenneth Stampp, Winthrop Jordan, Peter Wood, and Edmund Morgan have demonstrated, went to the heart of the South's social system, for slaves were everywhere, and everywhere their labor was essential.[20] Mark Tushnet has posited that the importance of slavery forced judges to create new categories in the state law of crime to allow masters to control slaves that would have never been acceptable in dealing with free persons.[21]

One would expect that the tensions involved in keeping slaves would automatically result in a violent society, but the linkage between slavery and crime is more complex. There was no wave of interracial crimes. With the exception of a handful of abortive slave rebellions, slaves are under-represented by population in the criminal court records. When they were brought to court, they were most often charged with thefts of necessities—food and clothing—and very rarely with rebellion.[22] It is not hard to explain the relative paucity of these prosecutions, for the plantation had a number of systems for controlling the behavior of defiant slaves without turning to the courts. Forms of bargaining and exchange, with some slaves acting for the master against other slaves, were commonplace. Corporal punishment, denial of privileges, and sale to another place (in effect a banishment) were also employed.[23] Whatever the real incidence of slave crimes may have been, the vast majority of them were summarily heard and handled on the plantation. This negative evidence of interracial crime is significant, for the relative absence of slave crimes from the courts' dockets in Richmond *should have* resulted in a *lower crime rate* there than in New York City or Massachusetts. In the North, the offenses of day laborers against each other and their petty thefts against their betters filled the county courts' records,[24] which returns us to our first puzzle: why were the Tidewater rates higher?

Who were the perpetrators of the excess of petty thefts, assaults, and batteries in Richmond, if not the slaves? The record provides an answer: the same day laborers, servants, and poor freeholders that one finds in other colonies' criminal records. As Richard Hofstadter, Gary Nash, and other scholars have reminded us, the lot of the poor, particularly the servant, was not a pleasant one in the colonies.[25] In Virginia, runaways and transported convicts were a noxious leaven in this class, and they appeared frequently in the criminal record. But why were the Virginia free poor so much more prone to crime than the free poor of New York and Massachusetts? Certainly there were more servants (by percentage of total population) in the Tidewater than in New York or Massachusetts, creating a potential problem of social control. As Gwenda Morgan has demonstrated, the majority of servants and laborers accused of misdemeanors were newcomers, vagabonds, runaways, and ne'er-do-wells.[26] What is more, these servants might and did consort with slaves in some of the offenses recorded by the clerk. Were the magistrates so concerned about maintaining their mastery of this society that they simply brought more cases of suspicious conduct to court than did their counterparts in Massachusetts and New York? This decision, a systematic extension of the magistrates' surveillance of deviant behavior, would result in an increased recorded crime rate.

To explain the difference in levels (not the total level, but its excess in Virginia), one may return to the actual pronouncements of law-keepers and law-makers in the Tidewater. What did they see as the prime movers of crime? In other words, what suspected or feared causes of crime led them to believe and investigate and so record a higher rate of crimes than did New England justices?

Editors, planters, and judges blamed servants, particularly transported convicts, runaways, and slaves, even as the number of these individuals was steadily growing in Tidewater. The increasing mass of convicted felons transported from England and slaves imported directly from Africa fueled the justices' anxiety about the conduct of all servants, white and black. As early as 1722, Robert Beverly warned his readers that convict servants in the colony would break down local justice: "Tho' the greedy planters will always buy them yet it to be feared they will be very injurious to the country which has already suffered murders and robberies [from them]."[27] Convict servants would corrupt other servants and slaves, join with them, hide with them, commit crimes with them. In 1724 the Rev. Hugh Jones inveighed against transported convicts precisely because they "spoil servants that were before very good."[28] A 1748 statute mandated the recording of prior English convictions of those arrested in Virginia, for "most" capital offenses were supposedly committed by convicts.[29] At the same time, another statute prohibited assemblages of more than five slaves, slaves' travels without passes, and other acts not criminal at all when done by free persons.[30]

Forced by the scarcity of labor and prior debt obligations to welcome slaves and convicts whose presence connoted crime and rebellion, the magistrates compensated by scouring the land for evidence of offenses. Fearing that every slave and every transported convict and every runaway was a potential criminal, the magistrates could allow no crime to go uninvestigated. Any crime inquiry might unveil a gang of thieves, a conspiracy among the slaves, or an epidemic-in-the-making of felony. This situation would motivate Virginia law-keepers to be more concerned with crime than their New England equivalents were. Concern of this sort would be translated into more arrests and indictments. Those individuals who proved to be implicated, but were not runaways, transported convicts, or slaves, could then be chastened and re-leased with a fine, on bond for future good behavior, or with a corporal punishment.

In the light of this hypothesis, it is necessary to examine the second paradox, for the two are closely bound; the key to the first unlocks the second. Despite the high rates of disorder in Richmond, the vast majority of defendants in minor criminal cases either confessed or did not contest the charges; between the years 1711 and 1754 only six of almost 200 put themselves upon the county. Why did only a few of those who were entitled to trial by jury actually ask for impanelment of a petit jury?

Virginians were proud that they shared with other Anglo-Americans the right to jury trial, but jury trial in criminal cases was costly and time-consuming. The county courts ordinarily met but a few days each session, seven or eight times a year, and extensive jury trials in criminal cases would extend these sessions indefinitely. The justices and potential jurors all had their own affairs to manage and cannot have relished the prospect of jury trials in every eligible criminal case.[31] Some did put themselves upon the court, if the clerk's notation that the defendant had or had not "something material to say in his own defense" connoted a bench trial, but this is speculation. Those defendants who pled guilty or were found guilty by the justices undoubtedly knew that it had been far cheaper to forego a jury trial, with the court costs that trial entailed, than to put themselves upon the court or even plead guilty and then to produce the sureties or fines assessed against them. Even if a jury found them not guilty of the offense charged against them, they might be ordered to bond themselves to the peace. Finally, as defendants probably knew, trial juries were likely to believe that grand juries and justices would not proceed to indict and try a suspect unless he or she were guilty as charged.[32]

But the absence of trial juries from the criminal record cannot be laid entirely to the aversion to time and expense. The Richmond County Order Books are filled with jury trials in civil actions. Summary criminal justice must have had a value, in addition to saving time and money, to induce defendants to forego jury trials. One notes that, without trial by jury, the disposition of criminal cases went so quickly that in many cases there could have been little attempt to establish guilt beyond any reasonable doubt. Justices and defendants must have realized and condoned this fact. The bar of Virginia, flourishing in this era, did not intervene in these hearings. Fair trial did not require counsel, except in extraordinary cases (usually entailing complex points of law).[33]

Recently, David Konig, and John Murrin and Greg Roeber, have argued that Virginia's first charter left an indelible mark upon criminal procedure in its courts—a unique aversion to jury trial.[34] The first grants of criminal jurisdiction were quasi-military, as befitted an outpost governed in martial fashion. Summary justice for all but the most serious offenses did persist through the seventeenth century. While the origin of the colony may have militated against the use of juries, other colonies with different origins shared the Old Dominion's experience. In New York, poor defendants willingly put themselves upon the court for judgment.[35] Through the end of the seventeenth century, Massachusetts defendants surrendered their right to jury trial in misdemeanor hearings.[36] Even in Pennsylvania, the county sheriffs rarely had to provide juries for trials of misdemeanors, for defendants ceded their right to be heard by their peers.[37] While this aversion to jury trial began to change in the eighteenth century, its persistence throughout the colonies during their formative years cannot be laid to the impact of quasi-military grants of criminal jurisdiction. A larger, deeper force was at work in defendants' submission to local criminal courts.

The conclusion suggests itself that these courts were viewed as agents of social control by those who lived in the county, criminal suspects included. In colonial Virginia, there were few institutions that could maintain order and harmony in society. The most prominent among these were the county courts. Defendants who made their permanent homes in the county must have been wary of challenging the authority of the grand juries and the justices for fear of bringing on the greater evils of social disruption that had in the past ripped through the colony. In return for suspects' submission to the justices' decisions, courts were patient and lenient. As with the established church, troublemakers were disciplined, but invariably readmitted to the community when they confessed and did penance. Guilt and innocence were not the sole issues for the county courts; the willingness of the accused to submit to authority was almost as important.

The almost automatic imposition of bonds for good behavior and to keep the peace typified the social-control function of the courts. Recognizances were an early and distinctive feature of local justice in England, preventing future misconduct by monetary penalties. Leaders of the community sometimes put up funds for the bonds and provided the sureties; ordinary yeomen and laborers could hardly have had the resources required. Under these conditions, the accused put himself under a pledge to the crown and to the community not to threaten its members or violate its laws. There are over 100 different persons named as sureties for such recognizances in the Richmond County records, a total that must have exceeded 10 percent of all free, propertied persons in the county. All of these men had a stake in keeping order and therefore in supporting the authority of the courts. The recognizance for "good behavior," issued at court, stated that the defendant would cease carrying on some unlawful activity and often required a return to the next session of court. A recognizance "to keep the peace against John Doe," which a single justice might impose, pledged the defendant not to harm a specific person. Both types were common in Richmond County. After 1722 the justices began to require bonds for good behavior from men and women presented by the grand juries. This form of pledge created a network of financial obligations that supported the authority of the justices and maintained order.[38]

Through 1729, bonds, fines, and other forms of reduction of charges for serious offenses and imposition of punishment at the county court were as common as bringing the offense to an examining or an oyer and terminer court. In these cases, again, offenders did not seek jury trials. Early in the 1700s, defendants agreed to reduction of charges, in effect renouncing the right to a trial in Williamsburg. The accused was recompensed for his relative incapacity to defend himself in county court by the knowledge that penalties would not exceed corporal punishment or fines nor require leaving the community.[39]

This flexibility of proceeding began to disappear in the 1730s, and by the next decade almost all of those men and women suspected of felonious offenses against property were examined in the called courts or tried in courts of oyer and terminer. The growing number of slaves put immense pressure upon the watch-and-warn system, for slaves had no financial attachment to it. The growing severity of the black codes bore witness to the creeping anxiety of authorities. Crimes by newcomers in bondage, men and women on the fringes of the community, ex-convicts, and servants dissolved the assumptions behind face-to-face justice. The accused did not live within the consensual network of personal and monetary ties that controlled anti-social conduct. To counter suspected crimes among runaways, transported convicts, and the slaves who shared their alienation, the justices turned increasingly toward examining and oyer and terminer courts.

Given this admittedly hypothetical psychological situation, the extent of voluntary renunciation of jury trial in misdemeanors has another explanation in addition to the deference paid to the person and authority of the magistrates, a reason fitting the solution to the first paradox. Cooperation went beyond a consensual interest in keeping order. The fears of the upper classes were shared by the free men and women, apprentices, and servants who wished to be safe in their own persons. They too suspected concerted evil among the strangers in their midst. They were therefore more willing to report and to provide evidence against runaways, transported felons, and slaves because the criminal justice system safeguarded their persons and property as well as the wealth and life of the wealthy. This hypothesis leads to an advanced understanding of the paradox of crime and order in the Tidewater. Interest and anxiety bound together rich and poor; free persons' deference was mingled with mutual dependence. Class differences were muted by shared fears, ironically growing out of the alliance against blacks that planters forged among whites at the end of the seventeenth century.[40] Thus, the victim and the potential victim of the higher crime rates of the Tidewater had themselves to blame in part for creating a separate society of permanently disadvantaged within the larger society of opportunity and freedom.

NOTES

[1] See, for example, Charles S. Sydnor, *Gentlemen Freeholders* (Chapel Hill, N.C., 1952), ch. 6; and Arthur P. Scott, *Criminal Law in Colonial Virginia* (Chicago, 1930), *passim*.

[2] The phrase "genetic legal history," coined by N. E. H. Hull, means that the history of the law is treated as a biologically closed system whose development is governed by a genetic code rather than by the interactive influence of environment. The finest example of this approach is Joseph H. Smith and Philip A. Crowl, eds., *Court Records of Prince Georges County, Maryland, 1696–1699*, American Legal Records Series, Volume 9 (Washington, D.C., 1964), xxiii.

[3] Rhys Isaac, *The Transformation of Virginia, 1740–1790* (Chapel Hill, N.C., 1982), 93.

[4] A. G. Roeber, *Faithful Magistrates and Republican Lawyers, Creators of Virginia Legal Culture, 1680–1810* (Chapel Hill, N.C., 1981), 78.

[5] Eugene D. Genovese, *Roll, Jordan, Roll: The World the Slaves Made* (New York, 1974), 25–49; Mark V. Tushnet, *The American Law of Slavery, 1810–1860* (Princeton, N.J., 1981), 71–156.

[6] Peter C. Hoffer and William B. Scott, eds., *Criminal Proceedings in Colonial Virginia, The Richmond County Record of Finds, Examinations and Trials of Slaves, 1711–1754*, American Legal Records Series, Volume 10, (Washington, D.C., forthcoming). All citations to the *RCP* refer to pages in the manuscript Introduction and document.

[7] The dark figure remains the most controversial issue in the history of crime—since unreported (or unpursued) crimes may be as important in their impact upon society as those cases that resulted in prosecution. If the dark figure hides a systematic bias (a deliberate leniency or, contrarily, a basic flow in the criminal justice system), reliance upon recorded figures may seriously mislead scholars. For reasons explored later, I do not believe that a systematic bias operated in Richmond.

[8] Tithables were recorded yearly in the Richmond County Court Order Books, Richmond County Courthouse, Warsaw, Virginia.

[9] Standardized population figures (dividing by the actual population and then multiplying by 10,000) facilitate comparisons with other regions. This is required practice in criminological research. The density of population *is* a factor in criminal activity, and Richmond's 2,000–3,000 adults, spread over 600 square miles, should not be confused with the far more compressed populations of Massachusetts' or New York's coastal counties. Differences in density do not bar the standardization necessary to make any comparison at all among jurisdictions and regions.

[10] *RCP*, 78–80 and after.

[11] Douglas Greenberg, *Crime and Law Enforcement in the Colony of New York, 1691–1776* (Ithaca, N.Y., 1976), table on 54. These are my computations based on tables in the Bureau of Census, *A Century of Population Growth* (Washington, D.C., 1909), 9.

[12] N.E.H. Hull, "Female Felons, Women and Serious Crime in Colonial Massachusetts, 1673–1774" (Ph.D. dissertation, Columbia University, 1981), data courtesy of author.

[13] *RCP*, "Introduction," notes 187 and 188.

[14] The vigilante tradition of western frontier communities is traced in Richard M. Brown, *Strain of Violence: Historical Studies of American Violence and Vigilantism* (New York, 1975).

[15] Criminologists generally concede that urban environments have higher crime rates than suburban or rural ones. The U.S. Department of Justice *Uniform Crime Reports* routinely supports this.

[16] Jackson Turner Main, *The Social Structure of Revolutionary America* (Princeton, N.J., 1965), 178–80.

[17] Daniel Horsmanden, *A Journal of the Proceedings in the Detection of the Conspiracy . . . [The Great Slave Conspiracy . . . (1744)]*, Thomas J. Davis, ed. (Boston, 1971), 33.

[18] Peter C. Hoffer and N.E.H. Hull, *Murdering Mothers, Infanticide in England and New England, 1558–1803* (New York, 1981), chapter 1.

[19] Michael Stephen Hindus, *Prison and Plantation: Crime, Justice and Authority in Massachusetts and South Carolina, 1767–1878* (Chapel Hill, N.C., 1980), 10.

[20] See Winthrop Jordan, *White Over Black: American Attitudes Toward the Negro, 1550–1812* ([1968] reprinted Baltimore, Md., 1969), 104–05; Kenneth Stampp, *The Peculiar Institution, Slavery in the Ante-Bellum South* (New York, 1956), 192–236; Peter H. Wood, *Black Majority: Negroes in Colonial South Carolina from 1670 through the Stono Rebellion* (New York, 1974), 271–84; Edmund S. Morgan, *American Slavery, American Freedom: the Ordeal of Colonial Virginia* (New York, 1975), 295–337.

[21] Tushnet, *American Law of Slavery*, 54–65.

[22] Data from Philip Schwarz, "Slave Criminality and the Slave Community, Patterns of Slave Assertiveness in 18th-century Virginia," unpub. paper, courtesy of author.

[23] Isaac, *Transformation of Virginia*, 332–46; Gerald W. Mullen, *Flight and Rebellion: Slave Resistance in Eighteenth-Century Virginia* (New York, 1972), 71–78.

[24] See, for example, Eli Faber, "Puritan Criminals: the Economic, Social, and Intellectual Background to Crime in 17th century Massachusetts," *Perspectives in American History*, XI (1978).

[25] Richard Hofstadter, *America at 1750, A Social Portrait* (New York, 1973), 33–65; Gary B. Nash, *The Urban Crucible: Social Change, Political Consciousness, and the Origins of the American Revolution* (Cambridge, Mass., 1979), 253–56.

[26] Gwenda Morgan, "The Hegemony of the Law: Richmond County, 1692–1776" (Ph.D. dissertation, Johns Hopkins University, 1980), 161–65.

[27] Robert Beverly, *The History and Present State of Virginia* (2nd ed., London, 1722), 287–88.

[28] Hugh Jones, *The Present State of Virginia* (London, 1724), 53.

[29] *RCP*, "Introduction," n. 91.

[30] W. W. Hening, comp., *Statutes at Large . . . of Virginia* (Richmond, Va., 1809–1823), VI, 105–11 (1748).

[31] *RCP*, "Introduction," 35–39.

[32] Warren M. Billings, "Pleading, Procedure, and Practice: The Meaning of Due Process of Law in the 17th-Century Virginia," *Journal of Southern History*, XLVIII (Nov. 1981), 580.

[33] *RCP*, "Introduction," n. 81.

[34] David Thomas Konig, "'Dale's Law' and the Non-Common Law Origin of Criminal Justice in Virginia," *American Journal of Legal History*, XXVI (Oct. 1982), 254–375; John M. Murrin and A.G. Roeber, "Trial by Jury: the Virginia Paradox," manuscript courtesy of the authors.

[35] Julius N. Goebel, Jr., and T. Raymond Naughton, *Law Enforcement in Colonial New York, A Study in Criminal Procedure, 1664–1776* (New York, 1944), 78.

[36] John M. Murrin, "Magistrates, Sinners, and a Precious Liberty: Trial by Jury in Seventeenth-Century New England" in David D. Hall, John M. Murrin and Thad W. Tate, eds., *Saints and Revolutionaries: Essays in Early American History* (New York, 1983).

[37] For example, between 1763 and 1790, 89 women stood accused of assault in Bedford, Berks, Bucks, Chester, Cumberland, Lancaster and Northumberland counties. Thirty cases were dismissed; 47 defendants pleaded guilty or put themselves upon the court; no one asked for a trial by jury; and the other cases simply disappeared.

[38] See, most recently, Bradley M. Chapin, *Criminal Law in the American Colonies, 1607–1660* (Athens, Ga., 1983), 27–28.

[39] Tushnet, *American Law of Slavery*, 33–34; Genovese, *Roll, Jordan Roll*, 25–26; and Genovese, *The World the Slaveholders Made* (New York, 1969), 151 and after.

[40] Morgan, *American Slavery*, 236 and after.

"He read it to me from a book of English law": Germans, Bench, and Bar in the Colonial South, 1715–1770

A. G. ROEBER

AN ESSAY ABOUT "Germans, Bench, and Bar in the Colonial South" brings to mind Ian McNeil's observation about the Lord Privy Seal: he is neither a Lord, nor a privy, and not yet a seal.[1] Scholars largely agree that there was no "South" in the colonial and Revolutionary era; everyone knows that there was no "Germany" then, only German-speaking territories and lands in Central Europe, and hence no "Germans"; legal historians are only now just beginning to ascertain what common bonds and distinctive procedures or traditions characterized judges and attorneys in colonial society. Therefore, the present explorations appear more than normally a fool's errand whose fortune will be dark and fame doubtful. Yet, several developments—recent work on the colonial Chesapeake, a symposium on the southern backcountry, the revival of interest in ethnicity, and the fact that 1983 is the tercentenary year of German immigration to the shores of North America—encourage an analysis of this important subculture of the middle and southern colonies.[2]

Certain perennial themes in southern history, especially the southerner's alleged uneasy relationship to formal legal institutions and procedures, are cast in a different light when viewed from within the various German enclaves. These central European settlers brought with them their own anti-lawyer biases. These suspicions about lawyers were matched by the Germans' desire for one of their own to sit as a justice in local courts. Both sentiments sprang from inherited experiences with legal officers in Europe;

both attitudes were shaped in part by Reformation attitudes—or at least popular lore about Luther's attitudes—toward lawyers.

This essay first examines both religious and institutional traditions in an effort to ground the German interaction with Anglo-American lawyers and justices in a somewhat common European soil. Then it proceeds to sketch the colonial pattern of interaction in the following manner: first, to look at the "imposed enclave" in Maryland; second, to keep in mind the "self-imposed enclave" of the Salzburgers in Georgia and among the Moravians of North Carolina; and third, to note that the majority of Germans in Pennsylvania, Virginia, and the Carolinas lived in "formal enclaves." That is, living in a self-consciously German area meant keeping the language and customs alive, but it also involved seeking contact with and use of Anglo-American legal institutions. In Pennsylvania and Virginia the Germans received full cooperation from provincial authorities; in the Carolinas, the picture was clouded by political and social upheaval in which the Germans played a key role.[3] What all these enclaves had in common by 1800 was a culture that was local. Unlike their Anglo neighbors who also distrusted lawyers, the Germans produced almost no members of the American bar. Far into the nineteenth century, their local and anti-lawyer culture kept alive the older eighteenth-century Anglo-American suspicions of lawyers, while state and federal benches and bars increasingly grew in influence. One begins to ascertain the degree to which Germans did or did not become "southerners" by first looking at the inherited values and attitudes they brought to the colonies.

Even scholars only remotely familiar with Martin Luther recognize him as a critic of lawyers. Some have speculated that the law career chosen for him by his father and then rejected by the young man lay at the heart of his censures against the profession. Whatever the rationale put forward by writers trying to explain Luther's strictures, all seem to agree that he had nothing good to say about lawyers. Strictly speaking, this is untrue. Though clearly one who favored the study of theology over law, Luther admitted more than once that lawyers who "help the prince to rule his land; advise cities and districts; help many a man guard his person, his wife, child, property, and honor" were worthy of respect, and parents ought to help a child who aspired to the law and "make the investment necessary for his study and advancement."[4] Luther loathed the baneful influence of legalism in church matters, and he made savage attacks against canon lawyers: they are "skinners, not of dead dogs, but of living humans"; their "ultimate end is money, not appreciation or knowledge"; anyone who aspires to be one "wants a steel head, a silver purse, and an ass made out of lead."[5] Nonetheless, what the ordinary German *thought* Luther had to say about lawyers probably was of more significance than what he did say, and for the period between 1546 and 1683, that is, between Luther's death and the migration of the first Germans to North America, ordinary Germans had little direct experience with the profession.[6]

Local courts and lawyers played both less and more important roles in Germany after 1400. In the early Middle Ages, the large landowners who had presided three times a year over public courts, the so-called general assemblies of inhabitants, proposed judgments for assembly approval. By the 1200s, the silence of the assembly was interpreted to mean assent to what these *Schoffen*, or presenting officers, had suggested. Between the thirteenth and fifteenth centuries, the old assemblies or public courts, disintegrated as feudal magnates, protected by imperial immunities as vassals of the Emperor from local court authority, increased their hold on legal matters in the localities. By the 1400s, the *Schoffen* had evolved into officers whose main allegiance was one of vassals to their overlord. To a limited degree, the law in small villages and on manors still tended to be communal as were land ownership patterns; the lowly still had some say in decisions. The *Schoffen*, given their traditional office as proposers of wise judgments, had presided over a legal tradition that was oral, local, and customary. The reliance on wise seers, rather than on complicated documents or legal specialists, then, typified German law, at least outside of imperial cities, until about 1500.[7]

The transformation of this traditional, communal law by the reception of Roman law is a complex and hotly debated story whose details must be omitted here. But one can summarize the development by stating that written pleadings came to displace both the *Schoffen*'s role and the oral traditions of lay-led law. By the 1500s, when Luther began fulminating against lawyers, he was criticizing an emerging profession. The shift from an oral tradition and the accompanying rise of professional lawyers came when enough lawyers existed to draft written pleadings, beginning in the late 1400s. In places like Frankfurt, the elderly merchants, the part-time holders of office who were not lawyers, increasingly deferred to a city attorney, "issuing judgments in their own names that had been actually drafted by their expert advisor."[8] Both in appellate courts, especially in the *Reichskammergericht* established in 1495, and in territorial appellate courts, written procedures pored over by members of the court who boasted doctorates in law created what one scholar has described as "one of the most complex and dilatory systems of written pleading that had so far appeared on the continent of Europe."[9]

Only in petty criminal causes did the tradition of the lay *Schoffen* survive into the seventeenth and eighteenth centuries. In local lay courts the practice of making accusations in public assemblies actually revived during these centuries. Thus, these petty misdemeanor courts were forums where the *Schoffen* made what in the Anglo-American colonial tradition would be grand jury presentments against citizens guilty of petty misdemeanors. The Germans who encountered justice of the peace courts in the colonies witnessed the presentments of grand jurors and heard the discretionary judgments of the justices and recognized the surviving traditions of wise, discretionary, and oral law, which had only managed to limp along after 1500 in the German territories as lawyers, written pleadings, and complex procedural argument squeezed aside the older role of the *Schoffen*. Naturally, since lawyers were expensive to hire, and since they operated largely in the appellate or imperial courts and under Roman procedural rules, the ordinary German would regard them as a species apart. There was nothing familiar about the profession, little to recommend it as an object of trust.[10]

Unfortunately, close analyses do not exist that probe the workings of the courts in the areas from which Germans emigrated.

Studies of areas in the general vicinity of the Palatinate, however, reveal something about local usages and how common people interacted with *certain* legal institutions and personnel. For example, ordinary men and women used the marriage tribunals (*Ehegerichte*) throughout the sixteenth and seventeenth centuries. Especially in Catholic territories such as Konstanz, where the *Offizialat* or tribunal dealt with disputes about marital agreements, women were able to establish their claims to hold a man to a promise of marriage; they were provided as well, at least in the city of Basel, with the statutory assurance that they could be accompanied by an attorney. Scholars believe these courts were declining by the seventeenth century, and such institutions exercised limited jurisdiction; they could not deal, for example, with the property aspects of family disputes. The city councils, acting in their judicial capacity, did so.[11]

In Strassburg, further to the west, the courts evolved along with the town as the formerly free city of the empire became in 1648 a part of France. Here, the *Magistrat* of Strassburg, the final authority in the city, sat as a supreme court of appeal, and under them a police court. Special tribunals, including an *Anmeister's* audience, which dealt summarily with minor affairs and petty claims, gave ordinary citizens access to the law. In rural areas, bailiffs performed a function similar to the *Anmeister's*, and even after 1648, when civil causes involving sums over 2,000 livres could be appealed to the sovereign council of Alsace in Colmar, older German customs and procedures survived.[12]

Although the German immigrants had access to the courts of their localities, most of the small disputes of local life would not have involved them in the higher courts' procedures; they would have had only minimal contact with the legal profession and the learned university law experts. It is perilous to make generalizations about "German" attitudes toward courts and legal officers because scholars know so little about the detailed, day-to-day workings of local institutions, particularly in the often-devastated and turbulent Palatinate. Even in the Swiss cantons and more stable areas from which many of the emigrants departed, research has only begun to reveal the relationship between bench and community. Still, the picture outlined above may fairly represent the ordinary German's contact with the law, though the details of that portrait must, for the moment, be left unfinished.

The German immigrants arrived in the New World beginning in 1683, settling in the colonies from New York to the Carolinas and later in Georgia. Different types of experiences shaped the relationship between Germans and English legal institutions because of distinct practices and attitudes exhibited by colonial governments, which had themselves developed in various fashions. The first type of relationship to note was that of the "imposed enclave," which evolved in Maryland.

Despite Maryland's and Virginia's supposedly similar histories, the two colonies differed both in their political constitutions and in Maryland's lack of an open western frontier. Moreover, the Proprietary government's policies regarding both bench and bar, distinctly different from the same institutions across the Potomac, retarded German participation in local court affairs far longer than in neighboring Virginia.[13] The Maryland bar was organized earlier under Proprietary instructions, was far more potent politically, and therefore emerged as a distinct profession earlier than in Virginia. Local county courts of Maryland were also far less powerful than their counterparts in the Old Dominion. Nevertheless, local justices were important in Maryland county life, and the Germans who began arriving in the mid-eighteenth century naturally might have sought the protection of a local justice or, at least, requested that someone who spoke their language be a member of the county judiciary. In fact, this did not happen until 1773 when John Stull became the first justice in Frederick County appointed from among the German settlers.[14]

The reasons for this retarded interaction of Germans with Anglo-American legal institutions were two-fold. The Calvert family, at odds with the Assembly almost constantly during the eighteenth century, was reluctant to inject non-English-speaking Germans into the fractious politics of the colony. In a colony where the Anglican clergy were urged not to get involved in any subject remotely "fractious" but to strive as indolently as possible for "complacency," dissenters, even of a quietistic sort, were viewed

with a certain nervousness. Second, the exclusion of even natu-
ralized Germans from sitting in the assembly, a restriction apparently imposed at the wish of the proprietors, coupled with less
attractive land policies than those in Pennsylvania and Virginia,
combined to restrict German development in the political arena.
Even though the Germans prospered in Frederick County, they
did so in isolation from the political life of colonial Maryland. This
enclave was not one that they chose to erect: they were forced into
it by the Anglo-American proprietary leaders.[15] Not until the
1800s did German-American lawyers and justices begin to appear
and achieve prominence and then primarily in the urbanized area
of the state.

It is tempting to compare Maryland's experience with Virginia's or Pennsylvania's since these two colonies bordered the Cal-
verts' province. However, just as Maryland played such a small
part in the on-going development of German immigrants' adaptation to English law, it is appropriate to turn next to a similar
community farther south, to the Salzburger immigrants in Georgia and their nearby neighbors in southern South Carolina. These
people, too, had only minimal contact with the bench and bar of
their provinces, but that decision was one of their choosing.

The Salzburgers, coming from an aggressively Roman Catholic territory of the Holy Roman Empire, had already experienced
the full terror of princely law when they were expelled from their
homelands, some fleeing to England and the colonies, others
seeking refuge in Brandenburg-Prussia. Both the Austrian origins
of the Georgia Germans and the Swiss background of the Purys-
burg, South Carolina, community distinguished these communities from their Palatine counterparts in the back-country who
had migrated down the Appalachian chain. Not surprisingly, the
Austrian immigrants, settling in the 1730s in the Oglethorpe ex-
perimental colony, depended upon their Lutheran pastors for legal guidance as well as spiritual shepherding. The Salzburger settlement at New Ebenezer relied solely upon the Reverend John
Martin Bolzius and Pastor Israel Christian Gronau for legal authority and advice. George Whitefield, on a visit to the settlement, commented that the Germans "are . . . blessed with two

such pious ministers as I have seldom seen. They have no courts of jurisdiction, but all differences are immediately settled by their pastors."[16]

Pastors meted out a more benevolent justice in the settlement at St. Mathew's Parish in Effingham County, Georgia, than that encountered by the less fortunate residents of Savannah. Until 1757, Bolzius held the power of attorney for the settlement in all its dealings with Lutheran authorities as well as the Trustees and, later, the Royal Government. In 1741, Benjamin Martyn's *An Impartial Enquiry into the State and Utility of the Province of Georgia* noted that the Salzburgers, a neat and industrious people, seemed to need no formal judicial institutions. "Though there is no regular Court of Justice, as they live in Sobriety, they maintain great Order and Decency. In case of any Differences, the Minister calls three or four of the most prudent Elders together, who in a summary Way hear and determine as they think just, and the Parties always acquiesce with Content in their Judgment."[17] Not until 1784 was a "Court-House and Gaol" ordered erected in Effingham County. By the 1790s the German community had removed into Scriven, Lowndes, Liberty, and Thomas counties, or into Savannah. These Germans sought almost no contact with an English bench and bar before the Revolution.[18]

Moreover, the history of both bench and bar in Georgia had not been one that would have encouraged the immigrants to seek out these institutions, even had they been so inclined. During the same decade that the Salzburgers were settling in, Francis Moore noted in his diary regarding Savannah that "there are no Lawyers allowed to plead for Hire, nor no Attornies to take Money, but (as in old times in England) everyman pleads his own Cause."[19] Though perhaps regarded as a boon by opponents of lawyers, this absence of a genuine bar meant that "everyman" who pleaded was best served when he both knew the English language and also had influential friends.

The local bench and bar did not begin to make a significant impact upon Georgia until very late in the colonial period, and even then, they did not affect the Germans to any degree. The only German names that appear on the rolls of lawyers and judges, ei-

ther at the circuit or superior court level from the Revolution onward, are Benjamin Skrine, who rode the middle circuit in the
early 1800s, and William Schley, a former Frederick County,
Maryland, lawyer who was admitted to the bar in Georgia in 1812
and practised in Augusta until he became a judge of the superior
court in 1825. Even though the influx of large numbers of slave-
owning planters altered Georgia life and society greatly after 1750,
there is little or no evidence indicating that the struggling bar and
the country benches of Georgia in the royal period made any significant impression upon the Germans of Ebenezer.[20]

The interaction of English local courts and lawyers with German immigrants in South Carolina is a more complex story and
presents modern scholars with a peculiarly difficult task because
of the absence of hard evidence. First, Charleston boasted some
impressive individuals with substantive legal training, but the up-
country produced few lawyers before the Revolution; its county
courts were commonly known to be of poor quality and little
power; there were no circuit courts in the province until 1769. Although many of the chief justices of the province were trained formally as lawyers, these men did little for the administration of
justice outside of Charleston proper. Furthermore, the justices of
the peace in South Carolina exercised only limited authority before 1750, and even with the cautious decentralization of legal institutions that occurred before the Revolution, they were never as
significant as their counterparts in North Carolina or Virginia.

There is no evidence that any person of German descent had
practiced before the colonial bar, but the German community of
post-Revolutionary Charleston did produce a modest number of
lawyers. George B. Eckhard, described as "the idol of the German population of Charleston," was admitted to the bar in 1816.
The son of Jacob Eckhard, the organist for the German Lutheran
Church as well as for St. Michael's, Eckhard was apparently the
first prominent lawyer produced by the Charleston German community. Even so, the Charleston bar produced no chief justices,
equity judges, recorders of the city court, attorneys general, solicitors, admiralty judges, or U.S. district attorneys of German
extraction in the first thirty years of the republic. The retarded

evolution of German practitioners is illustrated by the example of John M. Felder. Born in 1782 in the Orangeburg District, the eldest son of Samuel Felder, John attended Yale. Graduating in 1804, he obtained legal training at Tapping Reeve's Litchfield, Connecticut, school and was admitted to the bar in 1808. His grandfather, an immigrant from Switzerland in the late 1720s, had been killed in the Revolution, and his father Samuel had served as a justice on the General Sessions of the County Court in the 1780s. But Felder's ancestral connections to the legal offices of the province were atypical. Not until the post-Revolutionary era did South Carolina Germans begin to make significant contributions to the institutions of Anglo-American law, which until that time had been dominated by the small bench and bar in Charleston.[21]

The Regulator Movement best explains this slow interaction of German-speaking people with the Carolina bench and bar in the back-country. In both North and South Carolina, this episode in the years just before the Revolution deeply affected the Germans' attitudes about the bench and bar. But the actions of the German communities in the Carolinas toward the Regulation also reveal their interest in, and frustration with, these legal offices before the crisis itself broke. Since the history of the South Carolina back-country was tied to that of North Carolina in some respects, and since the Germans living in the Newberry, Orange, and '96 District areas were in part emigrés from North Carolina and Pennsylvania, it is necessary to examine North Carolina's peculiar policies with regard to justices and lawyers.[22]

North Carolina, unlike its neighboring colony to the south, based its eighteenth-century county courts on Virginia's. And, because it possessed a functioning county court system that provided some immediate access to legal process, the colony did not experience exactly the same resentment against remote courts and officers that South Carolina's centralized bench and bar provoked. Lawyers had been prohibited from the Carolinas under John Locke's *Fundamental Constitutions*, which stipulated in Article 70: "It shall be a base and vile thing to plead for money or reward; nor shall anyone (except he be a near kinsman no farther off than cousin german to the party concerned) be permitted to plead another man's cause till, before the judge in open court, he hath taken an oath that he does not plead for money or reward. . . ."[23] However, licensed practitioners did exist in North Carolina from the 1690s onward, though not in large numbers. Just as South Carolina had at first prohibited lawyers from practising by copying verbatim a 1658 Virginia statute, so too did North Carolina. As the Albemarle region began to evolve separately from South Carolina, it forbade lawyers to practice at first, and it restricted lawyers still later by setting fees in 1715 and by incorporating Virginia's practise of prohibiting justices, clerks, and sheriffs from pleading as lawyers in the courts where they officiated.[24]

Although the Swiss settlement at New Bern had briefly promised a German-speaking presence in North Carolina, both this short-lived experiment and another in the Cape Fear area in the 1730s, produced no noticeable interaction of Germans with Anglo-American legal institutions. Only in the 1740s, well into the royal period, did the Germans begin to flow down the mountain valleys from Pennsylvania and Virginia and come to comprise a sizeable percentage of the population in Rowan, Surry, present-day Cabarrus-Mecklenburg (often called "little Pennsylvania"), and eight other counties. As these German-speaking settlers moved into the western areas in the 1740s and '50s, they began to encounter the same problem their Anglo-American counterparts faced: the local courts were dominated by English-speaking friends of the governor, and hordes of merchants and lawyers swarmed around the new settlements. In one significant manner, North Carolina departed from the wise practice of its northern neighbor. Virginia's justices were chosen from families of standing, usually long-term residents, or if newcomers from Britain, of wealth and familial connections. The judicial officers of the court (in Rowan and Orange Counties, for example) were men such as Edmund Fanning and John Forock, who were either recent immigrants to the area or commonly reputed to be engaged in buying and selling of clerkships and lining their pockets by the exactions of exorbitant fees.[25]

A fundamental distinction existed at the time among the Germans who settled in North Carolina that materially affected their relationship with the bench and bar of the colony. The Moravians, the pietistic reform sect that had at first allied itself with and then had broken with the Lutheran church, was regarded by the government as peculiarly loyal and worthy of trust and office. Justices of the peace emerged in the 1750s among the Moravians in Rowan county. Jacob Loesch, Jacob Bonn, Georg Heinrich Barrager, Friedrik Miller, Heinrich Spoenhauer, a certain "justice Sporge," Jacob van der Merl, and Charles Holder all were appointed to serve on the bench in Rowan and in the new county of Surry between 1750 and 1771. These Moravians were staunchly loyal to the government in the Regulation Crisis, which erupted in the 1760s. By contrast, among non-Moravian Germans, justices of the peace were few in number and apparently not particularly influential. Walter Carruth had been a German justice in Anson County in 1749 and in Rowan after 1753 when the new county was created. Beyond this early and important German justice, however, the court records yield the names of only a few other men: Jacob Costner in Tryon, Johann Ludwig Bart (John Lewis Beard) in Rowan in the 1750s, and later, Joseph Shinn, Jacob Barnhardt, and Michael Braun in Mecklenburg-Cabarrus—the latter three men, however, only serving in the post-Revolutionary period.[26]

The Moravians' desire for their own justices sprang not from a desire to participate in the broader contours of provincial legal and political life, but from an honest and stated anxiety that if someone not a member of the community bore a grudge against the Moravians, an unsympathetic justice could do the pietists great damage. When confronted by the Regulators, the Moravians held fast, even though, as a subsequent report by a Moravian bishop revealed, they understood little of what the fracas was about. They admitted that rapacious lawyers and merchants were bothersome, but they sided with the government. In 1775, faced with a decision of whether to support the King or the Bostonians, the Moravians hoped that some "higher authority" than a revolutionary committee would instruct them about the proper course they should take, but Bishop Graff suggested that they could support independence but should "say nothing whatever about the points at issue, which we do not understand . . . it will probably be better to bear what cannot be changed, than to refuse and so come into a much worse position. Such a course brought us fairly well through the recent Regulator confusion."[27]

The Moravians, friendly with North Carolina lawyers such as John Dunn, were reluctant to confront these officers of the courts, and on at least one occasion when Jacob Bonn was on the bench, non-Moravian justices wanted to have some misbehaving lawyers arrested, "but Br. Bonn forbade that."[28] Such attitudes led the Moravians to condemn the Regulation, though they were approached for support. Somewhat smugly, the writer of the Moravian document, the *Bethabera Diary*, noted of the Battle of Alamance that the Regulators had fled, and "one party, especially the Germans from Abbots Creek, had stacked their arms and had been pardoned by the Governor."[29]

Perhaps it was the absence of Lutheran and Reformed pastors in sufficient numbers among the non-Moravian Germans or perhaps the fact that Governor Tryon overlooked the non-Moravians in his appointment of German justices in the western counties, which explains why German involvement in the Regulation outside of the Moravian community was widespread and intense. A mixture of two types of "enclaves" evolved in North Carolina. The Moravians choose a kind of self-imposed isolation in which their justices operated mostly to keep unsympathetic Carolinians at bay. In addition, there were the "formal" enclaves of non-Moravian Germans, clearly angered by lack of redress in the courts, taking up arms to protest their communities' need for succor.

Historians have detailed with care both the anti-lawyer aspect of the Regulation and the class dimensions of the conflict. But few have noticed that a substantial portion of the men involved in the Regulation were non-Moravian Germans. When Governor Tryon finally proclaimed a pardon in 1771 for the Regulators, he explicitly exempted Samuel Waggoner, John Winker, and Jacob Felker of Mecklenburg County for their part in the violence. The petition to the Governor for aid against lawyers who took exorbitant fees was signed by Jacob Fudge, Richard Cheek, and Charles Saxon, with Cheek identified on the petition as "a Dutchman."

Tryon noted in his journal in August of 1768 the antipathy exhibited against him in the German community in Mecklenburg
by writing: "Sunday the 21st the Governor attended divine Service when Mr. Suther (a swiss) tho' a dutch minister recommended with warmth a due abedience to the Laws of the Country. . . ." Even more pointed was the sermon of the Reverend
George Micklejohn, the Scots-Anglican pro-government minister, himself a recent arrival in the colony in 1766. His sermon,
which was ordered reproduced by the Governor, took as its text
the famous passage of Romans 13:1–2, which Luther translated
in German to mean "subjection" to the "higher powers" (*Obrigkeit*). Micklejohn's sermon, *On the important duty of Subjection to the
Civil Powers*. . . . was a subtle appeal to ethnic prejudice, not only
incorporating a key text that any German immediately would have
recognized, but also noting that "for an *Englishman* to oppose the
laws of his country, is an instance of the highest folly and contradiction we can conceive. . . ."[30]

Even more striking evidence of the disaffection of the Germans
in Surry, Rowan, and Mecklenburg counties can be obtained by
examining tax lists. Professor James Whittenberg has already
completed this survey and found that approximately 23 percent
of the Regulators were of German background.[31] Clearly, the relationship of the non-Moravian German enclaves in western North
Carolina counties to the lawyers and justices where they lived was
anything but positive. Moreover, the identical disaffection, but
for different reasons, existed right across the boundary line in the
back-country of South Carolina.

There, the absence of a functioning court and the grievances of
small enclaves of German settlers coalesced into opposition to the
dominance of the Charleston elite. However, in South Carolina,
there was little overt oppression from court officers since there
were no lawyers about, and the local courts had been in operation
for only a few years. Germans evidently were in the commission
of the peace in Newberry and Orangeburg counties, which may
explain why the Regulator crisis here, though clearly involving
some Germans, did not take on quite the aspect it did in neighboring North Carolina. For example, though both Jacob Frey and

Elisha Teiger lost their militia commissions for their role in the Regulation in the "Dutch Fork" area, which had been settled in the 1740s, Michael Dickert presided as a justice in the '96 District in the period just before the Revolution.[32] The destruction of Orangeburg County records makes an accurate estimate of German involvement in the Regulation impossible, but the presence of Germans like Christian Minnich and Jacob Motte on the local bench until 1768 and then their absence from 1768 to 1774 suggest that they, too, were perhaps not regarded as completely reliable. Only in 1775 does Henrich Felder reappear on the list of Quorum justices for the Orangeburg district. And not until 1772 did Isaac Huger manage to secure election to the Provincial Assembly for the St. Mathew's Parish, only to lose his seat to Tacitus Gaillard, in 1773, perhaps due to Gaillard's long-standing membership on the local court and family connection to the Huguenot merchants and planters in Charleston.[33]

Richard M. Brown's study of the Regulation in South Carolina pointed out that Germans were involved in the crisis, but few readers at the time seemed to find significant the disaffection of these "formal" or self-conscious enclaves. Certainly, the fact that the Regulation in South Carolina was fought to bring *more*, not less, institutional law to the back-country, unlike the aims of the North Carolina Regulation, helps to explain a lower profile of German participants in the more southern province. The skepticism of the Germans with regard to the Charleston establishment, rehearsed in the Regulation, came to be obvious by 1775. Even though Henry Felder, Isaac Porcher, and Jacob Christopher Zahn represented St. Mathew's Parish by the late 1770s, and William Gieger and Jacob Seyler the Saxe-Gotha Germans, the early stages of the Revolution proceeded without much German help. The letters sent to the Council of Safety in 1775 by William Tennent and William Henry Drayton reflect the reluctance of the Orangeburg and '96 residents to listen to Charleston explanations about the need for resistance to British rule. After a meeting had been called in which "to our great mortification not one German appeared . . . ," Drayton wrote back to Charleston, "The Dutch are not with us."[34]

Thus, in South Carolina, complaints against political and judicial policies of eastern authorities provoked Germans to participate in a Regulation movement, but they were far less prominent than their counterparts in the North Carolina dissent. Largely, this appears to have stemmed both from the fact that the judicial institutions in North Carolina were operative but unresponsive to non-Moravian German needs, as opposed to simply inoperative, as was the case in South Carolina. Moreover, from the fragmentary evidence it also appears true that at least some German settlers had been incorporated into the local judicial system in South Carolina, powerless though the local institutions were. On the other hand, in the neighboring colony, the non-Moravian Germans did not possess a significant influence on the local court system in Rowan, Tryon, Surry, or Mecklenburg counties, where they participated in large numbers in the Regulator Movement.

Finally, one must consider a similar but more successful integration of formal enclaves that emerged in Virginia and southern Pennsylvania. In these colonies, Germans appeared on the commissions of the peace sooner than in the Carolinas; the governments in Philadelphia and Williamsburg responded with alacrity to petitions from Germans who sought a justice for their precincts who understood their language. Here, as elsewhere, the motivation may well have been economic: the immigrants could not prosper if they did not know how to defend their property and their rights; without a justice who could serve as intermediary between the Anglo-American colonial legal system and their own Germanic communities, they were lost. In southwestern Pennsylvania, and in the Piedmont and Valley counties of Virginia, the immigrants encountered no difficulty in securing such men.

The present state of scholarship makes it impossible to determine precisely the relationship between Germans and bench and bar in Pennsylvania. To date, there is no adequate study of the local courts of Pennsylvania, much less sufficient work on the courts and their workings in the German settlements. Therefore, conclusions must be tentative and restricted to the evidence from the trans-Allegheny settlement in Bedford (today Bedford and Somerset) County, which was populated not only by Germans moving east, but also by immigrants out of Virginia and Pennsylvania, whose ancestors came directly from the Rhineland.[35]

From 1683 the Germans were aware of the need to master the strange ways of English law. The manuscript books of Daniel Pastorius, the Frankfurt lawyer, included three items entitled *The Young Country Clerk, Good Counsel for Bad Lawyers and Attorneys*, and *Law Terms Added to the Compleat Justice*.[36] The interaction between Germans and legal personae, however, remains dark until the 1740s when the surviving records began to reveal a pattern that appears to have been dominant. Jerome Wood's study of Lancaster, Pennsylvania, notes that this overwhelmingly German enclave required legal officers from the beginning to be capable of dealing not only with English law, but also with German litigants. Created in 1729, this county's court met first at the Postlethwaite Inn, with the court of Quarter Sessions sitting at Lancaster. Within the first decade, powerful German leaders like Sebastian Goff, one of the first two burgesses of the period, or Simon Kuhn, a physician, also sat as justices on the local court. However, though German justices existed in Lancaster, German lawyers did not. The legal profession in this community was dominated by Thomas Cookson, Edward Shippen, and George Rosse, all Anglo-Americans. Not until considerably later did John Hubly, a second-generation German, the son of an innkeeper, begin to practice law.[37]

This pattern applies as well to the trans-Allegheny settlement in Bedford County. Created in 1771 from Cumberland County, Bedford County immediately established its General Quarter Sessions of the Peace & Gaol Delivery and a court for holding pleas in the town of Bedford. The court appointed in 1771 was composed of men of British backgrounds, though familiarity with German was essential, at least for the court clerk; the very first will recorded for the township was written in German.[38] The western area of Bedford, known popularly as "Brothers' Valley" or *Brudersthal* because of its Dunkard and Amish settlement, clearly intended to keep its legal affairs in order. The courts had no sooner been constituted when Abraham Keble was put forward by the Germans as a man suitable for the bench who could deal with their legal affairs. Keble was added to the bench and began a long career in government offices. When Somerset County was created in 1795, Keble became one of the judges of the new county. In the township of Berlin, also located in the new county, Adam Miller, a former Maryland militiaman who had immigrated to the colonies in 1773, also served as a justice from 1791 to 1798 when he resigned to sit in the General Assembly. It is tantalizing, but necessarily speculative, to think that Keble and Miller were influenced to seek positions on the local bench due to conversations with Harmond Husband, the former North Carolina Regulator who fled northward, settling in Bedford (later Somerset) County in 1771.[39]

German justices existed in this southwestern area of Pennsylvania, but the circuit court bench created by the 1790 Constitution was exclusively an Anglo- or Scottish-American preserve. Moreover, of 34 members of the bar produced by the Somerset region between 1795 and 1820, only six were of German extraction, with four of the six admitted after 1803. While Germans functioned as jurymen and assessors and filled minor offices, major judicial posts and the bar were either beyond their grasp, or perhaps, their reach.[40]

The westward movement was not the only influence on the legal evolution of southwestern Pennsylvania. From Virginia, too, a substantial number of Germans moved northward into Bedford-Somerset in the years immediately before and after the Revolution, particularly from Loudon County and back up the Valley from Frederick and Berkeley counties. Whatever economic or social reasons these Germans had for leaving Virginia, discontent with the local courts was not one of them. In perhaps no other colony did the immigrants manage so quickly to secure a German justice of the peace on the bench. Partly the result of a perceptive policy on the part of governors like Sir William Gooch, partly the result of available, qualified men, the German enclaves east of the mountains in Spotsylvania (and its subsequent divisions) or in the Valley of Augusta (and its subsequent divisions) experienced the same phenomenon. In both regions there were German justices from the start, but in neither region did any German colonist practise before the bar until the 1800s.

East of the mountains, Orange County, created in 1734, was

the location of the Lutheran segment of the original group of settlers who had stayed in Virginia at the urging of Alexander Spotswood. The very first meeting of the county court in January of 1734 included the oath-taking by Justices Joist Hite and Benjamin Borden, both of German extraction. Hite, best known for his land speculations and contèsts with the Proprietors of the Northern Neck, did not apparently spend much time serving as a justice. But Borden, an agent of Lord Fairfax, a prominent merchant and recent immigrant from New Jersey, apologized in November for not attending the sessions of the court, explaining, "I have got a cold and a pain in my bones and next Cort I purpose to com if I am well . . . and if I should not com next Cort I desire the favour of the Cort to excuse me till I have got better settled and then I hope I shall perform my duty better. So genttle men I hope you are wise men and would consider the grate vantage of moving so far with a grate famaly and settleing all a new. . . ."[41]

Just as the colonial Council had responded to the petition presented in April of 1734 for justices on the northwest side of the Blue Ridge and had specified Borden and Hite, Hite's petition "on behalf of himself and divers others the inhabitants of Sherrando . . ." reflected the alacrity with which the colonial government continued to incorporate the Germans in August County and trans-montane counties, into the workings of the court. When Peter Scholl petitioned the court for better roads closer to the homes of Germans who had been ordered to repair the extant road thirty miles away, the court struggled to respond. And in 1745 the commission of the peace included Scholl. Though his identity is not entirely established, he appears to have been, like Borden, a New Jerseyman from the Raritan area. No sooner had Rockingham county been erected in 1777 (with an estimated German population of some 43 percent) than the Commonwealth appointed Isaac Hinckle as a member of the first commission of the peace. In no Virginia county before 1800, however, did any German practice law as an attorney.[42]

The patterns sketched previously for the various regions seem to confirm the conclusion that many Germans were anxious to have a justice in local courts and that they perceived themselves as belonging in those courts. Yet, they had little contact with the bar, and they produced no lawyers from their midst until the nineteenth century. Moreover, the significant participation of Germans in the anti-lawyer Regulator Movement seems to indicate a definite anti-lawyer attitude among these immigrants. Unfortunately, extensive literary evidence that might help to confirm these general impressions does not exist. Only from a few scattered comments of Heinrich Melchior Muhlenberg, the Lutheran pastor responsible for organizing his church in the colonies, does one gain a deeper perspective about this prejudice.

Both in his *Journal* and in reports to Saxony on the progress and problems of the congregations (*Hallesche Nachrichten*), the Lutheran leader made oblique reference to the bench and bar of the colony of Pennsylvania and to lawyers in general. In assessing a dispute between congregations and pastors, Muhlenberg explained to his Saxon superiors that "If we make an appeal to the civil authorities we thereby show disrespect to the duly constituted consistories and superintendents of the Church, expose our own infirmities, and give ourselves over into the hands of the lawyers, and then tedious and expensive law suits follow. The lawyers know well how to twist spiritual things into worldly shape. . . ." Bitter from his experiences with English courts, Muhlenberg even scorned justices by instructing his countrymen, "According to the English laws, when a disputed matter has long been before the court and the lawyers of both parties have grown tired of it, seeing perhaps that their clients have been already plucked bare, the judges usually refer the business to an arbitration."[43]

Reminding his superiors that "we know very well what difficulties are encountered in Europe, when . . . the authorities of the Government undertake to impose a restraint upon a community or upon a parish," Muhlenberg concluded that "when legal process is resorted to then confidence is gone." The preference for settling churchly disputes within the congregation itself, of course, had scriptural warrant, and Christians had been warned by St. Paul not to take each other to court. For the Germans in the colonies there were cultural and linguistic disincentives for going to English law for redress unless all other alternatives had been exhausted.[44]

Muhlenberg had been informed about the sharp legal practices that resulted in the loss of the Newburg, New York, patent of some early Germans granted the land by "the illustrious Queen Anne." His conclusion was that "this is what happens when preachers and congregations dispute and undermine each other and are thrown into disorder; they keep the shell of the mussel while the lawyer takes the pearl for his faithful services." Before Germans can understand how to defend themselves, "the English people [get] the jump on them. Why? Because they had influential patrons and money in their pockets."[45] Annoyed to be dependent upon even such a prominent lawyer as John Dickinson, Muhlenberg reluctantly concluded that "whenever there is something to be done for the honor of God without money, the lawyers are not at home. So . . . I . . . mollify his illness somewhat with *aurum potabile*. He told me quite frankly that the dose was not strong enough and he must have more if he was to get well."[46]

With Pennsylvania justices, Muhlenberg seemed to get on better. One wonders at his description of Ralph Schmidt as "the English justice of the peace," until Muhlenberg explains that he is a Presbyterian and "shares the secret prejudice of his fellow Presbyterians, that the German Lutherans retain too much of the papistical leaven." Muhlenberg grimly noted, "the English are very cunning in their ways. . . . We preachers do not have the time or the opportunity to study the English laws, and the English lawyers will give no advice unless they are paid in cash." Muhlenberg struggled to record exactly what the justice informed him of, regarding a deed of conveyance, numbering the points of law the justice put forward and his own responses, and noting the final, unassailable authority of the justice's position: "He read it to me from a book of English law. . . ."[47]

In conclusion, some Germans, such as those in Maryland, even had they wanted more active integration with legal and political life were prohibited from undertaking such activities and lived in imposed enclaves, which may have promoted the preservation of their language and traditional patterns of life. Both the Salzburger Lutherans and North Carolina Moravians chose to live in self-imposed enclaves, using Anglo-American legal officers and courts largely to keep others at bay and to provide a minimal nexus with the broader Anglo-American world. Last, and probably most representative of the majority of Germans in the colonies, were large, formal enclaves—self-conscious groups of Germans living in various counties who wanted to secure for themselves a German-speaking justice of the peace, but who saw themselves as a part of the larger province in which they lived. In none of the three types of community did Germans have many positive contacts with lawyers (with the possible exception of the Moravians), and Germans did not themselves become lawyers in large numbers before the nineteenth century. Even in the ante-bellum period, research on the higher benches of the South has revealed that the degree of accommodation reached by Germans with *local* benches and bars reflected a localism manifested in the absence of Germans on the Federal and high state benches of the southern jurisdictions.[48]

Clearly, the rising influence of the legal profession in the early republic, and particularly in the South, seems to have passed the Germans by. One would assume, in the absence of any clear evidence of prejudice systematically directed against them, that this resulted from decisions of their own making. Neither by religious nor ethnic legacy, nor by choices made in the colonial period, were the Germans inclined to look with favor upon a career at the bar. Further, their fondness for local, justice-of-the-peace law dispensed at the county level tied them to an older system that was increasingly superceded by more powerful state and federal courts in the nineteenth century. Perhaps, although this is pure speculation, their very distrust of secular legal disputes, their very suspicion of lawyers and powerful figures spared them the dislocation suffered by Anglo-American whites who resorted with increasing frequency to the "code of honor" as formerly meaningful local courts and rituals failed to provide satisfactory avenues of resolution for conflict in southern life. Perhaps only belatedly did the Germans of a later generation abandon their suspicions of the common law as interpreted by lawyers.

Only further research into the local records and surviving family papers in southern communities[49] where the Germans lived will confirm or contradict these initial conclusions. And only then will we be in a position to know exactly how these inhabitants of enclaves in the South, far from their original legal and linguistic world, helped to shape, or were excluded from shaping, a land molded by peculiar American institutions and by books of English law.

NOTES

The author would like to acknowledge the following for financial support of and comments on the research: Lawrence University Faculty Research Grant; American Council of Learned Societies Grant; Albert J. Beveridge Grants (American Historical Association); German Academic Exchange Grants; Institute for European History, Mainz, West Germany; Maxwell Bloomfield; Charles McCurdy; John Phillip Reid; Kermit L. Hall.

[1] Ian R. MacNeil, *The New Social Contract: An Inquiry into Modern Contractual Relations* (New Haven, Conn., 1980), p. xii.

[2] Aubrey C. Land, *et al.*, eds., *Law, Society, and Politics in Early Maryland* (Baltimore, Md., 1977); Thad Tate and David Ammerman, eds., *The Seventeenth Century Chesapeake: Essays on Anglo-American Society and Politics* (New York, 1979); "An Uncivil War: The Southern Backcountry During the American Revolution," March 18–19, 1982, Washington, D.C., sponsored by the Institute for Early American History and Culture; Wilfrid Prest, ed., *Lawyers in Early Modern Europe and America* (New York, 1981); Stephen Botein, *Early American Law and Society: Essay and Materials in Law and American History* (rev. ed., New York, 1983).

[3] My designation of various types of "enclaves" was stimulated by some comments of Professor McCurdy at the conference. However, see also "Anthropology and History in the 1980s" by Cohn, Adams, Davis, and Ginzburg, *Journal of Interdisciplinary History*, XII (1981–82), 227–78; Werner Sollors, "Theory of American Ethnicity," *American Quarterly*, XXXIII (1981), 257–83; Fredrik Barth, ed., *Ethnic Groups and Boundaries* (Boston, 1969), 9–38; Robert Redfield, "The Folk Society," *American Journal of Sociology*, LII (1947), 293–308; Milton M. Gordon, *Assimilation in American Life: The Role of Race, Religion, and National Origins* (New York, 1964). Obviously, I agree more with Barth than Gordon insofar as I am looking at "boundaries" rather than elaborating on the cultural "content" of the German enclaves.

[4] The anti-lawyer comments of Luther are scattered throughout the Reformer's works. The citations here are from *D. Martin Luthers Werke: Kritische Gesamtausgabe* (58 vols., Weimar, 1883–); the *Tischreden* (6 vols., Weimar, 1912–21). The translations used here are those by H. G. Haile, in *Luther: An Experiment in Biography* (New York, 1980), 87 (WA 30/2, 561).

[5] Haile, *Luther*, 286: *Briefwechsel*. Kritische Gesamtausgabe (14 vols., Weimar, 1930–), XI, 278, 1–2; *Tischreden* V, 290, 5–6.

[6] See Hans Leiermann, "Der unjuristische Luther," *Luther Jahrbuch* XXIV (1957), 69–85; Albert Stein, "Martin Luthers Meinungen uber die Juristen," *Zeitschrift Der Savigny-Stiftung fur Rechtsgeschichte, Kanonistische Abteilung* LIV (1968), 362–75; on later attitudes, Dietrich Rueschemeyer, *Lawyers and Their Society: A Comparative Study of the Legal Profession in Germany and the United States* (Cambridge, Mass., 1973), 146–84; Adolf Weissler, *Geschichte der Rechtsanwaltschaft* (Leipzig, 1905), 232.

[7] Konrad Zweigert and Hein Kotz, *An Introduction to Comparative Law*, trans. Tony Weir (2 vols., Amsterdam, 1977), I, 133–36; John P. Dawson, *A History of Lay Judges* (Cambridge, Mass., 1960), 94–115; Dawson, *The Oracles of the Law* (Ann Arbor, Mich., 1968).

8 Dawson, *Lay Judges*. 106.

9 *Ibid.*, 107.

10 *Ibid.*, 109–15. On grand jury use in England and Virginia, see A. G. Roeber, *Faithful Magistrates and Republican Lawyers: Creators of Virginia Legal Culture, 1680–1810* (Chapel Hill, N.C., 1981), 86–90. Germans in North Carolina's New Bern settlement were appearing as jurymen as early as 1710; see G. D. Bernheim, *A History of the German Settlements and of the Lutheran Church in North and South Carolina* (Philadelphia, 1872), 81. This same use of Germans for lesser county officials can be found in any of the types of settlement enclaves discussed. For South Carolina, Virginia, and Pennsylvania, see below; for Maryland, see Elizabeth Augusta Kessel, "Germans on the Maryland Frontier: A Social History of Frederick County, Maryland, 1730–1800" (Ph.D. dissertation, Rice University, 1981), 292–308.

11 Thomas Max Safley, "Marital Litigation in the Diocese of Constance, 1551–1620," *Sixteenth Century Journal*, XII (1981), 61–77; Safley, "Women in German Courts: Marriage Litigation as a Source of Women's History," Sixteenth Century Studies Conference, Iowa City, October, 1981, unpublished paper; Thomas Robisheaux, "Peasants and Pastors: Rural Youth Control and the Reformation in Hohenlohe, 1540–1680," *Social History*, VI (1981), 281–300.

12 Franklin L. Ford, *Strasbourg in Transition, 1648–1789* (Cambridge, Mass., 1958), 5–6; 13; 91–94. For further details on the structures of courts and the distinctions between private and public legal matters, Mack Walker, *Johann Jakob Moser and the Holy Roman Empire of the German Nation* (Chapel Hill, N.C., 1981), 125–45; see also the bibliography cited in Dawson, *Oracles of the Law*, 148–262.

13 See Robert Barnsley Kershaw, "The Development of the Maryland Bar, 1715 to 1830: 'The Road to Riches and Ye Highest Honors,'" (Senior thesis, Princeton University, 1974); Alan F. Day, "Lawyers in Colonial Maryland, 1660–1715," *American Journal of Legal History*, XXII (1973), 145–63; Carol Van Voorst, "The Anglican Clergy in Colonial Maryland, 1692–1775," (Ph.D. dissertation, Princeton University, 1978).

14 Kessel, "Germans on the Maryland Frontier," 1981, 292–93; 316–19. Maryland boasted an anomalous early German political figure in Casparus Hermann, the son of the Bohemian immigrant to the New World, Augustin Hermann. But both Hermanns' careers as either wealthy proprietors of Bohemia Manor, or in Casparus' case, a figure of some importance in Cecil County's history, provide no paradigm for understanding the relationship of German-speaking peoples to the provincial bench and bar of Maryland. Charles Payson Mallory, "Ancient Families of Bohemia Manor," *Papers of the Historical Society of Delaware*, VII (1888), 11–23.

15 Bernard Bailyn, *The Origins of American Politics* (New York, 1970), 121–23; Clarence P. Gould, *The Land System in Maryland 1720–1765*, Johns Hopkins Studies in Historical and Political Science (Baltimore, Md., 1913), 86–88; Van Voorst, "Anglican Clergy," 267–82. For later details of German settlement, see Dieter Cunz, *The Maryland Germans: A History* (Princeton, N.J., 1948); for an intelligent perspective on the various types of writings available on the German immigration, see Kathleen Neils Conzen, "The Writing of German-American History," *Immigration History Newsletter*, XII (1980), 1–14, and her essay "The Germans" in Stephan Thernstrom, ed., *Harvard Encyclopedia of American Ethnic Groups* (Cambridge, Mass., 1980), 405–25; and Don Yoder's assessment of the Pennsylvania Germans, *ibid.*, 770–72.

16 Samuel Urlsperger, *Detailed Reports on the Salzburger Emigrants Who Settled in America . . .*, George Fenwick Jones, ed., with an introduction, Hermann J. Lacker, trans. (5 vols., Athens, Ga., 1968–80); R. A. Strobel, *The Salzburgers and Their Descendants . . .* (Baltimore, 1855), 110, citing Whitefield's 1738 letter after his visit; see also *Henry Newman's Salzburger Letterbooks*, George Fenwick Jones, ed. and trans. (Athens, Ga., 1966), 405, which mentions the Salzburgers and the "Country Courts of Salzburg" before their expulsion; see the introduction to Vol. III of the *Detailed Reports*, xix, on Boltzius' role as a judge.

[17] Cited in Charles C. Jones, *The Dead Towns of Georgia* (Athens, Ga., 1974), 47; see also Warren Grice and E. Merton Coulter, *Georgia Through Two Centuries* (3 vols., New York, 1965), I, 14–18, on the five Salzburgers elected as delegates to the Provincial Congress in Savannah, some of whom refused to participate in the Revolution (John Stirk, John Adam Treutlen, Jacob Waldhauer, John Florl, and Christopher Craemer).

[18] The Germans did have two justices of the peace, John Adam Treutlen and Jacob C. Waldhauer, who were sitting in the 1770s. However, when a dispute arose between pastors Triebner and Rabenhorst within the community, the Rabenhorst faction was led by Justice Treutlen. Heinrich Melchior Muhlenberg, the leader of the Lutherans in the colonies, was called in to mediate the dispute, found for the Ravenhorst faction, but could not entirely reconcile the parties involved. See Library of Congress, Manuscripts Division, "Records of the Jerusalem Lutheran Church, 1754–1800," Box 628, entries for "Minutes of a Conference, 1774." On Muhlenberg, see below.

[19] Journal of Francis Moore, 1736, cited in Walter G. Cooper, *The Story of Georgia* (4 vols., New York, 1938), I, 178.

[20] James Ettridge Callaway, *The Early Settlements of Georgia* (Athens, Ga., 1948), 40–41; Stephen F. Miller, *The Bench and Bar of Georgia* (2 vols., Philadelphia, 1858), II, Appendix, 369–78. Significantly, though some Salzburgers had been sent to the Provincial Congress in Savannah in 1774, the 25 men elected to serve in the Continental Congress included 10 lawyers, none connected with the German settlements. See Grice and Coulter, *Georgia Through Two Centuries*, I, 405–07.

[21] On South Carolina's bench and bar, see Hoyt P. Canady, "Gentlemen of the Bar: Lawyers in Colonial South Carolina" (Ph.D. dissertation, University of Tennessee, 1979), 27–42, 72–6, 99–136, 169–205; on the justices and their roles in the courts, Jo Anne McCormick, "Civil Procedure in the Camden Circuit Court, 1772–1790," in Herbert A. Johnson, ed., *South Carolina Legal History: Proceedings of the Reynolds Conference* (Spartanburg, S.C., 1980), 241–54; for a contemporary (and not complimentary) assessment of the S.C. justices, Richard J. Hooker, ed., *The Carolina Backcountry on the Eve of the Revolution: The Journal and Other Writings of Charles Woodmason, Anglican Itinerant* (Chapel Hill, N.C., 1953), 126–28, 211–12, 214–18, 238, 244, 274–5; on the Germans and their relationship to the bar, John Belton O'Neal, *Biographical Sketches of the Bench and Bar* (2 vols., Charleston, S.C., 1859), I, 329–37; II, 325–42, 589–95; on Felder, A. S. Salley, Jr., *The History of Orangeburg County, South Carolina* (Orangeburg, S.C., 1898), 257, 260–69, 276; O'Neall, *Bench and Bar*, II, 325–29.

[22] Richard Maxwell Brown, *The South Carolina Regulators* (Cambridge, Mass., 1963), 2, 19–20, 103, Appendix 145–47, 204–05, details the relationship among the Germans and Regulators and Moderators.

[23] Cited in Ernest H. Alderman, "The North Carolina Colonial Bar," *James Sprunt Historical Publications*, XI-XV (1911–16), 5–6; on the establishment of the courts and the influence of the Virginia institutions, see Paul M. McCain, *The County Court in North Carolina Before 1750* (Durham, N.C., 1954).

[24] The attempt to regulate lawyers, however, was apparently not very successful. The 1715 statute setting fees and restricting sheriffs and justices from practicing was repealed in 1746, and controversy attended attempts from then on into the 1750s to do something about rapacious lawyers. For the statute, see James Walter, William L. Saunders, Stephen B. Weeks, eds., *Colonial and State Records of North Carolina* (Raleigh, N.C., 1886–1914), XXIII, 86; on the later controversies surrounding lawyers, see James P. Whittenberg, "Planters, Merchants, and Lawyers: Social Change and the Origins of the North Carolina Regulation," *William and Mary Quarterly*, 3d Ser., XXXIV (1977), 215–38; Marvin L. Michael Kay, "The North Carolina Regulation, 1766–1776: A Class Conflict," in Alfred F. Young, ed., *The American Revolution: Explorations in the History of American Radicalism* (DeKalb, Ill., 1976), 71–123; A. Roger Ekirch, *"Poor Carolina": Society and Politics in North Carolina, 1729–1776* (Chapel Hill, N.C., 1981), 178–89.

[25] See Whittenberg, "Planters, Merchants, and Lawyers," 229–34.

²⁶ In general on the Moravians of Wachovia, see Kenneth G. Hamilton, "The Moravians and Wachovia," *North Carolina Historical Review*, XLIV (1967), 144–53; Jery L. Surratt, "The Role of Dissent in Community Evolution Among Moravians in Salem, 1772–1860," *ibid.*, LLI (1975), 235–55; information on officers and frequent visits of lawyers to the Moravian community compiled from Adelaide L. Fries, ed., *Records of the Moravians in North Carolina* (2 vols., Raleigh, N.C., 1922–25), I and II, *passim*. See also Jethro Rumple, *A History of Rowan County, North Carolina* (Baltimore, 1981); J. K. Rouse, *The North Carolina Picadillo* (Salisbury, N.C., 1966), 31–35, 55–58; minute books, Court of Quarter Sessions for relevant counties, North Carolina State Archives; Joseph R. Nixon, "The German Settlers in Lincoln County and Western North Carolina," in *James Sprunt Historical Publications* (Chapel Hill, N.C., 1912), 30–62.

²⁷ Fries, ed., *Records*, II, 875–76.

²⁸ *Ibid.*, I, 393.

²⁹ *Ibid.*, I, 457.

³⁰ William S. Powell, James K. Huhta, Thomas J. Farnham, compilers and editors, *The Regulators in North Carolina: A Documentary History 1759–1776* (Raleigh, N.C., 1971), 477, 155–57, petition for the governor's aid against lawyers and exorbitant fees; see also letter of Edmund Fanning to Fudge, 1 May 1778 with copies sent to Saxon and Cheek, 106–07; Tryon's *Journal* for August, 1768, 129; Mickeljohn's sermon reprinted, 170–84, the specific quotation at 179. The doctrine of *Obrigkeit* is the subject of a vast literature in German, especially since the 1930s.

³¹ A communication with Professor Whittenberg, College of William and Mary, saved me the arduous duty of completing this task.

³² See Brown, *South Carolina Regulators*, Appendix, 145–47, 204–05; Thomas H. Pope, *The History of Newberry County, South Carolina: Volume I, 1749–1860* (Columbia, S.C., 1973), 6–7, 25–33, 41, 62–65, 77–79; Appendix A, 287–302, which demonstrates that Germans were used as jurymen; Appendix D on officeholders (1785–1800), 303–08, which indicates that no justices, county judges, clerks, or sheriffs, except possibly Samuel Kenner, 1791–1800, justice of the peace. See 93, ff. on lawyers in Newberry Village after 1789 (21 names to 1832); one German name, John Bauskert.

³³ See Salley, *History of Orangeburg*, 217–18, 246–49, 260–76.

³⁴ Ibid., 285, letter of August 7, 1775, by Tennent and Drayton; see also August 9, 1775, 291–92; also August 16, 1775, Drayton to the Council of Safety, partially reprinted in Hooker, ed., *The Carolina Backcountry* (Part Three: the Regulator Documents), 189.

³⁵ For a general survey of the courts and the bar, Frank M. Eastman, *Courts and Lawyers of Pennsylvania: A History, 1623–1923* (4 vols., New York, 1922); for the colonial period, Vols. 1 and 2, with sketches of early lawyers and judges. On the westward migration patterns of the Germans, see Homer T. Rosenberger, "Migrations of the Pennsylvania Germans to Western Pennsylvania," *Western Pennsylvania Historical Magazine*, LIII (1970), 319–35; LIV (1971), 58–76, at notes 322, 327, 332; heads of family list for Bedford, 61. For migration in general, Don Yoder, ed., *Pennsylvania German Immigrants, 1709–1786: Lists Consolidated from Yearbooks of the Pennsylvania German Folklore Society* (Baltimore, Md., 1980), 1–10, 141.

³⁶ Osward Seidensticker, *The First Century of German Printing in America, 1728–1830* (Philadelphia, 1893), 3–5.

³⁷ Jerome H. Wood, Jr., *Connestoga Crossroads: Lancaster, Pennsylvania, 1730–1790* (Harrisburg, Pa., 1979), 17, 29–30, 174–77.

³⁸ E. Howard Blackburn and William H. Welfley, *History of Bedford and Somerset Counties, Pennsylvania*, William H. Koontz, ed. (3 vols., New York, 1906), I, 1–7, 71, 79.

³⁹ *Ibid.*, II, 47–63; 160–63; 438; (no author), *The Berlin Area: Berlin, Pennsylvania, 1777–1977* (Berlin, Pa., 1977), 99–100.

⁴⁰ Blackburn and Welfley, *History of Bedford*, II, "Bench and Bar," 408–37; *Civil List*, 438–47.

⁴¹ Klaus Wust, *The Virginia Germans* (Charlottesville, Va., 1969), 93–94 on the movement

of the Virginians back into Pennsylvania; on the Orange County group, 22–25, 124; W.
P. Huddle, *History of the Hebron Lutheran Church* (New Market, Va., 1908); William Edward Eisenberg, *The Lutheran Church in Virginia 1717–1962* (Roanoke, Va., 1967) 5–18, 482–84. On Hite, see Robert D. Mitchell, *Commercialism and Frontier: Perspectives on the Early Shenandoah Valley* (Charlottesville, Va., 1977), 28–30; Borden's letter reprinted in John Frederick Dorman, compiler, *Orange County, Virginia Deed Books 1 and 2, 1735–1738; Judgments, 1735* (Washington, D.C., 1961), 72–73.

    [42] Joseph Kellogg, "Court Records of Augusta County, Virginia," *National Genealogical Society Quarterly*, XXVII–XXIX (1939–41), 30–34; Joseph A. Waddell, *Annals of Augusta County, Virginia, from 1736 to 1871* (Staunton, Va., 1902), 47; John W. Wayland, *A History of Rockingham County, Virginia* (Dayton, Va., 1912), 38, 65–67; John W. Scholl, *The Scholl, Sholl, Shull Genealogy* (New York, 1930), 8–9. Lyman Chalkley, *Chronicles of the Scotch-Irish Settlement in Virginia* (3 vols., Baltimore, Md., 1965): Vol. 1 reprints the Augusta County Order Book from 1745; by the 1750s there were only two practising attorneys in the area. In a pamphlet, *Historical Sketch of Bedford County, Virginia, 1753–1907* (Lynchburg, Va., 1907), a list of attorneys qualified in the county court from 1754 yields (to 1820) 92 men with only two possibly German names, Michael Vanstarem, qualified 1799; William Skillern, 1798. Besides checking county court order books (available on microfilm from the Virginia State Library, Richmond, Archives Division), I have used the lists of justices of the peace compiled and available as "Justices of the Peace of Colonial Virginia, 1757–1775," *Bulletin of the Virginia State Library*, XIV (1921).

    [43] *Hallesche Nachrichten, or, Reports of the United German Evangelical Lutheran Congregations in North America, Specially in Pennsylvania*, W. J. Mann and B. M. Schmucker and W. Germann, eds., C. W. Schaeffer, trans. (2 vols., Reading, Pa., 1882), I, 188 (letter of Muhlenberg to Halle, Dec. 12, 1745).

    [44] *Ibid.*, 199. The prohibitions against taking a fellow Christian to court are in Matthew 18:15–16; I Corinthians 6:1–7.

    [45] *The Journals of Henry Melchior Muhlenberg in Three Volumes*, Theodore G. Tappert and John W. Doberstein, trans. (Philadelphia, 1942), I, 337, 338.

    [46] *Ibid.*, II, 63 (April 11, 1764).

    [47] *Ibid.*, I, 361–62 (July 17, 1753).

    [48] I am indebted to Professor Kermit Hall, University of Florida, for sharing with me his research on the composition of the benches in the southern jurisdictions to the Civil War. There were no Germans among the members of the appellate benches in the southern states, nor were there federal judges of German extraction. One exception was Isaac Pennybacker (Pennypacker) of remote Pennsylvania origins, who served on the U.S. district court for the Western District of Virginia, 1840–1845.

    [49] German population in proportion to the whole was as follows: 1/3 of Pennsylvania, 100,000 Germans in 1776 and over 120,000 by 1790; 8.7 percent of the entire U.S. population in 1790 (a conservative estimate which does not control for anglicized names), distributed at 33 percent in Pennsylvania, 12 percent in Maryland, 9 percent in New Jersey, 8 percent in New York, 6 percent in Virginia, and in the Carolinas, between 3 and 5 percent with 1/6 of the population of Georgia (then at 45,000 persons). However, in western counties of Virginia (Frederick, Berkeley, Rockingham, and Page), the proportions were 30 to 60 percent; in western North Carolina, 23 percent. See Rosenberger, "Migrations," 321; Conzen, "Germans," 407; Mitchell, *Commercialism*, 42–55; Merrins, *Col. N.C.*, 61; Davis, *Fledgling Province*, 16; Coleman, *Colonial Georgia*, 224.

The "Route to Hell" Retraced:
The Impact of Popular Election
on the Southern Appellate Judiciary,
1832–1920

KERMIT L. HALL

THE MOST SUSTAINED development of popular partisan election of state appellate court judges stretched from the Jacksonian era of the 1830s to the demise of Progressivism during World War I. Mississippi in 1832 was the first state to elect all of its judges. After New York adopted the practice in 1846 every new state entering the Union did so as well.[1] The movement spread more gradually in the South than the North, and, in some southern states, it followed an oscillating course of adoption, recision, and readoption. During the 1850s Alabama, Kentucky, Louisiana, Maryland, Missouri, Tennessee, Texas, and Virginia mandated the election of judges to their highest appellate courts. During the tumult of Reconstruction, Louisiana, Virginia, Mississippi, and Texas abolished the elective system, but Arkansas and North Carolina embraced it. So too did Florida and Georgia somewhat later. Texas in 1876 and then Louisiana and Mississippi in the early twentieth century returned to the elective system. Only South Carolina clung throughout the period to appointment by joint vote of the legislature. Of the former states of the Confederacy in 1920 only South Carolina and Virginia did not elect their high court judges. In sharp contrast, throughout this period states in the North steadfastly retained the popular partisan election of judges.[2]

Despite the pervasiveness of this legal reform, scholars know relatively little about it. As James Willard Hurst observed three decades ago, and as is still the case today: "We have no broad historical studies concerning the selection of judges outside the great

cities . . . nor have we studies which single out the elective judiciary."[3] Coming to terms with this neglected phase of American
legal history raises questions about its variable impact throughout
the nation, especially differences between the South and North.
An assumption that the South had distinctive legal and political
institutions underlies much of the writing on southern history.[4]
Characteristics long associated with southern culture, especially
race, the development of post-Reconstruction one-party Democratic hegemony, and an oligarchical social order based on powerful kinship connections, may have uniquely shaped the election
and composition of the southern appellate judiciary.[5]

From 1832 to 1920, lawyer-politicians in the North and the
South dominated the state constitutional conventions and their all-
important committees on the judiciary. These reform-minded
lawyers, as Charles Cook and others have argued, pursued primarily professional and secondarily political goals.[6] Law reform,
despite all of its hoopla, was a limited affair. In the state constitutional conventions of the mid-nineteenth century, lawyer-delegates expected to professionalize the bench by bringing popular
will to bear on the influence exercised by party leaders over judicial patronage. Subsequent generations of lawyer-reformers in
the late nineteenth and early twentieth centuries chafed at what
they believed to be the limited successes of their predecessors.
They sought simultaneously to perpetuate the positive effects of
popular will on the selection process while reducing the continued influence of party leaders through the adoption of the direct
party primary and non-partisan judicial elections.[7] Throughout
this ninety-year period proponents and opponents of popular
election—North and South—returned again and again to four issues: the quality, accountability, independence, and social accessibility of the appellate judiciary.[8] The debate over these issues
discloses the expectations held by lawyer-delegates above and below the Mason-Dixon Line, but words reveal little about whether
the social and political differences that separated North from South
produced distinctive judiciaries.

Between 1832 and 1920, 552 judges served on the highest appellate courts of the eleven states of the one-time Confederacy and

Maryland.[9] This essay compares the characteristics of these judges' careers and, where applicable, their elections with data on 152 judges elected to the highest appellate courts of the Midwest from 1861 to 1899 and on 294 judges appointed to the federal district and circuit courts between 1829 and 1899.[10] Together the data reveal that on the issue of quality, southern and midwestern judges were similar, but on the matters of accountability, independence, and social accessibility, the southern appellate judiciary was distinctive.

Quality

Delegates to southern constitutional conventions sought to foster judicial quality. The lawyer-delegates who formulated the judiciary articles had professional reasons to place the most competent persons available on the appellate courts. They agreed on what constituted quality, but they disagreed about how best to promote it. They wanted honest, upright, and even-tempered judges possessed of demonstrated technical legal ability gained through education, training, and prior judicial service. They also agreed that party politics presented an obstacle to the fulfillment of these goals.

Disagreement arose, however, over how best to reduce the dangers of partisanship in the selection process. Critics of popular election charged that qualified lawyers would not stand for office because of the uncertainty of tenure and the expenses and indignities of the necessary canvassing. They also stressed that popular election allowed party organizations to repay political debts earned by loyal supporters.[11] "In an elective judiciary," a Louisiana delegate argued in 1864, "it makes little difference in the result whether we have a man of great mind and a high order of talent . . . if he runs against the political party which happens to be in power, no matter what the character of his competitor, he will be defeated."[12] Proponents of popular election rejected this view. They insisted that popular election would remove judges from partisan patronage struggles waged by governors and legislators.[13]

Judicial quality is an elusive concept. Quality, in a sense, remains in the eye of the beholder. An analysis of judicial opinions alone does not offer a sure grasp on these evanescent abilities.[14] For example, whereas one recent historian of slave law has concluded that most southern appellate judges suffered from "cognitive limitations," another has argued that these same judges had an impressive ability to adapt tort law to the exigencies of the system.[15] Contemporary evaluations of judges also pose problems. Southern Democratic lawyers following Reconstruction blasted the quality of Republican judges, yet recent historical scholarship has found much to praise in the efforts of these so-called carpetbaggers.[16]

Nevertheless, it is possible to measure some of the characteristics which contemporaries associated with judicial quality. Data drawn from biographical sources reveal how, if at all, various methods of selection resulted in different levels of academic and legal education, prior judicial service, and political activism on the southern appellate bench.

Simple statistical tests applied to these data reveal no meaningful association between method of selection and particular indicators of quality. Judges with formal higher education, formal legal education, and previous judicial service reached the appellate bench whether popularly elected, appointed by a governor, or selected by a legislature.[17] The absence of any meaningful association leads to the inference that specific methods of selection had slight influence on these characteristics of quality.

The South had the best formally educated appellate judiciary in the nation.[18] Almost three-fifths (57.6%) (Table 1) of its judges had graduated from a college or university. Their level of educational achievement more fully resembled that of the lower federal judiciary than it did their midwestern counterparts; about three-fifths (60.7%) of lower federal judges, compared with two-fifths (41.7%) of midwestern judges, earned a degree in higher education.[19]

Provincialism typified the higher educational experience of southern appellate judges. While almost three-fourths (72.1%) of them attended college in the state of their service, only about one-half (51.2%) of the midwestern and about one-third (36.2%) of

Table 1
Method of Selection by Judges'
Highest Level of Academic Education
1832–1920[1]
(Adjusted Percent)[2]

Method of Selection		Level of Education				Total Percent
	N	Grad College	Attnd College	Other	Little/None	
Southern State	(509)					
Pop. Elect	228	56.8	12.3	27.1	.4	
Appointed	146	58.3	14.5	22.4	.7	
Legis. Elect	130	58.5	8.9	25.9	2.9	
Midwestern State[3]	139	41.7	17.3	40.2	.7	
Federal[4]	351	60.7	8.5	29.9	.9	
Total Percent		57.6	11.7	29.6	1.1	
Number	(999)	(576)	(117)	(296)	(10)	100.0
Missing Cases	(79)					

[1] Data on midwestern judges for years 1861–1899, and data for federal judges, 1789–1899.
[2] All percentages in subsequent tables are on an adjusted basis.
[3] All midwestern judges popularly elected.
[4] All federal district and circuit judges appointed.

lower federal judges did likewise. Federal judges as a whole most often had received cosmopolitan educations in Ivy League institutions. Southern and midwestern appellate judges seldom (9.3% and 14.7%) attended these universities, but more than two-fifths (43.4%) of the lower federal judiciary had done so.

The persistent provincialism of the state appellate judiciary also appeared in its legal training. During these years most judges trained for the legal profession by reading law in the office of an

Table 2
**Method of Selection by Judges'
Highest Level of Legal Education
1832–1920**

Method of Selection	N	Level of Education			Total Percent
		Grad or Attnd Law School	Read Law	Other/None	
Southern State	(507)				
Pop. Elect	230	29.6	61.9	8.5	
Appointed	145	22.3	67.8	9.9	
Legis. Elect	132	10.9	78.8	10.3	
Midwestern State	138	23.9	76.1	—	
Federal[1]	252	30.1	69.9	—	
Total Percent		24.4	70.4	5.2	100.0
Number	(897)	(219)	(632)	(46)	
Missing Cases	(143)				

[1] Data on federal judges are for period 1829 to 1899. The inclusion of earlier data, given the few number of law schools, would have been misleading.

attorney or judge; seven-tenths (70.4%) (Table 2) of them entered the legal profession in this manner. The incidence of formal legal education climbed during the late nineteenth and early twentieth centuries as more and more law schools opened their doors. Yet as late as 1920 less than two-fifths (37.9%) of all state judges had received a law school education.[20] When state appellate judges did attend law school they tended to go to institutions in their states, although several southern judges also attended the famous Cumberland and Transylvania Law Schools. Southern appellate judges

Table 3
Method of Selection by Judges'
Elected Political Experience
1832–1920

Method of Selection				Nature of Experience						Total Percent
	N	Legis.	Judicial & Legal	Exec.	1+2	1+3	2+3	1,2+3	None	
Southern State	(507)									
Pop. Elect	234	24.6	21.6	2.1	26.3	1.3	1.7	2.5	19.1	
Appointed	151	40.0	14.2	3.2	17.4	1.3	.6	1.3	19.4	
Legis. Elect	134	49.3	10.3	—	18.4	6.6	—	.7	13.2	
Midwestern State	136	7.4	39.0	1.5	29.4	2.2	6.6	5.9	8.1	
Federal[1]	216	26.8	19.4	2.8	23.6	4.6	.5	1.8	20.4	
Total Percent		29.3	21.0	2.0	23.5	3.1	1.7	2.5	17.0	100.0
Number	(871)	(254)	(182)	(18)	(205)	(27)	(15)	(22)	(148)	
Missing Cases	(169)									

[1] Data only for period 1861–1899.

seldom strayed outside their section for legal training at one of the prestigious Ivy League institutions; less than one-tenth (9.7%) of them and only about one-fifth (20.3%) of midwestern judges had such an educational experience. Federal district and circuit court judges, on the other hand, had more cosmopolitan legal educations; fully two-fifths (41.2%) of them had attended an Ivy League law school.

State appellate judges' public careers reinforced their educational provincialism. Political and judicial experience on the local level complemented one another. Regardless of jurisdiction or section, the judges' quest for public office was a way of life; about four-fifths (81.15%) (Table 3) of southern and federal (79.9%) judges had held elected public office compared with nine-tenths

Table 4
**Method of Selection by Judges'
Highest Level of Previous Judicial
Service, 1832–1920**

Method of Selection	Highest Level of Previous Judicial Service					Total Percent
	N	Local	State	Federal/ Confed.[1]	None	
Southern State	(529)					
Pop. Elect	236	56.2	1.4	.8	41.6	
Appointed	156	39.9	1.0	2.0	57.1	
Legis. Elect	137	52.4	1.6	.7	45.3	
Midwestern State	136	65.4	1.5	.7	32.4	
Federal[2]	391	23.3	15.7	16.0	44.9	
Total Percent		42.0	6.6	6.5	44.9	100.0
Number	(1056)	(444)	(70)	(69)	(473)	
Missing Cases	(22)					

[1] Includes previous service on the federal territorial bench.
[2] Data for 1820–1899.

(90.9%) of midwestern judges. This political activism surely strengthened the judges' awareness of and commitment to the broad values of the states in which they served.

Political and judicial careers were compatible. Midwestern judges had the highest incidence of prior judicial service; more than two-thirds (67.6%) (Table 4) of them had served in a prior judicial capacity, compared with about one-half (52.4%) of southern and two-fifths (44.2%) of federal judges. The prevalence of judicial experience among midwestern judges reflected the stronger commitment in that section to partisan, popular election of lower court judges. This practice fostered a narrow career path for would-be midwestern appellate judges. While they concentrated their political activism in judicial and public legal careers, southern appellate judges most frequently developed their elected political careers in state legislatures. About two-fifths (38.6%) of southern judges had previously won elected judicial or public legal service, but more than double that number—four-fifths (80.0%)—of midwestern judges had such service. Based on campaigns for a lower court post, therefore, midwestern judges were far more likely than their southern counterparts to assume a gladitorial role in seeking an appellate judgeship.

Particular schemes of judicial selection had nothing to do with the quality of the appellate judiciary—North or South. Popular election, gubernatorial appointment, and legislative election produced judges with essentially similar qualitative characteristics. The lawyers in the state constitutional conventions who fashioned the articles treating the selection of judges shared an apparent consensus on the issue of quality. They simply had no wish to adopt any scheme that promised to make appellate advocacy more difficult by bringing unqualified judges to the bench.[21] That same concern ensured that appellate judges were aware of the political and legal contours of their states through previous experience.

Within the broadly similar backgrounds of the southern and midwestern judges there was an important difference in career patterns. Successful aspirants for high judicial office in the Midwest had followed a narrow career path that rewarded prior elected judicial and public legal service. These posts were an apprenticeship for subsequent higher judicial service. Southern appellate judges had more diverse public careers that included often extensive legislative experience. These differences suggest that matters of judicial accountability and independence rather than quality distinguished the impact of popular election in the Midwest and the South.

Accountability and Independence

From 1832 to 1920 advocates and opponents of popular judicial election clashed over two problems: the nature of judicial accountability and the extent of judicial independence.[22] Proponents of judicial elections argued that judges should remain sensitive to the social and political values of the communities they served, that they should be socialized into a judicial role that balanced community and professional values, that they should accept limits on their independence as a necessary function of democratic government, and that they should reflect a healthy pluralism in their social and career backgrounds. On the other hand, opponents contended that the method of judicial selection should keep the judiciary sensitive to the values of the legal culture—impartiality, due process, and technical legal pleading—and that judges should be socialized into roles that instilled an appreciation for these values. As Stephen Wasby has argued about contemporary America, the historical issue of judicial accountability turned on questions of whether judges would be more responsive to legal and professional or popular constituencies.[23]

The meaningful exercise of judicial accountability through popular election requires a sensitive, active, and informed electorate.[24] Two sets of conditions influenced the abilities of southerners and midwesterners to hold the appellate judiciary accountable. The first involved the structure of each section's politics; the second were constitutional and statutory provisions that either dealt specifically with judicial elections or, more generally, the conduct of judicial elections as part of the electoral process. Because these conditions differed in North and South, so too did levels of judicial accountability and independence.

The character of southern politics diminished the possibilities of holding appellate judges popularly accountable. Although the section had a robust two-party system in the antebellum years, it decayed during the post-Civil War period into what Morgan Kousser has termed a "reactionary revolution" of single-party Democratic hegemony.[25] Wholesale disenfranchisement of blacks and poor whites eliminated first the Republican and then the Populist parties as competitive threats. A sharp decline in voter turnout followed. These developments subverted the meaning of accountability since, as students of judicial elections have argued, party identification provides the single most important cue in voting.[26] Without a choice, of course, the cue itself became meaningless.

A host of constitutional provisions also influenced the accountability and independence of the appellate judiciary. The most important of these strictures involved length of tenure, staggered
terms of service, timing of elections, ballot form, and the power
of governors to fill vacancies.[27]

These provisions had contradictory consequences. Some of
them made the judiciary potentially more accountable and less independent. As judicial elections grew in popularity, tenure during good behavior waned. Even in states that retained gubernatorial appointment or legislative selection the practice of limited
terms of service took hold. Only one-tenth (11.2%) of all southern
appellate judges enjoyed tenure during good behavior; throughout the South after the mid-1850s the term of service ranged from
six to fifteen years.[28] As states shifted methods of judicial selection they invariably provided for staggered terms of office and this,
combined with the practice of filling vacancies for the unexpired
portion of a full term, meant that about three-fifths (59.1%) of all
judges not appointed with tenure for good behavior had initial
terms of service shorter than the constitutionally-mandated term.

Other constitutional and statutory provisions made the judiciary less accountable and more independent. During the 1850s
and 1860s southern states that elected their judges tried to keep
the process free from party politics by holding judicial elections
at times other than the general election. This practice declined
during the 1860s in favor of election dates which coincided with
balloting for other state-wide offices.[29] Thus, of the 239 elections
for which data are available, only one-tenth (10.4%) occurred at
the same time as the presidential contest. Until the mid-1890s
parties and individual candidates had responsibility for preparation of ballots. This practice essentially eliminated split-ticket
voting and meant that voters could only reject a candidate by
striking through his name on the ballot. Although Progressive reformers in most southern states by the early twentieth century had
established state responsibility for providing a general party-col-
umn ballot, disenfranchisement and the direct party primary subverted the popular basis of this reform.[30]

Because the character of southern politics and the constitutional provisions governing voting in judicial elections varied from

state to state, so too did levels of accountability. Yet a discernible pattern emerged: states on the South's periphery exercised the greatest degree of popular accountability over the judiciary.[31]

Uncontested judicial elections occurred most frequently in the Deep South. Of those elections for which data are available, more than three-fifths (61.5%) (Table 5) were uncontested.[32] Mississippi was the only exception. But since that state abandoned popular election in 1868 and did not readopt it until 1914, the more than two-thirds (68.4%) of contested judicial elections in it occurred during the competitive, two-party antebellum era.[33] When Mississippi resumed the practice of electing its appellate judges it did so under the terms of the all-white party primary. In Mississippi and elsewhere in the Black Belt the white primary and the generally late adoption of popular election combined to drive conflict over staffing the state appellate bench into the Democratic party. This eliminated competition and made lawyers within the Democratic party the judiciary's principal constituency.

Elsewhere in the South the incidence of contested judicial elections increased significantly. About eighty percent (79.1%) of all appellate court elections were contested in non-Black Belt states, and this level approached that reached in Ohio (98.0%), a representative midwestern state.[34] Contested elections, however, did not mean competitive elections. The intensity of competition, more than any other single variable, differentiated voting for judges in the South from elections in Ohio. Voters throughout the South decided only one-quarter (25.9%) of all judicial elections by five or fewer percentage points, while in Ohio more than three-quarters (76.2%) of all judicial elections were competitive. Even North Carolina, the southern state with the strongest tradition of participatory democracy and two-party competition, decided only about one-half (52.4%) of its judicial elections on a competitive basis.[35] The vigorous two-party system of Ohio promoted competition and heightened accountability. The single-party politics of the South, although beset by regional exceptions, had the opposite effect.

Levels of judicial independence also varied between the two sections. Historically, the western legal tradition has tipped the

Table 5
State of Judicial Election by
Level of Competition, 1832–1920[1]

State		Level of Competition			Total Percent
	N	uncontested	uncompetitive[2]	competitive	
Alabama	(22)	72.7	22.7	4.6	
Arkansas	(21)	52.4	28.6	19.0	
Florida	(7)	85.7	14.3	—	
Georgia	(9)	88.9	11.1	—	
Louisiana	(9)	100.0	—	—	
Mississippi	(19)	31.6	31.6	36.8	
Texas	(27)	18.5	66.7	14.8	
N. Carolina	(21)	23.8	23.8	52.4	
Tennessee	(30)	20.0	63.3	16.7	
Maryland	(40)	22.5	30.0	47.5	
Ohio	(54)	2.0	21.8	76.2	
Total Percent		39.5	34.6	25.9	100.0
Number	(205)	81	71	53	
Missing Cases	(34)				

SOURCE: see note 32.
  [1] Election returns are unavailable for all elections in Virginia and for scattered elections in Arkansas (11), Georgia (5), Louisiana (9), North Carolina (1), and Maryland (1).
  [2] An uncompetitive election was one in which the winner gained more than 55 percent of the vote.

balance in favor of insulating judges from politics and popular will. The rise of popular election and limited terms of office constituted an attempt to push the balance back in the other direction. Rapid turnover among judges diminishes the institutional cohesiveness, continuity of operations, and autonomy of courts. The independence of the judiciary, therefore, touches both the ability of judges to exercise their power and the institutional vitality of appellate courts.[36] The length of southern appellate judges' careers and the reasons for their termination of office reveal that they enjoyed relatively greater independence than did their midwestern counterparts.

Elected rather than appointed southern judges had a statistically greater persistence on the bench.[37] Moreover, the strength of this relationship increased as the term of service of elected judges increased.[38] An elected judge in the South averaged 10.2 years (Table 6) of service, while appointed judges averaged only 5.4 years. Southern elected judges had on the average two years greater longevity than did midwestern judges, although judges in both sections lagged significantly behind the average 18.2 years of service by federal judges. The diminished ability of popular election to hold southern judges accountable nourished these same judges' independence.

The judges' reasons for leaving office also underscore the greater emphasis on judicial independence in the South. Southern appellate and lower federal court judges most frequently left the bench (Table 7) because of resignation and death. Judicial removals accounted for about one-tenth (7.4%) of all vacancies in the South, and these occurred during the era of the Civil War and Reconstruction. The independence of southern appellate courts ebbed significantly during these years. Midwestern judges, in contrast, escaped removal from office, but the electorate in that section held a tighter rein over judges seeking reelection; about one-fifth (18.2%) of these judges failed to win either renomination or reelection, compared with slightly more than one-twentieth (6.9%) of southern judges. Furthermore, midwestern judges more frequently refused to seek reelection at the expiration of their terms than did southern judges, suggesting that the competitive, popular and partisan character of midwestern politics weighed more heavily on judges in that section.

Governors in both sections had important roles in structuring the composition of the elected appellate judiciary. Southern governors made a total of 115 interim appointments to the southern bench, and 63 of these occurred in states that relied on popular election. These interim appointees subsequently fared well at the polls; only one-tenth (9.5%) suffered defeat. In the Midwest governors appointed more judges (33.3% to 26.8%), but they subsequently enjoyed less electoral success. More than one-quarter (26.9%) of all interim appointees in the Midwest lost election, and interim appointees constituted almost three-fifths (58.3%) of all

Table 6
Method of Selection by Judges'
Tenure in Office, 1832–1920

Method of Selection		Years of Service				Total Percent
	N	4 or less	5–10	11–20	21 and above	
Southern State	(541)					
Pop. Elect	235	18.8	33.6	29.9	17.7	
Appointed	168	53.3	25.1	16.5	5.4	
Legis. Elect	138	29.7	25.4	31.1	13.8	
Midwestern State	153	20.3	36.6	30.7	12.4	
Federal[1]	396	19.4	20.2	31.3	29.1	
Total Percent		26.1	26.6	28.5	18.8	100.0
Number	(1090)	(285)	(290)	(311)	(204)	
Missing Cases	(11)					

[1] Data for period 1829–1899.

judges defeated for election in that section. The southern electorate exercised less vigilance, and it also granted governors greater discretion in composing the appellate bench than in the Midwest.

The weakened spring of democratic government resulting from single-party politics and massive disenfranchisement affected the accountabilty and independence of southern appellate judges. The electorates of the upper and lower South did exercise different levels of accountability over the judiciary, but throughout the South the elective regime, which had taken firm hold by the early twentieth century, promoted rather than retarded the persistence of appellate judges. The politics of the New South enhanced the

Table 7
**Method of Selection by Judges'
Reasons for Termination, 1832–1920**

Method of Selection	Reason for Termination						
	N	Removed	Death	Resigned	Change Selection Method	Refused To Run	Not Elec. Not Nominated
Southern State	(537)						
Pop. Elect	235	7.6	27.4	48.1	2.5	3.8	9.8
Appointed	165	6.6	8.4	53.6	15.1	7.2	8.5
Legis. Elect	137	8.0	29.2	54.7	7.3	—	—
Midwestern State	132	—	21.2	25.7	—	35.8	18.2
Federal[1]	217	—	41.3	58.7	—	—	—
Total Percent		4.5	26.7	49.7	4.6	7.6	6.9
Number	(886)	(40)	(237)	(440)	(41)	(67)	(61)
Missing Cases	(35)						

[1] Data on federal judges only for period 1861–1899.

institutional stability and cohesiveness of these southern appellate courts, but it also further isolated the appellate judiciary from popular control.

Access

Differences in social accessibility complemented these distinctive levels of judicial accountability. The concept of social accessibility has two meanings. First, it refers to the variable impact of more or less democratic methods of judicial selection on the social composition of the bench. Second, it involves the extent to which these methods of selection promoted traditional "chains of opportunity" through ties of blood and marriage.[39] For legal systems, the persistence of local connections, close family ties, and entrenched social elites usually means that innovation suffers.[40]

Historians differ sharply over the social accessibility of the state appellate judiciary. Mark Tushnet has argued that state appellate judges—apparently in all sections of the nation—were drawn from the ranks of "big capital" and were "affiliated by marriage and association with leading members of the capitalist class."[41] James Willard Hurst and Lawrence M. Friedman, while also ignoring geographical distinctions, have reached still other conclusions. Hurst emphasized the increasing social openness of the bench during the nineteenth century; Friedman insisted that judges were most frequently drawn from "good, solid middle-class backgrounds"—they were "elected,—not elite."[42] More recently, A. G. Roeber, in his study of Virginia's early legal profession, has speculated that the Country tradition, which perpetuated a class of powerful lawyers based on family oligarchies rather than talent, persisted well into the nineteenth century.[43]

Southern judges came from social backgrounds of marginal diversity; as Friedman has argued, most judges had roots in prosperous and ambitious families. Method of selection and section of service had no significant association with the judges' social origins.[44] By late twentieth-century standards these persons might best be described as middle class, but by nineteenth-century perceptions the nearly two-thirds (67.2%) (Table 8) of judges from "prominent" origins were in essence members at birth of the upper-middle class. They were the sons of successful professionals, planters, merchants, and bankers in the South.[45] Yet diversity existed; the remaining one-third of all southern judges were about equally from elite (15.0%) and modest (17.7%) origins. The sons of the powerful and the almost powerless did meet on the southern bench; to an important degree this socially top-heavy institution permitted some openness in the recruitment of judges. The courts of the Midwest and the federal government followed a similar pattern. The social bases of the South's appellate judiciary paralleled that of the nation as a whole.

Table 8
Method of Selection by Judges'
Social-Class Origins, 1832–1920

Method of Selection		Social Class Origin [1]			Total Percent
	N	Elite	Prominent	Modest	
Southern State	(453)				
Pop. Elect	211	12.8	72.0	15.2	
Appointed	127	15.7	63.8	20.5	
Legis. Elect	115	16.5	66.1	17.4	
Midwestern State	127	18.0	68.6	13.4	
Federal [2]	322	23.6	63.0	13.4	
Total Percent		18.3	66.4	15.3	100.0
Number	(902)	(165)	(599)	(138)	
Missing Cases	(188)				

[1] The bases for categorizing judges' social-class origins is discussed in Hall, "The Children of the Cabins: The Lower Federal Judiciary, Modernization, and the Political Culture, 1789–1899," *Northwestern University Law Review*, 75 (Oct. 1980): 423–71, esp. 466–71.

[2] Data on federal judiciary for period 1789 to 1899.

The existence of this limited social accessibility does not explain why some lawyers with essentially well-to-do backgrounds became judges and others with similar social origins did not. The concept of "chains of opportunity" provides an explanation.[46]

As persons move along career paths, formal institutional and informal personal connections create possibilities for advancement. No career develops entirely through self-choice; certain chains of opportunity make advancement possible. Supposedly, the absence in the United States of formal legal requirements for appellate judgeships has prevented the development of an institutionalized class of judges.[47] Party and professional associations have most often framed the selection process, and judicial aspirants have actively participated in these groups as an essential step toward the bench. Judges from modest social origins in both sections frequently engaged in partisan and professional activities as a means of compensating for their backgrounds.[48] Yet for many southern judges the Country tradition of advancement through chains of opportunity created by kinship remained and even grew in importance.

Ties of blood and marriage connected judges on the same southern state benches. Political activism among the general population of the South was unique; judicial office-holding was a rarity, a condition that makes these kinship ties all the more impressive. One-third (37.2%) (Figure 1) of all southern judges had kinfolk on the same state bench, triple the incidence for midwestern judges.[49] While modest levels of kinship ties remained constant in the Midwest, the incidence of family connections in the South followed an irregular course. These connections dropped during Reconstruction, with the influx of Republicans and carpetbaggers unrelated to the old or future power structure, and then rose quickly and steadily from the 1880s through the early twentieth century. The political redemption of the South had the impact of reformulating a traditional pattern of office-holding based on family alliances. This development, moreover, coincided with the full adoption of popular election of judges. The southern judiciary remained after Reconstruction firmly within the Country tradition described by Roeber.

Judges above and below the Mason-Dixon Line did share the common experience of family connections to persons with judicial service on any bench. The formulation of a judicial career apparently depended on these kinship connections. Of the southern appellate judiciary, about two-thirds (61.1%) (Table 9) had kinfolk who were also judges. These connections were marginally less significant on the lower federal courts (57.9%) and midwestern appellate bench (49.1%).[50] A strong statistical association existed in the South between appellate judges with kinfolk in public ser-

Figure 1
Incidence of Judges with Kinship Connections on the Same Bench, 1832–1920

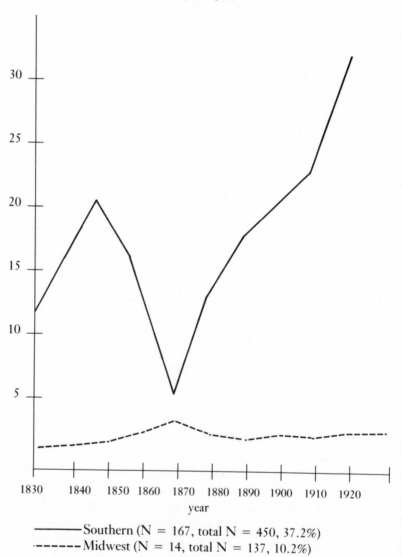

————— Southern (N = 167, total N = 450, 37.2%)
------- Midwest (N = 14, total N = 137, 10.2%)

Table 9
Method of Selection by Judges with
Kinfolk in Any Judgeship, 1832–1920

Method of Selection		Level of Kinship Connection					Total Percent
	N	(1) Blood	(2) Marriage	(3) D.K.	1,2 + 3	None	
Southern State	(496)						
Pop. Elect	227	14.4	15.9	7.6	19.8	42.3	
Appointed	144	20.1	12.5	3.5	14.6	49.3	
Legis. Elect	125	22.4	19.2	7.2	30.4	20.8	
Midwestern State	136	21.3	6.6	5.1	16.9	50.9	
Federal[1]	366	22.9	11.5	6.3	17.2	42.1	
Total Percent		20.4	12.9	6.0	19.0	41.7	100.0
Number	(998)	(203)	(129)	(60)	(190)	(416)	
Missing Cases	(105)						

[1] Data on federal judges for period 1799–1899.

vice and judicial office-holding. Differing methods of selection had no discernible impact in democratizing the selection process by bringing to the bench persons without such connections.[51] Regardless of the method of selection and section, most appellate judges apparently linked their careers to a chain of opportunity fashioned by fellow kinfolk who provided at least a model of and an incentive toward pursuit of judicial service. This pattern of career development necessarily narrowed accessibility to the bench.

Despite some limited diversity in the social foundations of the appellate judiciary, two themes remain constant: the importance of class and kinship. Of these themes class remained constant across sectional lines; the sons of the upper-middle class filled the appellate bench. The pervasiveness and intensity of kinship connections, especially after Reconstruction, made the southern appellate bench distinctive. The process of political and social redemption in the New South spurred the reinstitution of the Country tradition. This development occurred despite the South's movement toward popular judicial election. In terms of democratic practices, but not democratic forms, the accessibility of the appellate bench was a major casualty of southern social structure, especially in the era of New South politics.

Conclusion

"It is easy to take the route to hell," Robert Toombs warned the 1877 Georgia constitutional convention, "but few people ever returned from it." The former Confederate Secretary of State feared that popular election of the South's highest appellate judges would "forever pollute" the courts. Blatant racism propelled some of this hostility; Toombs, like other conservative southerners, feared that former Unionists and Republicans would use "fraud and force" to manipulate the votes of blacks for judges.[52] Yet Toombs, who persuaded the convention to reject popular election, spoke as more than a racist demagogue. He trusted in a vision of judicial accountability that stressed the importance of professional legal rather than popular constituencies. Toombs coupled with this a belief that the South should enshrine through an appointive judicial selection process the traditional values of social and political deference.[53]

Qualitatively, Toombs' fears proved groundless. Judges in the South and the Midwest had similar levels of academic achievement, legal training, prior judicial service, political activity, and social origins. Only in the provincial educational preparation of southern judges did the two judiciaries differ qualitatively.

Toombs also failed to appreciate the tenaciousness with which the values and style of southern politics and society shaped the appellate judiciary, regardless of the method of selection. The enshrinement of white political rule made southern democracy a contradiction in terms; it rendered the appellate judiciary substantially less accountable to and more independent of the population it served. As C. Vann Woodward observed years ago, Progressive reform in the South and the quest for white supremacy reinforced one another.[54] Single-party Democratic politics and the apparent reassertion of the Country tradition in southern society after Reconstruction restricted the popular accountability and social accessibility of the appellate bench. While important differences separated the upper from the lower South, southern judicial elections as a whole remained, in comparison with the Midwest, often uncontested and invariably non-competitive.

Southern politics and society combined to fashion a distinctive judicial culture. The values of that culture emphasized independence, prior education and training, provincialism, deference to authority, and respect for ties of blood and marriage. The greater stress in the South on judicial independence, as opposed to the midwestern commitment to judicial accountability, made the courts of the South more stable, cohesive, and entrenched.

The implications of this distinctive southern judicial culture for the relative prestige and legal innovativeness of these courts remains unclear. Certainly, students of southern legal history need to know more about the character of appellate justice, if for no other reason than the existing evidence is contradictory. Some studies suggest that at the beginning of the twentieth century many southern appellate courts enjoyed both national prestige and a reputation for innovation.[55] Others stress that the distinctive elements in the South's judicial culture itself pushed these courts toward mediocrity. After 1870 the appellate courts of the Northeast and the Midwest, with their twin commitments to legal professionalism based on merit and sensitivity to the problems of democratic legitimacy, set the pace for innovation in the law. The frequency with which judges throughout the nation cited the opinions of judges from these courts far exceeded the attention given to the work of southern appellate judges.[56] If this latter view is correct, then both moderate southern legal reformers, with their faith in the power of popular will to enhance the courts, and conservative spokesmen such as Toombs, with their trust in legal professionalism, misjudged the intensely corrosive character of traditional southern values on appellate justice. For better or worse the southern appellate judiciary was less the creature of a particular method of selection and more the image of the social order it served.

NOTES

The author acknowledges the helpful comments and criticisms offered by Charles Mc-Curdy, Maxwell Bloomfield, David R. Colburn, and Bertram Wyatt-Brown.
    [1] The relevant historical literature is discussed in Kermit L. Hall, "The Judiciary on Trial: State Constitutional Reform and the Rise of the Elected Judiciary," *The Historian*, XLVI (May 1983), 112–32. On the developments in each of the states see Evan Haynes, *The Selection and Tenure of Judges* (New York, 1944), 101–35.
    [2] Haynes, *The Selection and Tenure of Judges*, 101–35. Massachusetts was the most notable exception to the pattern in the North. On the highest appellate courts of the South, see Ralph Wooster, *The People in Power: Courthouse and Statehouse in the Lower South, 1850–1860* (Knoxville, Tenn., 1969), 64–80, and Wooster, *Politicians, Planters, and Plain Folk: Courthouse and Statehouse in the Upper South, 1850–1860* (Knoxville, Tenn., 1975), 75–96.
    [3] James Willard Hurst, *The Growth of American Law: The Lawmakers* (Boston, 1950), 173.
    [4] On the general problem of southern distinctiveness see C. Vann Woodward, *American Counterpoint: Slavery and Racism in the North-South Dialogue* (Boston, 1971), esp. 8–9 and on the nature of the southern legal system, and the healthy respect accorded the law in the South, Charles S. Sydnor, "The Southerner and the Laws," *The Journal of Southern History*, VI (Feb. 1940), 3–23.
    [5] Scholars are hardly of a mind about the impact of these peculiarly southern conditions on the appellate judiciary. See, for example, the conflicting assessments of Michael Meltsner, "Southern Appellate Courts: A Dead End," in Leon Friedman, ed., *Southern Justice* (Boston, 1965), 13, 138–39; Gregory A. Calderia, "On the Reputation of State Supreme Courts," paper presented at the 1982 Annual Meeting of the Midwest Political Science Association; and Rodney Mott, "Judicial Influence," *The American Political Science Review*, XXX (July 1936), 295–315.
    [6] Charles M. Cook, *The American Codification Movement: A Study in Antebellum Legal Reform* (Westport, Conn., 1981), 185–214; Hall, "The Judiciary on Trial;" and Maxwell Bloomfield, *American Lawyers in a Changing Society* (Cambridge, Mass., 1976), 136–90.
    [7] Glenn R. Winters, "The Merit Plan for Judicial Election and Tenure—Its Historical Development," *Duquesne Law Review*, VII (Fall 1968), 61–77.
    [8] Hall, "The Judiciary on Trial." On the continuing relevance of these issues see Philip L. Dubois, *From Ballot to Bench: Judicial Elections and the Quest for Accountability* (Austin, Tx., 1980), 3–36, 242–52.
    [9] Maryland serves as the border state representative in this analysis because of the availability in the Maryland Hall of Records of data on judicial elections. Neither Kentucky nor Missouri offered such rich voting data. The general problem of collecting data on judicial elections is discussed more fully below. The list of judges was compiled from several sources. The most important of these were state legislative manuals, court reports, and records held in the archives of all the southern states. This list includes only regular judicial officers; special justices have been excluded.
    [10] The data collection techniques and the weighing of specific kinds of data, especially those data relating to wealth, are discussed in Kermit L. Hall, *The Politics of Justice: Federal Judicial Selection and the Second American Party System, 1829–1861* (Lincoln, Neb., 1979), 179–

80; Hall, "The Children of the Cabins: The Lower Federal Judiciary, Modernization, and the Political Culture, 1789–1899," *Northwestern University Law Review*, LXXV (Oct. 1980), 423–71; and Hall, "Constitutional Machinery and Judicial Professionalism: The Careers of Midwestern State Appellate Judges, 1861–1899," in Gerard W. Gawalt, ed., *The New High Priests* (Westport, Conn., forthcoming). The debate over popular election of judges followed similar paths in North and South. The concern with and emphasis on quality was national. See, for example, Simon Fleischmann, "The Influence of the Bar in the Selection of Judges Throughout the United States," *American Law Review*, XXX (May-June 1905), 348–79; and Morton Keller, "The Politics of State Constitutional Revision, 1820–1930," in Kermit L. Hall, Harold M. Hyman, and Leon V. Sigal, eds., *The Constitutional Convention as an Amending Device* (Washington, D.C., 1981), 72–73.

11 Hall, "The Judiciary on Trial."

12 *Debates in the Convention for the Revision and Amendment of the Constitution of the State of Louisiana. Assembled at Liberty Hall, New Orleans, April 6, 1864* (New Orleans, 1864), 304.

13 Hall, "The Judiciary on Trial."

14 The rich literature on judicial process and judicial behavior underscores the difficulty of this enterprise. See, generally, Calderia, and, on the relationship of popular election to issues of quality, Dubois *From Ballot to Bench*, 6–20, 249–51, and Bradley C. Cannon, "The Impact of Formal Selection Processes on the Characteristics of Judges—Reconsidered" *Law and Society Review*, VI (May 1972), 579–93.

15 Mark Tushnet, *The American Law of Slavery, 1810–1860: Considerations of Humanity and Interest* (Princeton, 1981), 8, 39, 42, 53, 229. Tushnet's argument is an altogether remarkable set of assertions based on a present-minded view of what constitutes ability. See, on the other hand, Thomas D. Morris, "'As if the Injury was Effected by the Natural Elements of Air, or Fire': Slave Wrongs and the Liability of Masters," *Law and Society Review*, XVI (1981–82), 569–600.

16 See, for example, the Justice Oran M. Roberts' chapter, "The Political, Legislative, and Judiciary History of Texas for Its Fifty Years of Statehood, 1845–1895," in Dudley G. Wooten, *A Comprehensive History of Texas* (2 vols., Dallas, 1898), II, 168–210. For other literature see Wooster, *The People in Power*, 167–70.

17 The statistical measures used were Lamba and the uncertainty coefficient. Both are probability or proportional reduction of error statistics whose values range from 1 to zero, with a value of zero measuring no improvement in prediction. A value of .3 or above suggests a meaningful association. Both of these measures are appropriate for use with nominal level data. However, since some independent variables treated here could be viewed as ordinal in nature, the asymmetric statistic eta, also a measure of association, was computed. The computed values of each were as follows: college education (uncertainty coefficient: .024, Lamba = .1, eta = .12); formal legal education (u.c. = .029, lamba = .006, eta = .20); and prior judicial service (u.c. = .026, lamba = .003, eta = .057).

18 On the general level of education of appellate judges see Lawrence M. Friedman, *A History of American Law* (New York, 1973), 334–35.

19 As Edward Pessen has argued, access to higher education during these years was a product of social class, a point discussed at length below. See Edward Pessen, "Social Structure and Politics in American History," *The American Historical Review*, LXXXVII (Dec. 1982), 1297–98.

20 The somewhat higher percentage of popularly elected southern judges with formal academic training reflects the trend in the late nineteenth and early twentieth centuries toward law school preparation coupled with the larger number of judges brought to the bench in the first two decades of the twentieth century. Of course, the percentage also underscores that popular election was altogether compatible with the forces of legal professionalization. On this development see Robert Stevens, "Two Cheers for 1870: The American Law School," *Perspectives in American History*, V (1971), 405.

21 This argument had neither sectional nor temporal limits. See, for example, George

Winchester, *An Address to the People of Mississippi* . . . (Natchez, 1833), 12; *Albany Law Journal*, XVIII (July 1873), 11–12; and, more generally, Winters, "The Merit Plan for Judicial Selection and Tenure," 63–67.

[22] These essentially reciprocal themes have repeatedly surfaced in the historical debate over judicial power and various schemes of judicial selection. For a contemporary discussion of their multiple meanings see Stephen L. Wasby, "Accountability in the Courts," in Thomas Greer, *et al.*, eds., *Accountability in Urban Society* (Beverly Hills, Calif., 1978), 143–68. On the nineteenth century see Hall, "The Judiciary on Trial," and Hall, "Constitutional Machinery and Judicial Selection."

[23] Wasby, "Accountability in the Courts," 155.

[24] On judicial elections, see Dubois, *From Ballot to Bench*, 243–44, 51.

[25] J. Morgan Kousser, *The Shaping of Southern Politics: Suffrage Restriction and the Establishment of the One-Party South, 1880–1910* (New Haven, Conn., 1974), 262.

[26] Dubois, *From Ballot to Bench*, 96–100.

[27] Hall, "The Judiciary on Trial." For a full listing of these various positions, see Francis N. Thorpe, *The Federal and State Constitutions, Colonial Charters, and Other Organic Laws* (7 vols., Washington, D.C., 1909).

[28] Haynes, *Selection and Tenure of Judges*, 101–35.

[29] Hall, "The Judiciary on Trial." The same pattern developed in the Midwest. See Hall, "Constitutional Machinery and Judicial Professionalism."

[30] See Kousser, *The Shaping of Southern Politics*, 239–44, 269–70.

[31] There is a significant difference of opinion about the extent of competition in judicial elections. The data presented here suggests that there was more rather than less. See J. Willard Hurst, *The Growth of American Law: The Law Makers* (Boston, 1950), 143; and Friedman, *A History of American Law*, 323–24.

[32] Data on the 239 judicial elections were collected from a variety of sources, the most important of which were: 1) consolidated election returns, held in the state archives of Maryland, North Carolina, Georgia, Florida, Alabama, Tennessee, Mississippi, and Texas; 2) legislative manuals, "blue books," and reports by the secretaries of state published for Arkansas, Texas, Louisiana, and Mississippi. No election returns were found for Louisiana or Virginia in the 1850s. Only scattered returns were available for Kentucky in newspapers and the papers of some of the governors of Kentucky held in the Kentucky State Archives in Frankfort. The data gathered for this study of the eleven states of the Confederacy and Maryland embrace between 90 and 95 percent of all judicial elections.

[33] There was a good deal of substance to antebellum judicial politics. Moreover, the assertion by Henry S. Foote, in *Bench and Bar of the South and Southwest* (St. Louis, 1876), 59, that party affiliation was not a strong factor in appointing judges is largely wrong; over nine-tenths (92.69%) of judicial appointees in the South before the Civil War were members of the appointing governor's party.

[34] Data on judicial voting in Ohio were drawn from *Statistical Report of the Secretary of State of Ohio* (Columbus, 1853–1921).

[35] V. O. Key, Jr., *Southern Politics* (New York, 1949), 205–11.

[36] Hall, "Children of the Cabins," 425–27, 459. There are, of course, many variables that contribute to the institutional vitality of courts, not the least of which is the nature of cases and the quality of counsel.

[37] The eta computed for method of selection and length of service was .32.

[38] The eta computed for method of selection and length of service, controlling for statutory term, was .52. The Pearsonian product moment correlation for statutory term by length of service for all judges—state and federal—was .62.

[39] Harrison C. White, *Chains of Opportunity: System Models of Mobility in Organizations* (Cambridge, Mass., 1970), 298–316.

[40] See Alex Weingrod, "Patrons, Patronage, and Political Parties," *Comparative Studies in Society and History*, X (July 1968), 377–400; Kermit L. Hall, "The Perils of Prosopography—Southern Style," *Vanderbilt Law Review*, XXXII (Jan. 1979), 338.

[41] Mark Tushnet, "A Marxist Analysis of American Law," *Marxist Perspectives*, I (Jan. 1978), 99.

[42] Hurst, *The Growth of American Law*, 138–46.

[43] A. G. Roeber, *Faithful Magistrates and Republican Lawyers: Creators of Virginia Legal Culture, 1680–1810* (Chapel Hill, N.C., 1981), 239, 244, 258–61.

[44] The lamba (.004), uncertainty coefficient (.008), and eta (.07) revealed no association between method of selection and social origins. These data also do not reveal any significant association between social origins and region of service.

[45] Pessen, "Social Structure and Politics in American History," 1297–1300, 1312. Social-origins should not be confused with the judges' social class positions when brought to the bench. Most judges had been upwardly mobile in their careers; through education, politics, and professional accomplishments they enhanced their status, and in doing so they dramatically narrowed the range of social-class positions to elite (24.4%) and prominent (75.6%) backgrounds. The analysis of the data in this section is based on the same scheme developed in Hall, "Children of the Cabins," 466–71.

[46] White, *Chains of Opportunity*, 1–7, 298–316.

[47] Hall, "The Judiciary on Trial."

[48] Hall, "The Children of the Cabins," 464–65; Hall, "Constitutional Machinery and Judicial Professionalism." Much the same held true on the southern appellate bench. About one-fifth (22.5, N = 121) of these judges were classified as partisan activists; that is, they had not only run for office, but they also had records of significant participation as local party organizers, delegates to state and national party conventions, and presidential electors. Strikingly, the strongest eta (.42) produced in this study was for method of selection by partisan activism controlled for social-class origin.

[49] These kinship ties count persons who served on the same state bench at the same or different times. Moreover, each person in the connection was counted; thus, Richard Wilde Walker, Sr., and Richard Wilde Walker, Jr., who were father and son on the Alabama bench, formed one connection but were counted as two persons. Only in counting in this way is it possible to observe changes in patterns over time. Because of the difficulty in isolating family relationships, these data undoubtedly *underestimate* the true level of interconnectedness.

[50] The seeming anomaly of judges selected through legislative elections is explained by the persistence of this method of judicial selection in South Carolina, a state of extraordinary interconnectedness among the political and legal elite. This finding, as argued below, confirms once again the significance of regional differences in judicial backgrounds that were rooted in endemic social and cultural patterns. See Canon, "The Impact of Formal Selection Processes," 591–92.

[51] The eta was .41 for method of selection by level of kinsfolks' political activism controlled for judicial service.

[52] *Proceedings of the Constitutional Convention of the State of Georgia Held in Atlanta, 1877* (Atlanta, 1878), 223–24.

[53] *Ibid.*, 224.

[54] C. Vann Woodward, *Origins of the New South, 1877–1913* (Baton Rouge, La., 1951).

[55] Bradley C. Canon and Lawrence Baum, "Patterns of Adoption of Tort Law Innovations: An Application of Diffusion Theory to Judicial Doctrines," *The American Political Science Review*, LXXV (Dec. 1981), 975–87; Caldeira, "On the Reputation of State Supreme Courts;" and Mott, "Judicial Influence."

[56] Peter Harris, "Some Predictors of the Interstate Diffusion of State Common Law, 1870–1970," paper presented at the 1979 Annual Meeting of the Law and Society Association; and Harris, "Problematic Cases and the Judicial Search for Authority," paper presented at the 1980 Annual Meeting of the Law and Society Association. For a typical statement on southern judicial inability see Michael Meltsner, "Southern Appellate Courts: A Dead End," in Friedman, ed., *Southern Justice*, 13, 138–39.

Selected Bibliography

The selected bibliography includes books and articles which examine aspects of southern legal history. This listing is not intended to be comprehensive, but rather to serve as a guide to the existing literature. It is restricted to secondary studies and omits edited collections of papers or court records. Likewise, the selected bibliography does not include general works on American legal history which treat the South in only a peripheral manner. Nor have we mentioned important works in southern history, such as Eugene D. Genovese's *Roll, Jordan, Roll: The World the Slaves Made* (1974) and Bertram Wyatt-Browns's *Southern Honor: Ethics and Behavior in the Old South* (1982), which include passages on legal matters but deal primarily with social and economic issues.

Although there are helpful accounts of particular topics, many subjects remain unexplored. Thus, the treatment of paupers, the status of married women, the working of the criminal justice system, the nature of the southern bench and bar, and the relationship between legal culture and commercial growth suffer from neglect. Moreover, no work considers the broad legal development of the region.

Alderman, Ernest H., "The North Carolina Colonial Bar," *James Sprunt Historical Publications*, XIII, No. 1, 5–31 (1913).

Billings, Warren M., "The Transfer of English Law to Virginia, 1606–50," in K.R. Andrews, N.P. Canny, and P. E. H. Hair, eds., *The Westward Enterprise, English Activities in Ireland, the Atlantic and America, 1480–1650* (Detroit, 1979).

———, "Pleading, Procedure, and Practice: The Meaning of Due Process of Law in Seventeenth-Century Virginia," *Journal of Southern History*, XLVII (Nov. 1981), 569–584.

Bloomfield, Maxwell, *American Lawyers in a Changing Society, 1776–1876* (Cambridge, Mass. 1976).

———, "The Texas Bar in the Nineteenth Century," *Vanderbilt Law Review* XXXII (Jan. 1979), 261–276.

Bodenhamer, David J., "Law and Disorder in the Old South: The Situation in Georgia, 1830–1860," in Walter J. Fraser, Jr., and Winfred B. Moore, Jr., eds., *From the Old South to the New: Essays in the Transitional South* (Westport, Conn., 1981), 109–119.

———, "The Efficiency of Criminal Justice in the Antebellum South," *Criminal Justice History*, III (1983), 81–95.

Bowler, Clara Ann, "Carted Whores and White Shrouded Apologies:

Slander in the County Courts of Seventeenth-Century Virginia," *Virginia Magazine of History and Biography*, LXXXV (Oct. 1977), 411–426.

Bridwell, Randall, "Mr. Nicholas Trott and the South Carolina Vice Admiralty Court: An Essay on Procedural Reform and Colonial Politics," *South Carolina Law Review*, XXVIII (June 1976), 181–218.

Brown, Roy M., *Public Poor Relief in North Carolina* (Chapel Hill, N.C., 1928).

Brown, Richard Maxwell, *The South Carolina Regulators* (Cambridge, Mass., 1963).

————, "Southern Violence—Regional Problem or National Nemesis?: Legal Attitudes Toward Southern Homicide in Historical Perspective," *Vanderbilt Law Review*, XXXII (Jan. 1979), 225–250.

Bruce, Dickson, D., Jr., *Violence and Culture in the Antebellum South* (Austin, Tex., 1979).

Bryson, W. Hamilton, ed. *Legal Education in Virginia, 1779–1979: A Biographical Approach* (Charlottesville, Va., 1982).

————, *A Bibliography of Virginia Legal History Before 1900* (Charlottesville, Va., 1979).

————, ed., *Virginia Law Reporters Before 1880* (Charlottesville, Va., 1977).

————, ed., "The Reports of Charles Lee and of John Brown," *University of Richmond Law Review*, XI (Summer 1977), 691–741.

————, "The Abolition of the Forms of Action in Virginia," *University of Richmond Law Review*, XVII (Winter 1983), 273–284.

Calvani, Terry, "The Early Professional Career of Howell Jackson," *Vanderbilt Law Review*, XXX (Jan. 1977), 39–72.

Carter, Dan. T., *Scottsboro: A Tragedy of the American South* (rev. ed., Baton Rouge, La., 1979).

Censer, Jane Turner, " 'Smiling Through Her Tears': Ante-Bellum Southern Women and Divorce," *American Journal of Legal History*, XXV (Jan. 1981), 24–47.

Chapin, Bradley, *Criminal Justice in Colonial America, 1606–1660* (Athens, Ga., 1983).

Chitwood, Oliver P., *Justice in Colonial Virginia* (Baltimore, 1905).

Cullen, Charles T., "New Light on John Marshall's Legal Education and Admission to the Bar," *American Journal of Legal History*, XVI (Oct. 1972), 345–351.

————, "Completing the Revisal of the Laws in Post-Revolutionary Virginia," *Virginia Magazine of History and Biography*, LXXXII (Jan. 1974), 84–99.

Daniel, Peter, *The Shadow of Slavery: Peonage in the South, 1901–1969* (Urbana, Ill., 1972).

Dargo, George, *Jefferson's Louisiana: Politics and the Clash of Legal Traditions* (Cambridge, Mass., 1975).

Deen, James W., Jr., "Patterns of Testation: Four Tidewater Counties in Colonial Virginia," *American Journal of Legal History*, XVI (April 1972), 154–176.

Dewey, Frank L., "Thomas Jefferson's Law Practice," *Virginia Magazine of History and Biography*, LXXXV (July 1977), 289–301.

Dougan, Michael B., "The Doctrine of Creative Destruction: Ferry and Bridge Law in Arkansas," *Arkansas Historical Quarterly* (Summer 1980), 136–158.

Day, Alan F., "Lawyers in Colonial Maryland, 1660–1715," *American Journal of Legal History*, XVII (April 1973), 145–165.

"Early Statutory and Common Law of Divorce in North Carolina," *North Carolina Law Review*, XXXXI (1963), 604–621.

Eaton, Clement, "A Mirror of the Southern Colonial Lawyer: The Fee Books of Patrick Henry, Thomas Jefferson, and Waightstill Avery," *William and Mary Quarterly*, VIII (Oct. 1951), 520–534.

———, "Mob Violence in the Old South," *Mississippi Valley Historical Review*, XXIX (Dec. 1942), 351–370.

Ely, James W., Jr., *The Crisis of Conservative Virginia: The Byrd Organization and the Politics of Massive Resistance* (Knoxville, Tenn., 1976).

———, "American Independence and the Law: A Study of Post-Revolutionary South Carolina Legislation," *Vanderbilt Law Review*, XXVI (Oct. 1973), 939–971.

———, "Charleston's Court of Wardens, 1783–1900: A Post-Revolutionary Experiment in Municipal Justice," *South Carolina Law Review*, XXVII (Feb. 1976), 645–660.

———, " 'That no Office Whatever be Held During Life or Good Behavior:' Judicial Impeachments and the Struggle for Democracy in South Carolina," *Vanderbilt Law Review*, XXX (March 1977), 167–208.

———, "The Legal Practice of Andrew Jackson," *Tennessee Historical Quarterly*, XXXVIII (Winter 1979), 421–435.

———, Andrew Jackson as Tennessee State Court Judge, 1798–1804," *Tennessee Historical Quarterly*, XL (Summer 1981), 144–157.

———, "Negro Demonstrations and the Law: Danville as a Test Case," *Vanderbilt Law Review*, XXVII (Oct. 1974), 927–968.

Flanigan, Daniel, "Criminal Procedure in Slave Trials in the Antebellum South," *Journal of Southern History*, XL (Aug. 1974), 537–564.

Friedman, Leon, ed., *Southern Justice* (New York, 1965).

Green, Fletcher M., *Constitutional Development in the South Atlantic States, 1776–1860: A Study in the Evolution of Democracy* (Chapel Hill, N.C., 1930).

Gunderson, Joan R. and Gwen Victor Gampel, "Married Women's Legal Status in Eighteenth-Century New York and Virginia," *William and Mary Quarterly*, 3rd ser., XXXIX (Jan. 1982), 114–134.

Hackney, Sheldon, "Southern Violence," *American Historical Review*, XLLIV (Feb. 1969), 906–925.

Hall, Kermit L., "The Promises and Perils of Prosopography—Southern Style," *Vanderbilt Law Review*, XXXII (Jan. 1979), 331–339.

Hamilton, William B., *Anglo-American Law on the Frontier: Thomas Rodney and his Territorial Cases* (Durham, N.C., 1953).

Harrison, M. Leigh, "A Study of the Earliest Reported Decisions of the South Carolina Courts of Law," *American Journal of Legal History*, XVI (Jan. 1972), 51–70.

Haws, Robert J., and Michael V. Namorato, "Race, Property Rights, and the Economic Consequences of Reconstruction: A Case Study," *Vanderbilt Law Review*, XXXII (Jan. 1979), 305–326.

Higginbotham, A. Leon, *In the Matter of Color: Race and the American Legal Process: The Colonial Period* (New York, 1978).

Higginbotham, R. Don and William S. Price, Jr., "Was It Murder for a White Man to Kill a Slave? Chief Justice Martin Howard Condemns the Peculiar Institution in North Carolina," *William and Mary Quarterly*, 3rd ser., XXXVI (Oct. 1979), 593–601.

Hindus, Michael S., *Prison and Plantation: Crime, Justice, and Authority in Massachusetts and South Carolina, 1767–1878* (Chapel Hill, N.C., 1980).

———, "Black Justice Under White Law: Criminal Prosecutions of Blacks in Antebellum South Carolina," *Journal of American History*, LXIII (Dec. 1976), 575–599.

———, "The Contours of Crime and Justice in Massachusetts and South Carolina, 1767–1878," *American Journal of Legal History*, XXI (July 1977), 212–237.

Hogue, L. Lynn, "Nicholas Trott: Man of Law and Letters," *South Carolina Historical Magazine*, LXXVI (Jan. 1975), 25–34.

Holmes, William T., "Whitecapping: Agrarian Violence in Mississippi, 1902–1906," *Journal of Southern History*, XXXV (May 1969), 165–185.

Howington, Arthur F., " 'Not in the Condition of a Horse of an Ox': Ford v. Ford, The Law of Testamentary Manumission and the Tennessee Courts' Recognition of Slave Humanity," *Tennessee Historical Quarterly*, XXXIV (Fall 1975), 249–263.

Ireland, Robert M., The *County Courts in Antebellum Kentucky* (Lexington, Ky., 1972).

———, "Law and Disorder in Nineteenth-Century Kentucky," *Vanderbilt Law Review* XXXII (Jan. 1979), 281–300.

———, "Homicide in Nineteenth Century Kentucky," *Register of the Kentucky Historical Society*, LXXXI (Spring 1983), 134–153.

Johnson, Herbert A., ed., *South Carolina Legal History* (Columbia, S.C. 1980).

Kilbourne, Richard Holcombe, Jr., *Louisiana Commercial Law: The Antebellum Period* (Baton Rouge, La., 1980).

Kirtland, Robert B., "Keep Your Eye on the Bastards! or, Sobering Reflections on the 150-Year Record of Early Virginia's Attitude Toward Lawyers," *University of Toledo Law Review*, XIV (Spring 1983), 685–705.

Kluger, Richard, *Simple Justice: The History of Brown v. Board of Education* and *Black America's Struggle for Equality* (New York, 1976).

Konig, David Thomas, " 'Dale's Laws' and the Non-Common Law Origins of Criminal Justice in Virginia," *American Journal of Legal History*, XXVI (Oct. 1982), 354–375.

Landon, Michael de L., *The Honor and Dignity of the Profession: A History of the Mississippi State Bar, 1906–1976* (Jackson, Miss., 1979).

Laska, Lewis L., "A Legal and Constitutional History of Tennessee, 1772–1972," *Memphis State University Law Review*, VI (Summer 1976), 563–672.

Lebsock, Suzanne D., "Radical Reconstruction and the Properly Rights of Southern Women," *Journal of Southern History*, XLIII (May 1977), 195–216.

Lee, Charles R., Jr., *The Confederate Constitutions* (Chapel Hill, N.C., 1963).

McCain, Paul M., *The County Court in North Carolina before 1750* (Durham, N.C., 1954).

McMillen, Neil R.,"Black Enfranchisement in Mississippi: Federal Enforcement and Black Protest in the 1960's," *Journal of Southern History*, XLIII (Aug. 1977), 351–372.

Mackey, Howard, "The Operation of the English Old Poor Law in Colonial Virginia, *Virginia Magazine of History and Biography*, LXXIII (Jan. 1965), 29–40.

Magrath, Peter C., *Yazoo: The Case of Fletcher v. Peck* (New York, 1967).

Martin, Charles H., *The Angelo Herndon Case and Southern Justice* (Baton Rouge, La., 1976).
Mays, David J., *Edmund Pendleton, 1721–1803* (2 vols., Cambridge, Mass., 1952).
Merrill, Boynton, Jr., *Jefferson's Nephews: A Frontier Tragedy* (Princeton, N.J., 1976).
Morris, Thomas D.," 'As If the Injury was Effected by the Natural Elements of Air, or Fire': Slave Wrongs and the Liability of Masters," *Law and Society Review*, XVI (1981–82), 569–599.
————, "Equality, 'Extraordinary Law,' and Criminal Justice: The South Carolina Experience, 1865–1866," *South Carolina Historical Magazine*, LXXXIII (Jan. 1982), 15–33.
Nall, James O., *The Tobacco Night Riders of Kentucky and Tennessee, 1905–1909* (Louisville, Ky., 1939).
Nash, A. E. Keir, "Reason of Slavery: Understanding the Judicial Role in the Peculiar Institution," *Vanderbilt Law Review*, XXXII (Jan. 1979), 7–218.
————, "The Texas Supreme Court and the Trial Rights of Blacks, 1845–1860," *Journal of American History*, LVIII (Dec. 1971), 622–642.
————, "Negro Rights, Unionism, and Greatness on the South Carolina Court of Appeals: The Extraordinary Chief Justice John Belton O'Neall," *South Carolina Law Review*, XXI (1968), 141–190.
————, "Fairness and Formalism in the Trials of Blacks in the State Supreme Courts of the Old South," *Virginia Law Review*, LVI (Feb. 1970), 64–100.
Nelson, Margaret V., *A Study of Judicial Review in Virginia, 1789–1928* (New York, 1947).
Nolan, Dennis R., "The Effect of the Revolution on the Bar: The Maryland Experience," *Virginia Law Review*, LXII (June 1976), 969–997.
Novak, Daniel A., *The Wheel of Servitude: Black Forced Labor After Slavery* (Lexington, Ky., 1978).
Preyer, Kathryn, "Crime, the Criminal Law and Reform in Post-Revolutionary Virginia," *Law and History Review*, I (Spring 1983), 53–85.
Rankin, Hugh F., *Criminal Trial Proceedings in the General Court of Colonial Virginia* (Williamsburg, Va., 1965).
Robinson, William M., *Justice in Grey: A History of the Judicial System of the Confederate States of America* (Cambridge, Mass., 1941).
Roeber, A. G., *Faithful Magistrates and Republican Lawyers: Creators of Virginia Legal Culture, 1680–1810* (Chapel Hill, N.C., 1981).
————, "Authority, Law and Custom: The Rituals of Court Day in

Tidewater Virginia, 1720 to 1750," *William and Mary Quarterly*, 3rd ser., XXXVII (Jan. 1980), 29–52.

Rowland, Dunbar, *Courts, Judges and Lawyers of Mississippi, 1798–1935* (Jackson, Miss., 1935).

Salmon, Marylynn, "Women and Property in South Carolina: The Evidence from Marriage Settlements," *William and Mary Quarterly*, 3rd ser., XXXIX (Oct. 1982), 655–685.

Saunders, Robert M., "Crime and Punishment in Early National America: Richmond, Virginia, 1784–1820," *Virginia Magazine of History and Biography*, LXXXVI (Jan. 1978), 33–44.

Scott, Arthur, P., *Criminal Law in Colonial Virginia* (Chicago 1930).

Semmes, Raphael, *Crime and Punishment in Early Maryland* (Baltimore, 1938).

Senese, Donald, "Building the Pyramid: The Growth and Development of the State Court System in Antebellum South Carolina, 1800–1860," *South Carolina Law Review* (1972), 357–379.

Shepard, E. Lee, "Lawyers Look at Themselves: Professional Consciousness and the Virginia Bar," *American Journal of Legal History*, XXV (Jan. 1981), 1–23.

———, "Breaking into the Profession: Establishing a Law Practice in Antebellum Virginia," *Journal of Southern History*, XLVII (Aug. 1982), 393–410.

Smith, Joseph H., "The Foundations of Law in Maryland: 1634–1715," in George A. Billias, ed., *Law and Authority in Colonial America* (Barre, Mass., 1965), 92–115.

Smith, Stephen A., "Arkansas Advocacy: The Territorial Period," *Arkansas Law Review*, XXXI (Fall 1977), 449–476.

———, "Impeachment, Address, and the Removal of Judges in Arkansas: An Historical Perspective," *Arkansas Law Review*, XXXII (Summer 1978), 253–268.

Spindel, Donna J., "The Administration of Criminal Justice in North Carolina, 1720–1740," *American Journal of Legal History*, XXV (April 1981), 141–162.

Spindel, Donna J., and Stuart W. Thomas, Jr., "Crime and Society in North Carolina, 1663–1740," *Journal of Southern History*, XLIX (May 1983), 223–244.

Stealey, John Edmund, III, "The Responsibilities and Liabilities of the Bailee of Slave Labor in Virginia," *American Journal of Legal History*, XII (Oct. 1968), 336–353.

Sydnor, Charles S., "The Southerner and the Laws," *Journal of Southern History*, VI (Feb. 1940), 3–23.

Tachau, Mary K. Bonsteel, *Federal Courts in the Early Republic: Kentucky, 1789–1816* (Princeton, N.J., 1978).

Tushnet, Mark V., *The American Law of Slavery, 1810–1860: Considerations of Humanity and Interest* (Princeton, N.J., 1981).

Vanderwood, Paul J., *Night Riders of Reelfoot Lake* (Memphis, Tenn., 1969).

Watson, Alan D., "Public Poor Relief in Colonial North Carolina," *North Carolina Historical Review*, LIV (Oct. 1977), 347–366.

Wiecek, William M., "The Statutory Law of Slavery and Race in the Thirteen Mainland Colonies of British America," *William and Mary Quarterly*, 3rd ser., XXXIV (April 1977), 258–280.

Williams, Jack Kenny, *Vogues in Villainy: Crime and Retribution in Ante-Bellum South Carolina* (Columbia, S.C., 1959).

Wyatt-Brown, Bertram, "Community, Class, and Snopesian Crime: Local Justice in the Old South," in Orville Vernon Burton and Robert C. McMath, Jr., *Class, Conflict and Consensus: Antebellum Southern Community Studies* (Westport, Conn., 1982), 173–206.

Notes on Contributors

JAMES W. ELY, JR., is Professor of Law at Vanderbilt University. Author of *The Crisis of Conservative Virginia: The Byrd Organization and the Politics of Massive Resistance*, he also has written widely in southern legal history, especially during the Revolutionary and early national periods.

DAVID J. BODENHAMER, Associate Professor of History at the University of Southern Mississippi, is author of numerous articles and papers on crime and criminal justice in the antebellum United States, including the Old South.

LAWRENCE M. FRIEDMAN, Marion Rice Kirkwood Professor of Law at Stanford University, is author of the prize-winning book, *A History of American Law*, coauthor of *Roots of Justice, Crime and Punishment in Alameda County, California, 1870–1920*, and has written numerous other books and articles on law and legal history.

TONY A. FREYER is Associate Professor of History at the University of Alabama in Tuscaloosa. Author of numerous articles and papers, his books include *Forums of Order: The Federal Courts and Business in American History*.

HARRY N. SCHEIBER is Professor of Law and History at the Jurisprudence and Social Policy Center, School of Law, University of California at Berkeley. A specialist in law and economic policy, he coedited *Law and the American Constitutional Order* and has written books, articles, and papers in legal history.

JOHN V. ORTH, Professor of Law at the University of North Carolina at Chapel Hill, is author of numerous essays and articles on English and American constitutional and legal history.

PHILIP J. SCHWARZ is Associate Professor of History at Virginia Commonwealth University and author of *The Jarring Interests: New York's Boundary Makers, 1664–1776*. He is at work on a book-length study of the criminal law of slavery in the colonial South.

THOMAS D. MORRIS is author of *Free Men All: The Personal Liberty Laws of the North, 1780–1861*, as well as several articles on the law of slavery. He is Professor of History at Portland State University in Oregon.

MARK V. TUSHNET, author of *The American Law of Slavery*, is Professor of Law at Georgetown University Law Center. He is currently at work on a book about the NAACP's litigative strategy during the 1930s and 1940s.

PETER C. HOFFER, Associate Professor of History at the University of Georgia, is coauthor of *Murdering Mothers: Infanticide in England and New England, 1558–1803*, and author of *Revolution and Regeneration*.

A. G. ROEBER is Assistant Professor of History at Lawrence University in Wisconsin. In addition to several articles on legal history, he wrote *Faithful Magistrates and Republican Lawyers: Creators of Virginia Legal Culture, 1680–1810*.

KERMIT L. HALL is Associate Professor of History at the University of Florida. He is author of *The Politics of Justice* and is editor of the four-volume *Comprehensive Bibliography of United States Constitutional and Legal History*.

Index

Adoption laws, 32, 43
Adultery, as crime, 38–39
Anti-alien landholding legislation, 82
Anti-drummer legislation, 82–83
Anti-foreignism, 72
Antoni v. Greenbow, 113
Appellate judiciary, 229–52
  judicial accountablity and indepen-
    dence, 238–44; contested/uncon-
    tested elections and, 240; constitu-
    tional provisions, effects of, 239;
    elected versus appointed judges, 241–
    42; governors' role and, 242; south-
    ern politics and, 238
  judicial quality, 231–37; judges, educa-
    tion of, 232–35; judges, political ca-
    reers of, 235–37; selection process
    and, 237; southern versus midwest-
    ern judicial careers, 237
  popular elections, development in
    South, 229
  popular elections, fear of, 250
  social accessibility of judges, 244–50;
    chains of opportunity concept, 246–
    47; kinship connections and, 247,
    249, 250; social accessibility, mean-
    ings of, 244–45; social class and, 245,
    249–50
  southern judicial culture and, 251

Banking reform, 88–90
Bankruptcy:
  antebellum period, 56–57
  federal receiverships of railroads, 78–80
Bar, southern, 14–16
Benefit of clergy for slaves, 128; abolition
  of, 128–29, 133, 134; death sentence,
  reduction of, 132; manslaughter and,
  134
Board of Liquidation v. McComb, 110–11
Bonds:
  century bonds, 115
  consols, 107–08
  Louisiana state bonds, 110
Boner v. Mable, 154
Bourbons, 110
Brooke, Francis Taliaferro, 148, 149, 160
Brown v. Board of Education of Topeka, 6,
  171, 181
Bryan v. Robert, 162

Campbell, John A., 61–62
Carpetbaggers, 110
Caveat emptor, 8
Charles River Bridge opinion, 8–9
Chattel mortgages, 147–66
  beginnings of, 150–51
  conditional sales and, 152
  equity of redemption, 158, 162–63
  fugitive slaves, 161
  possession problems, 156–58
  price paid/market value issue, 154–55
  slave sales, registry of, 155–56
  slave sales, in gross, 163
  social position of whites and, 159–60
  trust deeds and, 153
Chicago Vice Commission Report of
  1911, 39
Child labor law, 41–42
  southern opposition to, 91, 92
City of Mobile v. Bolden, 181
Civil War, antebellum debts of South, 106
Civil rights litigation, NAACP organiza-
  tion of, 171–81
Clark, Walter, 81
Cobb, T.R.R., 160
Code Duello, 23
Collins v. State, 38
Compromise of 1877, 110, 111, 116
Conditional sales, 152
Consols (consolidated bonds), 107–08
  coupons of, 107–10
  "Pealers," 109
Constitution of 1879 (Louisiana), Debt
  Ordinance, 110
Contract law, 147–48
  will theory of contract, 148, 153
Coupon Killers, 106
  purpose of, 112–13
Coupons, tax-receivable, 107–10
Coverture, 11
Credit, 55–59
  farmer's credit cycle, 54–55
  free black creditor/white debtor, 62
  law of insolvency/bankruptcy and, 56–
    57
  legal system and, 7–8
  merchants and, 56
  negotiability principle, 58
  personal interdependence and, 55–56
  preferential creditors, 57–58

Louisiana:
   antebellum state bonds, 110–12
   Debt Ordinance, 110
Louisiana ex rel. Elliot v. Jumel, 111
Lynching, 22

Married women's property acts, 12, 33,
   61
Marshall, Thurgood, 178, 179
Marshall, John, 148
McCulloch Act, 109
McGahey v. Virginia, 115
"Money Trust," 88
Morality, legal system and, 20–21, 38–40
Mortgages:
   legal history of, 149–50
   See also chattel mortgages.
Murray v. South Carolina Railroad, 31–32

Nat Turner Revolt, 134
National Association for the Advancement of Colored People (NAACP),
   171–81
   desegregation litigation, effects of, 179
   direct attack on segregation, 171–72,
      177
   salary equalization, 174, 176–77
Negotiability, rule of, 58
Negro Seamen's Acts, 5
New Deal, 93–97
   agriculture, national management of, 94
   emergency powers, 93
   impact on the South, 95–97
   Tennessee Valley Authority, 94
New Hampshire v. Louisiana, 111
North Carolina, state debt, 112

O'Neall, John Belton, 6, 17
Outlying slaves, 129, 130
Overton v. Bigelow, 150
Oyer and terminer courts, 128, 130–31,
   198

Parochialism, antebellum, 71–72
Paternalism, southern, 34–35
Paupers, 13
"Peelers," 109
Pensacola Telegraph Company case, 74
Peonage, 84
Philips, John, 75
Pine Barren Act of 1785, 7
Plea-bargaining, 37
Plessy v. Ferguson, 174

Poor relief, 13–14
Populist-Progressive reform response, 87
Priestly v. Fowler, 31, 32
Prisons, southern, 21–22
Prohibition, 39
Property, 59–64
   distributive nature of law, 61–63
   eminent domain, 62, 63
   herdsmens' interests, 59–61
   married women's property laws, 11–12,
      63
   mass ownership of land, 43
   race relations and, 61–62
   stock-law, 60, 63
Prostitution, 39

Railroad Commission Act, 85
Railroads, 50–54
   federal receiverships, bankruptcy cases,
      78–80
   freight rates issue, 80–81
   government aid, 50–51
   herdsmens' interests and, 59–60
   local interests in, 51–52, 53–54
   population changes and, 52–53
   social class interests, 52
   state aid and, 72
Readjusters, Virginia, 110, 112–14
Reagan v. Farmers Loan and Trust, 79
Receiverships, federal, railroad bank-
   ruptcy, 78–80
   South Carolina Railroad, receivership,
      79
Reconstruction, Virginia state debt and,
   107–20
Redeemers, Virginia, 107
Reform, southern response to, 88–93
Regionalism and southern legal history,
   3–4
Registry of slave sales, 155–56
Regulator Movement, 211, 213, 214, 215–
   17
"Riddlebergers," 113
Robertson Law of 1907, 82–83
Royall, William L., 114, 115
Ruffin, Thomas, 6, 155, 157, 159
Rural Electrification Administration, 84–
   95

Salaries, discrimination and, 174, 176
Scalawags, 110
Schoeffen, 204–05